PASCAL
FOR
PROGRAMMERS

PASCAL
FOR
PROGRAMMERS

Olivier Lecarme
Professor of Computer Science
University of Nice, France

Jean-Louis Nebut
Assistant Professor of Computer Science
University of Rennes, France

McGraw-Hill Book Company
New York   St. Louis   San Francisco   Auckland
Bogotá   Hamburg   Johannesburg   London   Madrid
Mexico   Montreal   New Delhi   Panama   Paris
São Paulo   Singapore   Sydney   Tokyo   Toronto

Library of Congress Cataloging in Publication Data

Lecarme, Olivier.
  Pascal for programmers.

  Bibliography: p.
  Includes index.
  1. PASCAL (Computer program language) I. Nebut,
Jean-Louis. II. Title.
QA76.73.P2L39 1984   001.64′24   83-16205
ISBN 0-07-036958-5

1 2 3 4 5 6 7 8 9 0   DOC/DOC   8 9 8 7 6 5 4

ISBN 0-07-036958-5

The editors for this book were Stephen Guty and Ursula
Smith, the designer was Elliot Epstein, and the production
supervisor was Thomas G. Kowalczyk. It was set in Caledonia
by ComCom.

Printed and bound by R. R. Donnelley & Sons Company.

CONTENTS

The incentive for writing this book was the observation, made some time ago, of a surprising fact: while the number of introductory computer programming texts that used Pascal as a primary language was growing, there was a definite need for a book that would introduce and describe the entire language to someone already familiar with computer programming. Among the best available Pascal textbooks, several described programming per se, with little stress on the programming language used as a vehicle. Many others described programming only in terms of Pascal, using the language as a frame for discussing the most basic and fundamental concepts of the matter. All were intended to be used in conjunction with a first course in computer programming.

We made the above observation in mid-1979. Now, several years later, many more textbooks invoking Pascal in their titles have been published, but the general state of affairs remains largely unchanged. We still feel that a book is needed to explain everything about Pascal to somebody who knows programming, somebody who does not have to learn what a computer, a program, an expression, or a procedure is.

It will be assumed that the reader has previously used some higher-level programming language such as Fortran, Cobol, Basic, or PL/I, or even some assembly or machine language. The reader is expected to be conversant with the most basic concepts of computer programming, so no time need be lost in explaining them.

As a consequence, this book is *not* intended for use in conjunction with an introductory course in computer programming, since there are many satisfactory textbooks intended for such a purpose. It can be used for an intermediate course by those writing more advanced programs, but its major aim is to serve as a self-teaching textbook. Since it offers an exhaustive treatment of Pascal and a faithful and precise description of the language standardized by ISO and the national standardization institutes, our intention is also that it should be used as a reference book. With this in mind, we have allocated a separate chapter to each of the main features of the language and have provided numerous appendixes at the end of the book, should specific details be required.

We scrupulously respect the ISO *Standard,* even when we do not completely agree with some minor options taken during its preparation. We think that the language defined by this *Standard* is the only one that deserves to be called standard Pascal. Any modifications, restrictions, or extensions made in the course of specific implementations of the language, whatever their inherent qualities may be, should be described and documented by the implementors themselves in an accompanying reference text. We think such modifications have no place in a general purpose book, however popular they may be. Moreover, we think that to describe and explain local variations or extensions of Pascal is to promote and perpetuate them, thus impeding the main goals of international standardization, which we think essential for the future of Pascal.

The authors of this book have been involved with Pascal for several years. We are both university teachers, and for many years we have taught Pascal or have used it as a tool for teaching programming to various audiences with various backgrounds. We both participate in working groups interested in Pascal and in programming methodology. Jean-Louis Nebut recently completed a Pascal textbook of the already well-represented category, but in French, which has proved very useful, as there is little written on the subject in that language. Olivier Lecarme was advocating the use of Pascal as early as 1972 (in an IFIP working conference). He contributed to several Pascal implementations, and he is an active member of the French and international standardization committees on Pascal.

Our many-faceted experience has forced us to examine this language closely. We consider it to be as well suited to its original goals today as it was when it was first designed.

We divided the task of writing this book in the following way: Olivier Lecarme wrote all the chapters and provided most of the examples; Jean-Louis Nebut outlined three chapters and supplied the remaining examples, all the exercises (with their solutions), and several appendixes. All the programming examples and all the solutions to the programming exercises have been thoroughly tested by Jean-Louis Nebut at the university computing center in Rennes. This was done with the aid of the Pascal implementation for Multics, made in Grenoble by CRISS-IREP with financial support from INRIA. In return, the tests made by Nebut have been very useful for the Grenoble team, especially as an incentive for keeping their implementation as consistent with the ISO *Standard* as possible.

Of course, this book has not been written without any influence from preceding textbooks. It is our pleasure to acknowledge our specific debt to the

ISO *Standard* (1983)* and to Jensen and Wirth (1974) as reference texts; to Wirth (1973, 1976) and Alagič and Arbib (1978) as sources of examples; to Nebut's aforementioned book and to a course given by Jean-Claude Boussard and Olivier Lecarme in a 1977 summer session in Montreal as models for the organization of the book and the order of presentation of the various concepts and topics.

We also wish to thank our families and professional colleagues for their endurance and sympathy throughout the realization of this project. Without their constant help and moral support, this book would not have been possible.

Olivier Lecarme, Nice
Jean-Louis Nebut, Rennes

*References in the text correspond to the bibliography in App. V.

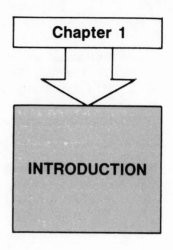

Chapter 1

INTRODUCTION

When compared with Fortran, Basic, Cobol, or PL/I, Pascal is not simply another language that allows the writing of equivalent programs. Rather, it is a new tool that encourages the writing of *better* programs. It would not be very useful to begin with an example of a program written in Pascal. The qualities of the language could not be shown clearly in a toy program one page long. Thus we describe in this chapter only the main principles that govern the design of Pascal and its resulting main characteristics. As in a stepwise-refinement process, readers will find that their grasp of Pascal will develop with each chapter, and they should not be surprised if it takes the whole book to get the whole idea.

1.1 SOME GENERALITIES CONCERNING PASCAL

The Pascal programming language was designed by Niklaus Wirth, professor at the Federal Polytechnical School of Zurich, Switzerland, in 1969. The main motivation of its author was to define a tool for teaching basic computer programming in a systematic way. The languages then used for this purpose were, in his opinion, either too primitive, or too complicated, or based on ill-defined principles, or all those things at once. The need for a language based on simple, logical, and natural principles was especially evident, as witnessed by the increasing popularity of the new philosophy of programming, named *structured programming* and initiated by Edsger Dijkstra, C. A. R. Hoare, and others.

Of course, it is possible in any language, even in machine language, to write well-structured programs that are reliable, readable, maintainable, portable, and efficient. However, it seemed really absurd, especially in teaching an introduction to programming, to have to use the existing tools with so many

1

precautions that the writing of even a simple program became a boring and tedious task. The main idea used in the design of Pascal, consequently, was that a good programming language should encourage the building of good programs.

The second idea was that such a language should be implemented easily and efficiently on present-day computers, instead of needing bulky, unreliable "optimizing" compilers, or new utopic computer architectures, or drastic subsetting in order to be reasonably efficient. As a consequence, when the definition of the language was published, a full compiler was available and used—a very infrequent practice indeed among language designers.

Several basic principles were used to attain these two main goals. For example, it was decided that:

- A concept should be introduced in the language only if it was both necessary and well understood by all. New, untested features should be introduced only in experimental languages.

- Useful redundancies should be employed as much as possible, i.e., redundancies that could be checked by the compiler or implementation system. Mandatory declarations are the best example of such redundancies.

- Because it would be counterproductive to give the user several different means for doing the same thing, the language should make only the best means available and eliminate the others.

- Since the prevention of errors always involves some cost, the necessary checking should be done at compilation time, in which case the checking is done only once, instead of at run time, in which case it is done for each execution of the program. The design of the language should allow for this as much as possible.

- Though two different concepts may exist in the language, there is not always need for their composition. For example, if a function may be defined using an expression, that does not mean that the substitution of an expression for a function name should be allowed everywhere. It would be better to forbid a useless generalization than to allow it to add to the cost of programs that do not use it.

- Universal languages tend to be huge and baroque, and no normal user can understand them in their entirety. A language that is intended to be simple and efficient must necessarily have limitations to its use.

As a consequence of these basic design principles, Pascal is indeed a simple and systematic language. It is much simpler than PL/I or Cobol, and even simpler than Fortran. However, it has much more expressive power, generally speaking, than Basic or Fortran, and, in many situations, than Cobol. Not being universal, Pascal has not the same field of applications as PL/I, and cannot be used, for example, in the handling of direct-access files or in asynchronous tasks.

The field of management data processing has been so much identified with Cobol that it may be somewhat difficult to transpose a particular application from Cobol to Pascal without entirely redesigning it—but maybe this burden will also be worth the trouble. Readers accustomed to Cobol will have to be more enduring than others, and will have to wait until Chap. 12 for examples of the kind they are accustomed to.

Readers familiar with any programming language will probably be frustrated when they cannot discover one or several of their favorite features in Pascal. Every time such lack is particularly evident, we shall try to explain why the feature is absent from Pascal. The answer, generally, will be that this feature is not well understood by users, is not very useful, is easily replaced by other parts of the language, or is too costly to implement.

Another difference that should strike the reader is a difference in style. Defensive programming, the avoidance of GOTOs, the choice of well-designed data structures, a hierarchical program structure, the shunning of clever tricks, all these rules of good style are stressed more and more in books about computer programming. Such rules may be applied to programs written in any language, but they tend to be entirely natural in Pascal. For example, avoiding GOTOs in Basic or Fortran is simply a fiendish source of frustration. Proper use of that invaluable tool, the procedure concept, in Cobol or even in PL/I, generally produces cumbersome, error-prone, and inefficient programs. In Pascal, on the contrary, after the user has acquired some experience, the use of such programming styles will seem perfectly natural, as will be demonstrated, we hope, in the examples and the exercises in this book.

1.2 A BRIEF HISTORY OF PASCAL

Pascal was designed in 1969 and named in honor of Blaise Pascal, a French scientist, philosopher, and writer of the seventeenth century. ("Pascal" is not an acronym; hence it need not be written in uppercase letters.) The language itself has its roots in Algol 60, in Algol W, a derivative of Algol 60 designed by Niklaus Wirth and C. A. R. Hoare in 1965, and in the ideas stated in the paper "Notes on Data Structuring" by Hoare (Dahl, Dijkstra, and Hoare, 1972), published a long time after it had been written and presented in seminars.

The first Pascal compiler was written from scratch by Wirth and his assistants, especially Urs Ammann, for a CDC 6000 computer. It was originally written in Pascal and bootstrapped using a copy of itself translated by hand into a low-level language. The first official definition of Pascal was published in January 1971 (Wirth, 1971) as a 28-page paper, extremely concise and somewhat difficult to read, with its syntax formalized but its semantics described only informally in plain English.

An attempt to formalize the semantic definition resulted in a paper by Hoare and Wirth, published in 1973 and describing almost all the semantics in only 13 pages. The paper also suggested some slight revisions to the language, which were incorporated in a revised report written in the same year but not published.

Much interest in the language had been aroused, together with some criticisms and controversy that resulted from the conciseness and brevity of the describing report, from apparent weaknesses of the language, or from ambiguities in its description. In the meantime, the CDC implementation was entirely redone by Urs Ammann and widely distributed, especially in universities, all around the world. This implementation served as a basis and tool for implementations on other computers, especially for a portable implementation built in Zurich that used an interpreter and was known as Pascal-P. This one was soon used to implement Pascal on almost every existing computer, from the smallest micro to the largest supercomputer.

With Kathleen Jensen, Niklaus Wirth wrote a user's manual, which was published together with the revised report (Jensen and Wirth, 1974) and rapidly became a best-seller. However, the official definition of the language remained ambiguous and incomplete, and there was extremely strong pressure from various sources for extending the language in several incompatible directions. Moreover, the ease of implementing the language and the fact that almost all its compilers were written in the language itself made it all too easy to implement ill-designed deviations and poorly motivated extensions—especially by those people who had not fully understood the basic overall design of the language or some of its most original features. And Pascal was being more and more widely used in the writing of production software, even more for that purpose than as the tool for the teaching of basic programming.

The time was clearly ripe for a standardization of the language if the community of its users wished to keep it as a common language and not let it become a collection of loosely related dialects—as had happened before to Basic. The impulse to standardize was given by many people, but especially by the Pascal Users Group, an informal international group of Pascalers created for the purpose of exchanging ideas and information about the language by means of a quarterly bulletin. The official initiative was taken by the British Standards Institute, member of the International Organization for Standardization (ISO). Under the direction of Tony Addyman, several successive drafts of reports on Pascal were written and submitted to the international community of users, then to the official committees of ISO and of its national members. ANSI and IEEE for the United States, DIN for Germany, AFNOR for France, and the Dutch association were the main contributors. The difficult and cumbersome process of international standardization is now completed, and the international standard may be considered as frozen.

The Pascal *Standard* (ISO, 1983) is mainly a clarification of the original revised report written by Niklaus Wirth. It removes ambiguities, solves contradictions, and fills gaps, thus leaving no room for different interpretations by different people. Moreover, it makes one slight modification and one important extension to the language, both judged absolutely necessary by the international community and approved by the original author of the language. A validation suite was developed during the process of standardization, and it constitutes an invaluable tool for determining whether a given implementation conforms to the *Standard,* and where it deviates if it does so.

The present book is based upon the international ISO *Standard* on Pascal, not on any particular implementation. It uses the terminology of the *Standard* as far as possible, but not its descriptive method, nor its sequence of presentation, which are systematic but not pedagogic. In fact, like all other standards, although it is shorter and more readable than most, the Pascal *Standard* is difficult and tedious to read and understand, and it cannot serve as a describing document. It is only the ultimate reference, meant to give the official answer to all possible questions (one possible and not infrequent answer being that there is no answer to the question).

In retrospect, one can wonder what brought about the success of Pascal, a success not anticipated at all when its first describing report was published. Reasons for very limited prospects were evident: the defining report was published in the first issue of a somewhat obscure journal; no supporting organization, agency, or vendor made any effort to promote it; the first implementation was done on a machine not widely used; and it was deliberately not an ambitious language.

In our opinion, the success of the language results from the conjunction of several very different factors:

- The initial implementation was surprisingly good and efficient, written in the language itself, readable, understandable, and available at no cost.

- The portable Pascal-P implementation made it possible to use the language on microcomputers, which were just beginning to sweep the market.

- The Pascal Users Group gave invaluable, cheap, and friendly support to numerous people interested in the language.

- No political or economic conflicts were involved, precisely because of the absence of official support.

Most of all, the language appeared exactly when it was needed, in the midst of the turmoil of the software crisis, as the natural tool for implementing the principles of structured programming, which were so controversial when they were applied to languages like Fortran or Cobol. Although Pascal was still completely unknown outside academic circles five years after its initial definition, five years more proved enough to make it a successful challenger to both Fortran and Basic for the title of the most popular programming language. After all is considered, it may be that the success of the language is simply the result of its intrinsic qualities.

1.3 HOW TO USE THIS BOOK

This book is intended for people who already know about programming, either from a good introductory course or from having learned by themselves. It is a book about Pascal and not a book about programming, although we have tried throughout the text to promote the design and construction of good programs. We took the option of presenting these ideas by means of examples and pragmatic remarks, not by the exposition and development of great and general principles.

Consequently, a person with no previous experience in programming will not be able to read this book profitably, and he or she should first read one of the numerous introductory textbooks available. We can wholeheartedly recommend the little introductory book by Niklaus Wirth (1973), which uses Pascal as a support language. Those who not only know about programming but also have a superficial knowledge of Pascal could read the first chapters of the present book very rapidly, checking what they already know with the help of the examples, and studying the text more closely only when the exercises begin, i.e., with Chap. 6. We hope that even those who know Pascal well may find this book worthwhile, that it may add to their knowledge of standard Pascal, and even present some unknown aspects of the language and some new ways to use it.

The sequence of presentation we use is somewhat unusual because of the unusual purpose of our book. A formal description of the language would present successively all data structures, then all control structures, with the unfortunate drawback of requiring an iterative reading. An introductory programming book would try to pack as many simple concepts as possible at the beginning to allow the immediate presentation of simple examples. Then it would present the remaining concepts progressively, from simpler to "advanced" (i.e., complicated), thus mixing things and hiding the logical structure of the language. But in this book we have tried to use a logical and systematic sequence to describe a logical and systematic language.

Chapters 2 to 5 present the basic building blocks that constitute programs. Programs are made of actions that process objects; consequently, the building blocks are statements for elementary actions and types for elementary objects. The remaining chapters present, one after the other, the different structures that make it possible to construct programs from these basic building blocks. Each chapter deals with one particular structure, either for actions or for objects. The sequence of these chapters is progressive; i.e., more difficult concepts tend to be at the end, but otherwise the chapters are somewhat independent. They should be read in order, however, since examples and exercises generally use all the concepts previously presented.

Examples are an integral part of the text and should never be skipped—they are the only way the purpose and function of the concepts can be fully understood. They are followed in most cases with remarks, which add information of a pragmatic and practical nature about matters that could not be explained *in abstracto*. As the book progresses, examples and remarks get progressively longer, since they use more and more of the language's expressive power.

The exercises proposed here are substantial—not drills, but real programming exercises. Solutions to selected exercises (one per chapter) appear in App. I. These solutions follow the logic of the examples. Of course, serious readers are strongly encouraged to try their own solutions before looking up the ones we suggest—and to analyze and criticize ours, which are by no means supposed to be the only "right" ones.*

The Pascal language that we describe is exactly the language described by the ISO *Standard*. As such, it differs from the languages accepted by nonstandard implementations. Since the *Standard* is new, nonstandard implementations are presently the rule, but we hope that all serious implementors will upgrade their products to the *Standard* as soon as possible. As a modest incentive, we try not to describe current deviations from the *Standard,* whatever their popularity may be.

With regard to compliance to the *Standard* of a given implementation, some important notions must be defined. In most situations, when the *Standard* states something, a program that deviates is simply illegal, and must be rejected by a *Standard*-complying implementation. For example, the declaration of all variables is mandatory in Pascal, and a program that forgets to declare some variable is simply wrong: no serious Pascal implementation will accept it.

In other situations, the problem may be more difficult and will not be detected without running the program. This is the case, for example, if a divisor is zero or if the value of an array index falls out of the bounds specified for the array. Such a situation is called an *error,* and although implementors should do their best to keep a good check on these conditions, some especially difficult cases or some adverse host computers may make such checking impossible or extremely costly. The Pascal language was designed for minimizing the

*If you're interested in further solutions, contact the publisher.

number of such situations, and the remaining difficulties are emphasized in this book.

In some situations, the *Standard* cannot specify what must be done and leaves some decisions to the implementor. This leads to the two notions of *implementation-defined* and *implementation-dependent* concepts. A concept is implementation-defined if it must be defined, but in a way that may differ from one implementation to the other. Simple examples are the precision of real arithmetic, the range for whole numbers, and the set of characters. A portable program should not rely on a particular specification of an implementation-defined concept.

A concept is implementation-dependent if it is not necessarily defined in a given implementation, which implies that its definition, if any, may differ from one implementation to the other. A simple example is the order of evaluation of the terms of an expression. A portable program should not rely on an implementation-dependent concept, whatever its possible definition may be; for example, it should not assume any particular order of evaluation of expressions, nor should it even assume the existence of any order at all. A list of all implementation-defined and implementation-dependent concepts may be found in App. VII.

Finally, the ISO *Standard* distinguishes two classes of *Standard*-complying implementations, depending on their acceptance or rejection of one specific extension made to the original language by the standardization process. Implementations complying at level 1 implement the concept of a conformant array parameter, as described in Sec. 10.7, while those complying at level 0 do not. (The ANSI Standard defines only level 0.)

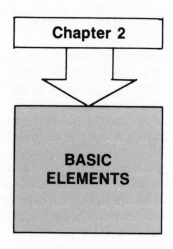

Chapter 2

BASIC ELEMENTS

A program is a sequence of executable statements that computes and processes values. The statement sequence constitutes the control structure of the algorithm described by the program; values are arranged in data structures suited to the given problem. Every programming language establishes some codified way for writing the various possible statements and data structures. The way in which the grammar is presented varies from one language to the other, and the particular way that is used in this book is somewhat different from the more traditional kinds of formalism derived from the Backus Normal Form (or the Backus-Naur Form). It is hoped that our presentation will be more easily understood by Pascal beginners.

The present chapter explains the way in which the various language constructs will be described in the rest of the book, as well as the rules for constructing lexical items. Then it presents the basic notions of a Pascal program, a constant and a variable, and it introduces the elementary statements of the language, i.e., the basic building blocks of structured statements, procedures, and, ultimately, programs.

Since the present book is intended for use as a complete reference manual as well as for use as an introduction to Pascal, it is necessary, in this chapter and the next three, to make forward references to some points that must be mentioned immediately but cannot be explained until the necessary concepts have been covered. As the book progresses, this will be less and less of an inconvenience, and every forward reference may be skipped on first reading.

2.1 METHOD OF PRESENTATION

The presentation of each simple or structured statement in subsequent chapters is preceded by a discussion of its function and by a brief comparison with similar statements, if any, in four widely used programming languages: Fortran, Cobol, Basic, and PL/I. The syntax is formally described with a graphic metalanguage, then in English comments, and illustrated in subsequent examples. The semantics are formally described with deduction rules and/or assertions, then restated in plain English. These two parallel methods of presentation both reflect the same goal, i.e., a clear, precise, and unambiguous description. The explanations in English will be (hopefully) more useful when the book is used as an introduction to Pascal, and the formal syntax and semantics will be more useful when it serves as a reference text.

For each means of data structuring, a formal description of the underlying concept is first presented, followed by a definition of the corresponding data structure in Pascal. Thus it is possible to distinguish clearly the abstract concept from its corresponding implementation, and to compare Pascal more easily with other languages. Moreover, operators applicable to the data structure can be clearly defined.

For both statements and data structures, each construction, after being defined syntactically and semantically, is used in a small illustrative example, followed by clarifications and pragmatic remarks on possible variants and improvements bearing on fault-tolerance, portability, and so on. As soon as enough has been learned (from Chap. 8 on), these explanations are followed by more general and useful examples, which show in action the notions just introduced. Dogmatism is avoided as much as possible, so no formal description is presented if it is assumed to serve no practical purpose—for example, when the formal description would be much more complicated than the notion being described, as would be the case for the **goto** statement in Sec. 2.8.

The metalanguage for specifying the syntax uses three graphic descriptors. A circle (or a figure made with two half circles linked with two horizontal segments) such as

encloses a symbol of the language: a special symbol, built with punctuation characters, or a keyword or word-symbol, built with letters. A rectangle encloses the name of another syntax rule, described elsewhere. Arrows link circles and rectangles, defining the order in which they follow each other.

A syntax rule is defined in a diagram which contains an arrow showing the entry point and an arrow issuing from the exit point. The title of the diagram is the name of the defined syntax rule. A sentence built by concatenation of all items encountered during a particular rule traversal (following the arrows and choosing one direction when there is a switch) is a sentence conforming to the rule. The diagram that defines some token may be substituted for any occurrence of this token enclosed in a rectangle. A sentence which contains no more rule names (all have been replaced by a particular sentence using the corresponding rule) is (a fragment of) a syntactically correct Pascal program.

All rule names in the present book are identical to the corresponding names in the ISO *Standard,* but the metalanguage used here greatly reduces the number of necessary names.

The purpose of the syntax diagrams which appear in the text is to describe locally the concept being presented. The collected syntax diagrams that appear at the end of this book (App. II) give a concise but comprehensive syntactic description of the full language. Because of these two different purposes, the diagrams are not identical in both situations; several diagrams appearing in different chapters may be brought together in one diagram in App. II.

Example 2.1

The following sentences conform to the syntactic rule illustrated in Fig. 2.1.

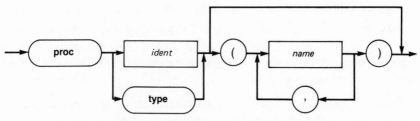

Fig. 2.1 Example of a syntax diagram.

proc *ident*
proc *ident* (*name, name, name*)
proc type (*name*)

Since *ident* and *name* are enclosed in rectangles, they are rule names, and they will be defined elsewhere.

The axiomatic rules that specify the semantics are written as *assertions* or as *deduction rules*. The effect of a statement, or the status of a data structure, is described by initial conditions (the *antecedent*), which precede the statement or the data operator, and final conditions (the *consequent*), which are verified after executing the statement or applying the operator to the data structure.

An assertion of the form $\{P\}$ S $\{Q\}$, where P and Q are logical formulas and S is a Pascal statement, means that if P is true before executing S, then Q is true after execution. In other words, the effect of S, when P is true, is to make Q true: S transforms P into Q.

The special notation P_y^x represents the formula obtained by systematically replacing every free occurrence of x (not linked to P by the universal quantifier) with y.

Example 2.2

The semantics of the Fortran or PL/I assignment statement is defined by the assertion:

$$\{P_y^x\} \; X = Y \; \{P\}$$

This means that, if we know a particular consequent of an assignment statement, we can deduce its antecedent using this rule. If, after the assignment statement

$$A(I) = B(J) * C(K)$$

we know that $A(I) = 1$, this means that before the statement,

$$B(J) * C(K) = 1$$

The deduction rules have the following form:

if < one or several assertions which link the components of the data structure or of the control structure with some predicates >
then < an assertion which links the data structure or the control structure to the same predicates >

This means that if some assertions about the structure are verified then an assertion can be defined about the structure itself.

Example 2.3

The semantics of the Fortran logical IF is defined by the deduction rule :

if $\{P \wedge B\} \; S \; \{Q\}$ and $\{P \wedge \neg B \supset Q\}$
then $\{P\} \; IF \; (B) \; S \; \{Q\}$

Suppose, for example, that assertion P is that $X = COS(Y)$, and that we want to make true assertion Q, i.e., $X = ABS(COS(Y))$. We can write the following statement:

$$IF \; (X.LT.0.0) \; X = -X$$

The condition B is that $X < 0$.

2.2 PROGRAM ELEMENTS

A Pascal program is built with lexical tokens which are either language symbols or basic entities constructed by the programmer: identifiers, numbers, strings, labels, directives, and comments. The symbols and the basic entities are made with characters: letters, digits, and punctuation characters.

The numerous discrepancies between the various character sets available on different computers, or even on different input-output devices on the same computer, constitute an irritating problem. The character set that one can reasonably expect to find on any device is extremely restricted and almost impossible to use as the only available set in a modern programming language. Consequently, the representation of Pascal programs assumes a sufficient character set, and some rules are given for using supplementary characters, if available, or alternative representations, if some other characters are missing.

A preferred representation is provided by the ISO *Standard* and is mandatory when programs are intended for interchange between computer installations. All the expressiveness of the available character set may be used when programs are written for any other purpose, especially to be read. The following description makes a distinction between the standard representation for program interchange, accepted by any *Standard*-conforming compiler, and the more liberal representation used throughout the present book.

The first rule is that the particular representation of any given letter (uppercase or lowercase, italics, bold, etc.) has no significance outside character strings. An uppercase X and a lowercase x are the same symbol, and Begin, begin, BEGIN, and bEgIn all are the same word-symbol. Thus, the letters are described to be only:

$$a\ b\ c\ d\ e\ f\ g\ h\ i\ j\ k\ l\ m\ n\ o\ p\ q\ r\ s\ t\ u\ v\ w\ x\ y\ z$$

The digits are:

$$0\ 1\ 2\ 3\ 4\ 5\ 6\ 7\ 8\ 9$$

In the syntax diagrams that define basic lexical tokens, letters and digits are considered words of the language vocabulary, and are enclosed within circles. They do not appear in subsequent diagrams.

The language symbols are either special symbols or word-symbols. In the present book, the following special symbols are used:

$$+ \ - \ * \ / \ < \ \leqslant \ \neq \ \geqslant \ > \ = \ \wedge \ \vee \ \neg \ . \ , \ .. \ : \ ; \ [\ ] \ (\ ) \ := \ \uparrow$$

(Note that only the two symbols, := and .., need two characters.) Word-symbols (called keywords in other languages) are always printed in boldface; they are:

array	**begin**	**case**	**const**	**div**	**do**	**downto**
else	**end**	**file**	**for**	**function**	**goto**	**if**
in	**label**	**mod**	**nil**	**of**	**packed**	**procedure**
program	**record**	**repeat**	**set**	**then**	**to**	**type**
until	**var**	**while**	**with**			

In the standard representation for program interchange, no boldface is used, and word-symbols are written with ordinary letters.

The following special symbols are represented in a different way, using characters more frequently available in ordinary character sets.

Symbol	$\neq$	$\wedge$	$\vee$	$\neg$	$\leqslant$	$\geqslant$	[	]	↑
Standard representation	< >	**and**	**or**	**not**	< =	> =			^
Standard alternative							(.	.)	@

As this table shows, a few standard alternatives are provided for situations where more acceptable characters are not available. A particular implementation which could not provide, for example, angle brackets would have to define a nonstandard alternative for all comparison operators using these characters. Two other standard alternatives, which are not language symbols, will be defined for comment delimiters (see below).

Identifiers are defined by the rule illustrated in Fig. 2.2. That is, an identifier, called a "name" in several other languages, is a sequence of letters and/or digits, beginning with a letter. No other character may be used in an identifier (no space, no special character like #, @, or $). An identifier may be of any length (subject only to some maximum line length), and all its characters are significant. Word-symbols are reserved keywords; i.e., an identifier cannot have the same spelling as any word-symbol. All these rules and conventions differ significantly from those of Fortran, Basic, Cobol, and PL/I, which are each themselves different.

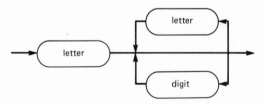

Fig. 2.2 Syntax diagram for an identifier.

Identifiers are chosen freely by the programmer, subject only to the restriction concerning word-symbols; they are used for naming the various objects defined in the program (constants, types, variables, field names, procedures, functions, parameters, or array bounds), and it must be emphasized that the choice of meaningful identifiers has an important effect on program readability. Unfortunately, several compilers set a nonstandard restriction on the number of significant characters of an identifier. The most frequent limit is eight, and for such a compiler, the two distinct identifiers *setconstituent* and *setconstant* cannot be distinguished. What is worse, the keyword **procedure** is sometimes recognized in an identifier like *procedur* or *procedural*.

Example 2.4

The following character sequences are identifiers:

i index number1 EndOfFile QuickSort OUT

The following character sequences are not identifiers:

Begin 3times Printer-output **IN**

The first one is a word-symbol, the second begins with a digit, the third contains a character different from a letter or a digit, and the last is a word-symbol.

In syntax diagrams and syntax descriptions which appear in this book, the symbol *identifier* occurs only infrequently as such; i.e., it is very often qualified as being some particular identifier, for example, a constant identifier, a function identifier, etc. This always has the same meaning; that is, such a qualified identifier is an identifier which has been previously defined or declared as having this qualification.

Numbers are represented in decimal notation only; they denote integer or real values (see Sec. 3.4). A number which contains a decimal point and/or the letter "e" (meaning "times 10 to the power") is a real number; otherwise it is an integer number. The rules for unsigned integers and numbers are illustrated in Fig. 2.3.

Example 2.5

Unsigned integers: 0 2 83 0210

Unsigned numbers: 0 0.0 3.14159 0.3e−08 3E2 1e+4

The following character sequences are not numbers:

.0 0. 1. e+4 E−10 .e5

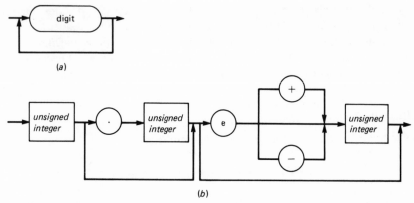

(a)

(b)

Fig. 2.3 Syntax diagram for (a) an unsigned integer and (b) an unsigned number.

Note that this definition is more restrictive than in many other programming languages, in which some or all of these character sequences are legal numbers. This restrictive definition avoids many lexical problems.

Labels are unsigned integers in the closed interval from 0 to 9999. They are used for prefixing statements, if necessary. They are distinguished by their integral value. Their use is very restricted by the language, and is defined in Sec. 2.8.

Strings are constants whose value is denoted by a character sequence enclosed within quotes. The rule for character strings is illustrated in Fig. 2.4. The set of all available characters is implementation-defined. A string which contains only one character denotes a constant of type *char* (see Sec. 3.4.3). If quotation marks must appear within a string, the marks are duplicated.

Fig. 2.4 Syntax diagram for a character string.

Example 2.6

The following character sequences denote constant values of type *char*:

$$\text{'a'} \qquad \text{'A'} \qquad \text{''''}$$

The first one is the lowercase first letter of the alphabet, the second is the corresponding uppercase letter, and the last is the single quote (").

The following character sequences denote character string constants:

'Pascal for Programmers' 'That''s wrong, try again'

Directives have the same syntax as identifiers and may appear in place of the body of a subprogram. Their use will be considered in Secs. 2.3 and 5.1. The only standard directive is "forward."

Comments are character sequences occurring outside character strings. They are enclosed within curly braces and cannot contain a right curly brace. The symbols (* and *) are standard alternative representations for { and }, respectively. Comments are used abundantly in a well-written program, for explaining the internal working of procedures and functions or the use of variables, parameters, and constants; for stating assertions before and after compound statements or subprograms; for linking the end of a subprogram or of a compound statement with its beginning; and so on.

Spaces, comments, and ends-of-line are token separators. Any number of separators may occur between two tokens (symbols, identifiers, numbers, strings, labels, and directives). At least one separator must occur between two tokens which are identifiers, numbers, labels, directives, or keywords. Note, however, that no separator may occur within a token.

All the preceding rules described in this section are somewhat similar to those of PL/I, but are very different from those of Fortran or Basic. Generally speaking, the input format of Pascal programs is entirely free. However, a correct presentation of the program text is essential for program readability, and there are several Pascal programming systems that contain a program paragrapher (or "prettyprinter"), which automatically formats programs according to some logical rules.

All the programs or program fragments that appear in this book comply with a set of implicit layout rules, including suitable indentation for each line, reflecting its place in the program structure, and systematic use of comments in compound statements. Taking into account the fact that a given letter character is unique, whatever its case, font, or thickness (i.e., a, A, *a*, *a*, or *A* all denote the first letter in the alphabet), we shall use different type fonts for different parts of the programs: word-symbols appear in **boldface**, identifiers in *italics*, and comments in this font. The first two conventions are the rule in most texts about Algol 60, Algol 68, or Pascal.

2.3 PROGRAM STRUCTURE

In several traditional programming languages, a program is a compilation unit (i.e., the unit processed in one execution of the compiler) in the same way that a subprogram is. This is true in Fortran and in Cobol (when subprograms exist), and partly true in PL/I. An execution unit (i.e., a self-contained executable text) is produced by linking the program with the subprograms it uses. Linking conventions between compilation units are defined, at least partly, within the language; for example, Fortran defines the COMMON statement and its use in data sharing.

The notion of a compilation unit is not defined in Pascal and is generally supposed to be implementation-dependent. The ISO *Standard* leaves open the option of naming and describing a subprogram external to the program (by way of an implementation-dependent directive; see Chap. 5), but it provides no tool for sharing data between several compilation units. All objects referenced in a program must be defined within it.

For all complete programs which appear in this book, and as a rule of wide applicability, a Pascal program is both a compilation unit and an execution unit at the same time. A link-edit phase has only to search and incorporate library subprograms of the Pascal execution-support system, which contains about 30 subprograms. Making possible the completely independent compilation of a subprogram would mean that the use of parameters could not be checked, and this would be contradictory to one of the basic points of Pascal philosophy, i.e., the use of full static type checking for the improvement of program security and reliability.

In Cobol, a program is identified with many details in the IDENTIFICATION DIVISION. Fortran does not require program identification, and in PL/I only the MAIN option specifies that some procedure constitutes the main program. In Pascal, a program is composed of a program heading (its identification) that is followed by a block (definitions and declarations of all objects used in the program, and statements) and is terminated by a period. See Fig. 2.5.

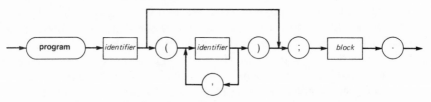

Fig. 2.5 Syntax diagram for a program.

The identifier that follows the symbol **program** is the program name, which has no meaning within the program (but may have outside, of course). The optional identifier list that follows is a parameter list for the program. Program parameters are distinct identifiers, which must be declared in the program block (with an exception explained in Sec. 9.2). The most frequent use of parameters is as file identifiers to be used in the program, and their occurrence in the program heading makes it possible to bind them with physical files or data sets in the program environment. However, the method and the meaning of this binding is implementation-defined. Only one point is specified by the ISO *Standard*: a program which reads data on the standard input device, represented by the predefined file identifier *input*, must specify this identifier as a program parameter; similarly, it must specify the predefined file identifier *output* if it writes on the standard output device. Details will be given in Sec. 9.2.

Other identifiers may appear as program parameters, but their meaning and the way in which they are bound to corresponding external entities are implementation-dependent; i.e., some implementations may allow the use of some sorts of identifiers which are not legal in other implementations. In fact, the program heading constitutes the interface between a Pascal program and its environment, and this is the reason why this part of the language depends most on that environment. In some implementations, program parameters can be constants, and they constitute a way of parameterizing the program just before execution. In others, they can be subprogram identifiers for procedures or functions external to the program (only their heading appears in the program, followed by the nonstandard directive "external"). The same method is sometimes used even with ordinary variables.

A block is roughly equivalent to the couple DATA DIVISION—PROCEDURE DIVISION of Cobol. The correspondence to the body of a procedure in PL/I or of a subroutine in Fortran is looser, since both languages allow the use of several forms of implicit declarations, and do not establish a clear dividing line between declarations and executable statements. In Pascal, all objects used in the program must be defined or declared before their use (except those objects which are predefined or predeclared in the language). These objects include files and variables, as in Cobol, but many other things too.

The order in which the different parts occur is imperative (see Fig. 2.6): it corresponds to a logic of progressive program construction (labels excepted), each declaration or definition part needing the preceding ones in order to be built. All parts except the last one may be empty, as can be observed in the label declaration part illustrated in Fig. 2.7.

Constant definitions and variable declarations will be covered in Sec. 2.4. Type definitions begin in Chap. 3, and continue in Chaps. 8, 10, 12, 13, and 14. Procedure and function declarations are explained in Chap. 5.

The statement part (Fig. 2.8) is also called the body of the block; it is its executable part, constituted by a sequence of statements separated by semicolons and enclosed within the symbols **begin** and **end**. This construct is also called a compound statement; see Sec. 2.7.

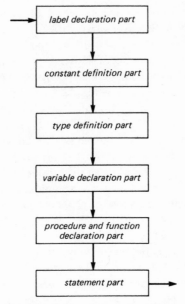

Fig. 2.6 Syntax diagram for a block.

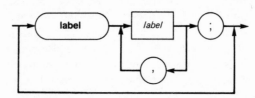

Fig. 2.7 Syntax diagram for the label-declaration part.

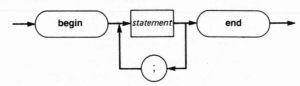

Fig. 2.8 Syntax diagram for the statement part.

The symbol **begin** in the program block marks the entry point of the program. Some operations are automatically made when this entry point is activated (see Sec. 9.2).

Example 2.7:   Two Very Simple Pascal Programs

program *TheZeroth* {a minimal, empty program};
begin
end {TheZeroth}.

program *TheFirst* (*output*)
{This is a complete Pascal program.};
begin
writeln ('*This is a very simple Pascal program*')
end {TheFirst}.

REMARKS

1. *TheZeroth* is a good test for measuring the time spent by a Pascal compiler and by a Pascal run-time executive in doing nothing (i.e., the Pascal system overhead). This program reads no data, computes nothing, and prints no result.

2. The heading of program *TheFirst* contains the standard file identifier *output* as a parameter because this program prints onto this file (without ever naming it); the character string enclosed within parentheses is printed by the predefined procedure *writeln*, called in the only statement of the program.

3. In both programs, all definition and declaration parts are empty; *output* and *writeln* are predefined identifiers and must not be declared. In both programs, the statement part contains only one statement, which in *TheZeroth* is an empty statement.

2.4   CONSTANTS AND VARIABLES

A constant is a denotation of some value in a set of universal values: *1* denotes the integral value "1"; *true* denotes the logical value "true." In Fortran, Cobol, Basic, or PL/I, constant denotations are only denotations for universal values. In most modern programming languages, the programmer can also establish an identity relation between an identifier and a universal value; i.e., constants may be named.

In Pascal, these identity relations are established in constant definitions in the constant-definition part of a block. See Fig. 2.9.

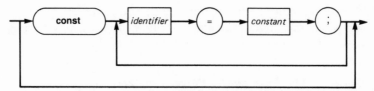

Fig. 2.9 Syntax diagram for the constant-definition part.

The designated values may be integers, reals, characters, or strings (see Fig. 2.10), but an additional way for introducing nonuniversal constants will be seen in Sec. 3.3. Only the constants that denote integer or real values may be signed. An important and regrettable deficiency of Pascal must be noted here: a constant cannot be defined as a combination of other constants, either universal or named (except by identity or with sign inversion). For example, it would be extremely useful to define some constant *area* as being the product of two other constants, *length* and *width*. These combinations can only be described in comments, with no guarantee of validity.

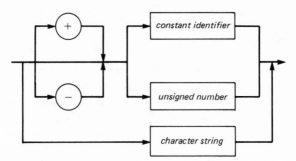

Fig. 2.10 Syntax diagram for a constant.

Example 2.8:   Constant-Definition Part

const
   pi = *3.1415926536* {universal value; a real};
   theend = '*** *End of program* ***';
   nbplaces = *4*; *nbcolors* = *6*;
   nbpins = *24* {nbpins = nbplaces * nbcolors};
   endcharacter = '.';

REMARKS

1. The denotation of a constant value implies its type: *pi* is a real constant, *theend* is a string constant, *endcharacter* is a char constant, and the three others are integer constants.

2. Nothing prevents a comment from being a lie; if *nbpins* is defined as being 25, the preceding constant-definition part would remain a perfectly valid one.

Variables are objects whose value can change during program execution. In contrast to Fortran, Basic, or PL/I, the declaration of all variables is compulsory in Pascal. (This is true also in Cobol, but in Pascal all objects must be defined or declared.) There is no implicit or explicit relation between the spelling of a variable identifier and the type of value it possesses. The declaration of a variable associates it with a type, i.e., a set of values which can be assigned to the variable (Fig. 2.11). According to its type, a variable may be *simple* (simple types are described in Chap. 3) or *compound* (structured types are discussed in Chaps. 8, 10, 12, 13, and 14). After its declaration, and before any assignment is made to it, the value of a variable is undefined; i.e., it is an error to try to use it.

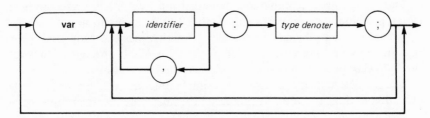

Fig. 2.11 Syntax diagram for the variable-declaration part.

Except for the case when it occurs in a variable-declaration part (or possibly in the program parameter list), all occurrences of a variable identifier are confined to the statement part, and constitute references to the variable: *read* accesses if the identifier occurs in an expression, *write* accesses if it occurs on the left side of the assignment symbol in an assignment statement or in some subprogram calls (actual variable parameter, some parameters for several predefined procedures).

Example 2.9

program *TheSecond* (*input*, *output*);
    var *x,y*: *integer* {two integer variables};
    begin {Here x and y have undefined values.}
        read(*x,y*) {Two values are read from the standard input device and assigned to x and y, respectively.};
        writeln ('*the sum of*', *x*, '*and*', *y*, '*is*', *x+y*)
    end {TheSecond}.

REMARKS

The predefined identifier *integer* is the name of the type that contains the set of integral values; x and y are two variables declared in the variable-declaration part of the program block and referred to by the *read* statement (a *write* access to the variables) and the *writeln* statement (a *read* access).

2.5 STANDARD PROCEDURE CALLS

Standard procedures are subprograms which are predefined in the language, and consequently are known by every *Standard*-conforming compiler. Such subprograms exist in all languages, and the most frequent example is that of the input-output subprograms: READ and WRITE in Fortran, Basic,* and Cobol and GET and PUT in PL/I. However, in these languages, the corresponding subprograms are generally called using special syntactic constructs instead of the ordinary procedure call statement. In Pascal, the construct has the general appearance of a procedure call, except for a few minor details.

The input-output subprograms of Pascal must be briefly presented here, even if procedures are fully covered later in Chap. 5 and input-output is treated in general in Chaps. 8 and 9. Examples 2.7 and 2.9 have already used input-output, and we cannot wait until Chap. 8 to write usable programs. However, the following presentation will provide just the bare outlines.

The call of a standard procedure is a simple statement which commands the execution of this procedure. It comprises the procedure identifier followed by a list of parameters within parentheses (except for *writeln*, which may be called without parameters).

2.5.1 INPUT: *read*($v1,v2, \ldots , vn$)

Parameters vi are references to variables. This procedure call causes the reading of the n values $val1, val2, \ldots, valn$ on the standard input device, and assigns these n values to the n variables denoted by $v1, v2, \ldots, vn$. The type of $vali$ must be the same as the type of vi: integer, real, or character. When a vi is a reference to an integer or real variable, reading proceeds as follows: all leading spaces and line ends (carriage return, end of card) are skipped; as soon as a nonblank character is encountered, $vali$ begins to be built if this character is a sign or a digit (otherwise it is an error, and the program stops with an error message); reading stops as soon as a character is encountered that cannot occur in an unsigned number (according to the syntax diagram of Sec. 2.2). When a vi is a reference to a character variable, $vali$ is the value of the first character not already read by the preceding reading, whatever it is.

*Basic uses PRINT instead of WRITE.

2.5.2 BUFFERED OUTPUT: *write(e1,e2, . . ., en)*

Parameters *ei* are expressions (a reference to a variable is an expression, the simplest one) whose value may be that of an integer, a real, a character, a Boolean, or a string. The values of the parameters are appended, in a standard format, to an output buffer associated with the standard output device. The physical writing of the buffer is not done by the predefined procedure *write*.

2.5.3 ACTUAL OUTPUT: *writeln(e1,e2, . . ., en)*

If its parameter list is empty, *writeln* causes the buffer associated with the standard output device to be actually output (printed, online or offline) and resets it. If a parameter list is present, *writeln* works as *write* (appending the parameters to the contents of the buffer), then as if it had no parameter (flushing the buffer). Writing an empty buffer prints a blank line.

Example 2.10

```
program TheThird (input, output)
  {This program demonstrates how read and write work on the standard
      devices.};
  var a,c,f: integer;
    b, e: real; d: char {standard type for characters};
begin {TheThird}
  read(a,b,c,d,e); read(f)
  {This is strictly equivalent to read(a); read(b); . . .; read(f), or to
      read(a,b,c,d,e,f).};
  write('The three integer values are'); writeln(a,c,f);
  writeln('The sum of the two real values', b, ' and', e, ' is', b+e);
  writeln('The character value of d is printed between two',
      'stars: *', d,
      '*')
end {TheThird}.
```

If the standard input device contains the following character sequence:

First line: 1 1.0 −1−0.1e−2

Second line: 4

and if the implementation-defined default format writes integers in eight positions and reals in floating-point notation with six fractional digits, the following lines are printed on the standard output device:

The three integer values are   1   −1   4

The sum of the two real values 0.100000e+01 and 0.100000e−02 is 0.101000e+.01

The character value of *d* is printed between two stars: • •

With the following data on the standard input device:

First line: 1   1.0

Second line: −1

Third line: −0.1E−2   4

the following lines are printed on the standard output device:

The three integer values are   1   −1   4

The sum of the two real values 0.100000e+01 and −0.100000e−02 is 0.999000e+00

The character value of *d* is printed between two stars: • •

REMARKS

1. The sequence of two procedure calls

   write('The three integer values are'); writeln(a, c, f)

   is exactly equivalent to the single statement

   writeln('The three integer values are', a, c, f)

2. When a character string does not fit on one line in the program, as in the last call to *writeln*, it can be cut into two lines, which are juxtaposed in the output buffer.

3. With the first set of data, the reading of the value −1 into c stops at the minussignthatfollowsthe1; d, of type *char*, thus takes the value '−'. With the second set of data, the reading of −1 stops at the end of the line. The corresponding character value, a space, is then assigned to d.

4. There is no relation between the format of calls to *read* and that of input data: reading is only driven by the type of the variables to which data must be assigned.

5. Of course, output results could be presented in other ways, with full control by the programmer. This will be explained in Sec. 9.4.

2.6 ASSIGNMENT STATEMENTS

The assignment statement causes a (new) value to be given to a variable (or to a component of a compound variable) or to a function identifier within the body of this function. Only the first case is considered presently.

Syntax

The rule for the assignment statement appears in Fig. 2.12. The term "variable access" is the shorthand used in the ISO *Standard* for "access to a variable," which could also be called "reference to a variable." A variable access is a variable identifier in the case of a simple variable, or of a compound variable considered as a whole. Otherwise, it denotes a variable component which depends on the structure of the variable, and that will be considered in the corresponding chapters. Note that Pascal does not use the equal sign for denoting the assignment. This avoids confusion with the comparison operator for equality (a notation like $I = I + 1$, although legal in Fortran or PL/I, hurts common sense), and the chosen symbol, $:=$, has been traditional in many languages since Algol 60.

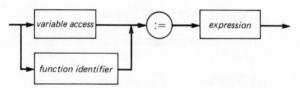

Fig. 2.12 Syntax diagram for an assignment statement.

Semantics

If x is a variable access of type T and y an expression whose value is assignment-compatible with T (see below),
then $\{P_y^x\}\ x := y\ \{P\}$

This means that the antecedent of the assignment statement may be deduced from its consequent by substituting the right-hand side expression for all free occurrences of the left-hand side variable access, as, for example, in

$\{x + 1 = 10\}\ x := x + 1\ \{x = 10\}$

REMARKS

1. The order in which the two sides of the assignment statement are evaluated is implementation-dependent; i.e., a correct program must not de-

pend on this order. This is important only if the variable access contains an expression whose value may be modified by the evaluation of the right-hand side expression, or vice versa. Such a dangerous situation can only occur if functions modify their parameters or some global variables, by a so-called side effect.

2. The value of the variable is undefined immediately after its declaration, and remains so until a value of the needed type is assigned to it, either by an assignment statement or by a call to an input procedure.

3. Like Fortran and Basic, but unlike Cobol and PL/I, Pascal contains no multiple assignment.

Although we have not yet explained exactly what the concept of a type is in Pascal, and although the various available data types are presented much later in this book, it is necessary, for the sake of completeness here, to define the meaning of *assignment-compatible*.

A value of type *T2* is assignment-compatible with a type *T1* if:

- *T1* and *T2* are the same type and are not file types (or do not contain file components); or

- *T1* is the type *real* and *T2* is the type *integer*; or

- *T1* and *T2* are ordinal types and the value of type *T2* is in the closed interval defined by *T1* (see Sec. 3.5); or

- *T1* and *T2* are compatible set types and all elements of the value of type *T2* belong to the closed interval defined by the base type of *T1* (see Chap. 13); or

- *T1* and *T2* are compatible string types (see Sec. 10.5).

For the present time, it is sufficient to remember that if x is declared of type *integer* and y of type *real*, the assignment $y := x$ is legal, while the assignment $x := y$ is illegal, because the type *real* is not assignment-compatible with the type *integer*. This is because there would be a loss of information in the conversion of a real value into an integer value and because there are at least two sensible ways to do this conversion: by rounding or by truncation. Consequently, this must be explicitly specified in the program by way of a predefined type-transfer function (see Sec. 4.4).

2.7 COMPOUND STATEMENTS

A compound statement combines several statements which are to be executed in sequence and are considered as a unique statement. It is the first and simplest structuring for statements that we present for Pascal. In Fortran and Basic, the sequentiality of executed statements is denoted by the end of statement at the end of a line; PL/I denotes this with the semicolon that terminates every statement. The grouping of several statements does not exist in Fortran and Basic (at least in the standard versions of these languages), which have no control structures. It is done in a very limited way in Cobol by the grouping of statements in a sentence terminated by a period; however, a grouping cannot be used inside another grouping. In PL/I, the compound statement structure is the DO group in its most simple form (without loop control), and it has almost the same properties as in Pascal. It is a necessary structure in these two languages because statements structures are generally not fully parenthesized.

Syntax

Note in Fig. 2.13 that the semicolon is a statement separator in Pascal, as in the languages of the Algol family, and not a statement terminator, as in PL/I; moreover, **begin** and **end** are not statements, but only statement parentheses.

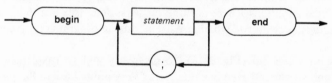

Fig. 2.13 Syntax diagram for a compound statement.

Semantics

Given the compound statement

> **begin** $S1$; $S2$; . . .; Sn **end**
> if, for all i from 1 to n, $\{Pi-1\}$ Si $\{Pi\}$,
> then $\{Po\}$ compound statement $\{Pn\}$.

This means that every statement Si may be considered as an assertion transformer (Si transforms $Pi-1$ into Pi) and that in sequential execution the consequent of one statement constitutes the antecedent of the following statement. This allows us to deduce the antecedent and consequent of the compound statement itself, and then to consider it as a "black box," described only as another assertion transformer. This works pretty well for the whole of Pascal, except for one statement only, the **goto** statement, because it breaks the sequential execution order.

2.8 OTHER SIMPLE STATEMENTS

Simple statements are the basic building blocks of the executable part of a program. They can be combined, by various means, in larger structured blocks. We have already considered in Sec. 2.6 a first simple statement, that is, the *assignment statement.* Another fundamental simple statement is the *procedure call statement*, which will be studied in Chap. 5. Let us examine here two more simple statements in Pascal.

The *empty statement* has an extremely austere syntax; see Fig. 2.14. Its semantics is in the same vein:

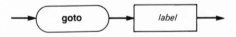

Fig. 2.14 Syntax diagram for an empty statement.

{P} empty statement {P}

That is, an empty statement contains nothing and does nothing. It serves only (1) to simplify some syntactic descriptions; (2) to allow a semicolon in front of a statement terminator such as the symbol **end**; (3) to describe explicitly some normal situations where nothing must be done (see Sec. 6.1); or (4) to define dummy procedures, which are useful during program construction and debugging.

The **goto** statement (Fig. 2.15), so necessary and so frequently used in Fortran and Basic (and even in Cobol), is of very limited use in Pascal because of the richness of control structures, and **goto**-less programs constitute the rule. Note that the symbol **goto** is a single word-symbol.

$$\longrightarrow \left(\quad \text{goto} \quad \right) \longrightarrow \boxed{\quad \textit{label} \quad} \longrightarrow$$

Fig. 2.15 Syntax diagram for a **goto** statement.

The **goto** statement indicates that further processing must continue at the program point specified by the label (i.e., at the statement prefixed by the label; see Sec. 5.1.3). Important restrictions must be satisfied, and they limit the use of the **goto** statement, considered a source of anarchy in programs. The label that is specified in a **goto** statement may prefix only:

1. One of the constituting statements of a compound statement which contains the **goto**.

2. A structured statement which contains the **goto**.

3. A statement at the outmost level in the statement part of a block embedding the block that contains the **goto**. Thus it is permitted to exit from

a procedure to an embedding procedure or to the main program, but this cannot cause branching into a structured statement.

In this last case, all blocks thus left have their activation terminated (this point will be considered again in Chap. 5).

Consequently, a **goto** statement cannot be used for jumping into a structured statement or a subprogram from outside, or even from one branch of a conditional statement to another one. Its normal use is limited to error handling within loops or subprograms, when the current processing cannot reasonably continue and must be terminated prematurely and definitely. As a further way of discouraging the programmer from using them, labels are not attractive things: they are neither variables nor constants nor values; they have hardly any mnemonic quality; and they must be declared at the very beginning of their block, as if to make the programmer feel ashamed. It is left as an exercise for the reader to count the number of **labels** and **gotos** that appear in all the examples of the present book (the following example excepted).

Example 2.11

{This program has no other meaning than to be an inventory of all the constructs already seen.}
program *TheFourth* (*input*, *output*);
   Label *13*;
   var *x*, *y*: *integer*;
begin {The statement part is in fact a compound statement.}
   read(*y*);
   x := *y* {an assignment statement};
   writeln('*value of x* =', *x*);
   goto *13* {a goto statement, within a compound statement};
{The following statement will never be executed.}
   y := *x*;
13: {This is an empty statement between the colon and the left brace.}
end {TheFourth}.

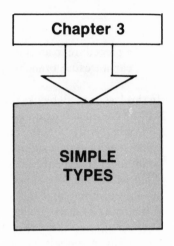

Chapter 3

SIMPLE
TYPES

Programs to be run on computers use three different classes of universal values:

- Numbers, for doing computations
- Logical values, for doing logical tests
- Printable characters, for communication with humans

These three classes should appear in all programming languages, but some problems of computer representation for these values interfere, and the situation is not so clear. Although only two logical values exist, they are not always explicitly present: Fortran has a type LOGICAL, with values .TRUE. and .FALSE., but Basic has nothing comparable, PL/I uses bit strings of length 1, and Cobol offers only a substitute for logical values with its condition variables.

In the case of characters, the situation is complicated by the wide variety of existing character sets. In Cobol, the mode DISPLAY denotes a character representation for a variable, but the chosen character set is supposed to be implementation-defined. Fortran has no notation for a variable which denotes one character (or more), and it is only in input-output formats that a particular interpretation may be defined for a character-valued variable.

For numbers, the architecture of arithmetic units prescribes several different representations: integer numbers are a bound subrange of N; real numbers are a finite and bound subset of R; fixed-point numbers may have also a decimal representation, packed or not. Fortran has integers, reals, and double-precision numbers; Basic has integers and reals; Cobol allows all possible specifications, although it does not know reals, at least in its standard definition; PL/I allows a mix of Fortran and Cobol, plus other possibilities for fixed-point binary numbers. For increasing the precision of computations, multiple-length real numbers exist in Fortran and PL/I, and are implemented either by hardware, if available, or by software (packages or microprogramming).

Thus, numbers are generally overspecified in classical programming languages, but these languages offer little or no means for classifying data in distinct categories. In contrast, Pascal simplifies the specification of universal values, while also providing tools for defining additional sets of elementary values and for building structured values from simple ones, using type constructors. In this chapter, we present the definition and properties of types in general; then we detail simple types.

3.1 TYPE DEFINITIONS

A type specifies the domain of the values that can be assigned to variables of this type, and implicitly determines the set of operators that apply to these values. As a general rule, both operands of a (binary) operator must be of the same type, or of compatible types (an exception is shown in Chap. 13). This gives the compiler many tools for verifying the coherence of expressions and for determining the exact meaning of several ambiguous operators. The partition of all values into distinct classes, provided by the type concept, is one of the most essential contributions made by Pascal to programming languages. To declare a variable of some given type is to state about this variable a permanently valid assertion, which the compiler can verify automatically, generally at compilation time or in some cases by cheap run-time checks. This is one of the best tools given to programmers for increasing their confidence in the programs they write.

A type is described in a *type denoter*, which may appear either in the type-definition part of a block, in which case the type is given a name for identifying it later, or in a variable declaration, in which case the type is anonymous and cannot be referenced elsewhere. Every type denoter introduces a completely new type, distinct from the others, even if this new type happens to have a domain of values identical to that of another type. Two types are identical only if they are the same type, or if one type is defined as being the other one, which thus becomes known under two distinct names. Note that this capability of naming types does not exist at all in the four programming languages taken as bases for comparison.

For the sake of completeness, we define here the concept of *type compatibility*, although it uses some notions covered only in subsequent chapters. Two types, *T1* and *T2*, are said to be compatible if:

1. *T1* is the same type as *T2*, or

2. *T1* is a subrange of *T2*, or vice versa (see Sec. 3.5), or

3. *T1* and *T2* are subranges of the same host type, or

4. *T1* and *T2* are set types with compatible base types (see Chap. 13) and *T1* and *T2* are both unpacked, or both packed, or

5. *T1* and *T2* are strings with the same number of components (see Sec. 10.5).

The type-definition part of a block has the syntax shown in Fig. 3.1. The type-definition part ends when a new declaration part or the statement part of the block begins. It defines all type identifiers that are local to the block.

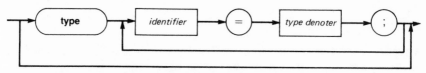

Fig. 3.1 Syntax diagram for the type-definition part.

Pascal types are distributed in three classes, as illustrated in Fig. 3.2. The three classes each specify one or several forms of type descriptions, or come down to a type identifier. *Simple types*, with their associated operators, are covered in subsequent sections. *Structured types* are in fact type constructors, and appear in Chaps. 8, 10, 12, and 13. A *pointer type*, described in Chap. 14, is also a type constructor, but with some properties that make it distinct from structured types.

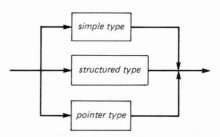

Fig. 3.2 Syntax diagram for a type denoter.

3.2 SOME GENERALITIES CONCERNING SIMPLE TYPES

Simple types are provided as several basic predefined types for the universal values and a type constructor for new, nonuniversal values, defined by enumeration. A value of a simple type is simple, i.e., atomic or scalar; it cannot be split into components. Simple types may be classified as shown in Fig. 3.3. The first line of the diagram allows the definition of a new simple type as being identical to an existing one, already defined.

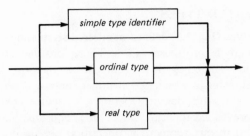

Fig. 3.3 Syntax diagram for a simple type.

Ordinal types (see Fig. 3.4) are types whose values may be enumerated: they constitute ordered, bound sets, and their domain of values is finite. Three universal operators, denoted as *predefined functions*, exist for every ordinal type.

1. *succ(x)*: If x is an expression of some ordinal type T, *succ(x)*, if it is defined, is an expression of the same type, which denotes the value that immediately follows x in the domain of values of T (the successor of x), according to the order relation defined in T. It is an error if this value does not exist, i.e., when x is the maximum value in T.

2. *pred(x)* is defined in a way similar to *succ(x)*, as the predecessor, if it exists, of x in the domain of values of T. It is an error when x is the minimum value in T.

3. *ord(x)* is an integer expression, which denotes the ordinal number associated with x. Ordinal numbers are defined for each ordinal type in the subsequent sections.

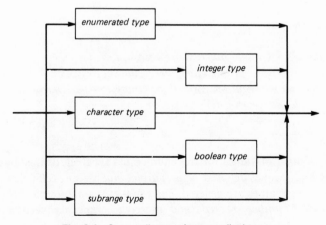

Fig. 3.4 Syntax diagram for an ordinal type.

3.3 ENUMERATED TYPES

An enumerated type (Fig. 3.5) defines an ordered set of values by enumerating the identifiers that denote these values. These identifiers become constant identifiers, and are defined by their occurrence in the type denoter (see Sec. 2.4). The textual order in which the identifiers appear determines the order relation for the values they denote. Operators for enumerated types comprise only the three predefined functions *succ*, *pred*, and *ord*, which apply to all ordinal types, and the six comparison operators. The ordinal number of the first value is 0, and the ordinal number of any other value is 1 plus the ordinal number of its predecessor.

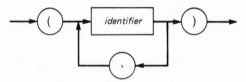

Fig. 3.5 Syntax diagram for an enumerated type.

Enumerated types, introduced by Pascal, are used mainly for avoiding esoteric representations for information local to a program, which do not constitute universal values. The resulting explicit representation is much better than the traditional use of integer values, and constitutes an important step towards more readable programs, much as do named constants. The skeptical reader is invited to inventory, in the examples appearing in the present book, all uses of integer representations or of anonymous constants (except 0, 1, *true*, and *false*).

Example 3.1

{type-definition part}
type
    civilstatus = (*single, married, divorced, widowed*);
    rainbow = (*violet, purple, blue, green, yellow, amber, red*);
    iostatus = (*timeout, busy, watchdog, emptystore, parityerror, addresserror,-*
        cadenceerror, nomorepaper);

REMARKS

1. The domain of values for the enumerated type *rainbow* is made of the only seven values denoted *violet, purple, blue, green, yellow, amber,* and *red*. These values are ordered; i.e., *violet* < *purple* < *blue* < *green* < *yellow* < *amber* < *red*, and moreover, *violet* = *pred*(*purple*) =

$pred(pred(blue))$ = . . . ; or $yellow$ = $succ(green)$ = $succ(succ($
$succ(succ(violet))))$; and so on.

2. The constant identifiers that denote values of an enumerated type are
   local to the block in which the type denoter occurs. Consequently,

   a. These constant identifiers cannot be redefined in the same block.

   b. They are not known outside the block in which they are defined nor,
      by implication, outside the program; i.e., their values cannot be read
      or written.

   If, in the preceding example, the following type definition is added:

   $primarycolor$ = $(blue, yellow, red)$;

   it is erroneous because the three constant identifiers $blue$, $yellow$, and
   red are already defined in the same context in type $rainbow$.

3. Enumerated types are completely tight; i.e., two different types have
   nothing in common, and two values of different types cannot even be
   compared.

3.4 PREDEFINED ORDINAL TYPES

Predefined types are simple types, proceeding from universal values. They
are called $required\ types$ in the ISO $Standard$, and we avoid the term "standard types" because of the possible confusion with what is standard and
what is not. Of course, all that appears in the $Standard$ is standard. The
corresponding identifiers are supposed to be defined in the environment of
the program.

3.4.1 THE TYPE $INTEGER$

The predefined type identifier $integer$ denotes the ordinal type whose domain
of values is a subset of integral numbers, bound by values $-maxint$ and
$+maxint$; $maxint$ is a predefined positive integer constant whose value is
implementation-defined. Normally, $maxint$ is the greatest integer that can be
represented on the computer. Values of type $integer$ are denoted using the
syntax diagram of Sec. 2.2. Operators on objects of type $integer$ include all
relation operators, appropriate arithmetic operators (see Chap. 4), and, of
course, the three predefined functions usable for every ordinal type. The ordinal number of an integer is this integer itself.

The type $integer$ may be considered as a particular enumerated type, whose
values are not denoted using constant identifiers, but with the usual notation
for decimal numbers. One reason this type is predefined is that it cannot be

defined in the language; the other reason is the existence of operators which need integer operands.

3.4.2 THE TYPE *BOOLEAN*

The predefined type identifier *Boolean* denotes the ordinal type whose domain of values is made up of only two values, denoted *false* and *true*. Operators defined on Boolean objects include logical operators (see Sec. 4.2), all relational operators, and the three predefined functions *pred*, *succ*, and *ord*. All this works as if the type *Boolean* were defined as

$$Boolean = (false, true);$$

i.e., *false* < *true*, *ord*(*false*) = 0 and *ord*(*true*) = 1.

However, the type *Boolean* must be predefined, because all comparison operators, whatever the type of their operands, yield a value of type *Boolean*, and because some control structures of Pascal need an expression of type *Boolean* (see Chaps. 6 and 7). These two situations account for most occurrences of implicitly boolean expressions or values. However, the explicit declaration of an object of type *Boolean* is less frequent in Pascal than in many other languages, because enumerated types provide a more general feature. As will be demonstrated in several examples in this book, the use of a multiple-valued status indicator is generally preferred to the use of several boolean flags.

3.4.3 THE TYPE *CHAR*

The predefined type identifier *char* denotes the ordinal type whose domain of values is an implementation-defined character set. Some of these values may have no printable representation. Remember that a constant of type *char* is denoted by the character, enclosed within quotes.

Since Pascal does not define a particular character set (nor does it assume the presence of some well-known or standardized set), the particular set of characters that may be supposed available, and their order relation, are implementation-defined. However, an implementation-independent Pascal program may rely on the following relations, which must be verified in any implementation:

- Digit characters are always present, ordered, and contiguous, so that

$$'0' = pred('1') = pred(pred('2')) = \ldots$$

- Letter characters exist, but possibly in only one case, lower or upper; lowercase letters, if they are present, are ordered, but not necessarily contiguous, i.e., '*a*' < '*b*' < '*c*' < . . . ; similarly, uppercase letters, if they are present, are ordered, but not necessarily contiguous, i.e., '*A*' < '*B*' < '*C*' < . . . .

These relations are verified by all currently used character sets, but nothing more can be said, for example, about the order relation between a lowercase letter and the corresponding uppercase one, or about the respective positions of letters and digits, or about the position of the space within the character set, and so on. The weak relation stated about letters comes from the EBCDIC set, where *succ*('*I*') ≠ '*J*', for example. Although the Pascal standard has been established by ISO, it does not use the ISO standard character set, whose American variant, called ASCII, is probably the most widely available set, with many desirable properties.

Operators defined by the type *char* are the ordinary predefined functions *succ*, *pred*, and *ord*. The ordinal number of a character is implementation-defined and is such that the order relation between two characters is the same as that between their ordinal numbers. An additional predefined function, *chr*(x), yields the character whose ordinal number is x, if this character exists. Like the type *integer*, the type *char* may be considered as a particular enumerated type whose values are not denoted by identifiers, but by use of a special notation.

3.5   SUBRANGE TYPES

A subrange type defines a new type whose domain of values is a subrange of the domain of values of another ordinal type, called its *host type*. The type denoter specifies the lower and upper bounds of the subrange as constants of the same type, which is the host type of the subrange type. (See Fig. 3.6.) They are part of the domain of values of the subrange type. The lower bound must not be greater than the upper bound.

Fig. 3.6   Syntax diagram for a subrange type.

Variables of a subrange type inherit all the properties of the host type, i.e., the order relation, the operators, and functions. The definition of a subrange type is a particularly important case of a permanent assertion stated about a variable, because

1. It is self-documented and manifest.

2. It is automatically verifiable: either the compiler checks at compile time that, for every assignment whose left-hand part is of a subrange type, the assigned expression does not fall outside the declared bounds, or it produces some code (generally simple and cheap) which checks this property at run time.

Subrange types are especially useful whenever the host type is the pre-defined type *integer*, because they constitute one of the simplest and safest tools for detecting logic errors in programs. In fact, it is extremely infrequent that a program uses the type *integer* in itself, and its occurrence in a declaration generally can be considered as a symptom of lazy or even sloppy programming. Of course, to exactly define the subrange that will be necessary for a given variable generally requires some thought from the programmer, but it is really worth the trouble.

As a secondary effect, the declaration of a variable in a subrange type is a hint for the compiler that some storage may be economized. This can be very important in large structured types whose components are of a subrange type.

Example 3.2

```
{type-definition part with subranges}
type
    index     = −10..+10 {host type = integer};
    hexaletter = 'A'..'F' {host type = char};
    rainbow   = (violet,purple,blue,green,yellow,amber,red);
    warmcolor = yellow..red {host type = rainbow};
```

REMARKS

1. The host type of each subrange type is implicitly the type of the subrange bounds.

2. It would be much better for the type *index* to define some integer constant with value *10*, and to use it in the type denoter. Otherwise, what is the meaning of this value *10*? Does it have a relation to the base of decimal numbers, or to the number of characters in a name, or to something else?

3. If a subrange type is defined as *lowerbound..upperbound*, *pred*(*lowerbound*) and *succ*(*upperbound*) may well exist, but they do not lie in the subrange. In fact, *pred* and *succ* yield a value which is an expression of the host type, if it exists. With a variable *w* of type *warmcolor*, for example, if *w* = *yellow*, *pred*(*w*) exists but is not of type *warmcolor*; it is of type *rainbow*, and cannot be assigned to a variable of type *warmcolor*. If *w* = *red*, *succ*(*w*) does not exist, and its evaluation is an error.

3.6 THE PREDEFINED TYPE *REAL*

The predefined type identifier *real* denotes the simple type whose domain of values is a bound and finite subset, implementation-defined, of real numbers.

Values of this type are denoted according to the syntax diagram of Sec. 2.2. This type is atomic, but not ordinal, and functions *pred*, *succ*, and *ord* do not apply.

Operators defined by the type *real* are the relational operators and the arithmetic operators. Two conversion functions are provided for transforming a value of type *real* into a value of type *integer* (see Sec. 4.4). Other usual arithmetic functions are predefined.

Note that Pascal, which does not pretend to be a universal programming language, does not provide several different precisions for reals, since one cannot guarantee a compatible implementation on different computers. Because the type *real* is not ordinal, it cannot serve as the host type of a subrange type. This is because, in contrast to subranges of the type *integer*, the corresponding concept would be costly to implement.

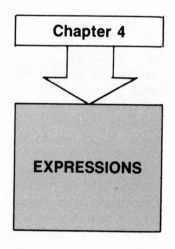

Chapter 4

EXPRESSIONS

An expression consists of one value or of several values and valid operators to be evaluated as a single value. The values used can be denoted by constants, variables, or variable components, or can be returned by functions. When several values are to be evaluated as an expression, they must be of a simple type or of a set type. Set expressions and operators will be covered later in Chap. 13.

4.1 PRECEDENCE AND ASSOCIATIVITY OF OPERATORS

An expression is evaluated according to rules defined in the language (*operator precedence*) or by mathematics (*operator associativity*). Four precedence levels are displayed in the syntactic diagram shown in Fig. 4.1. Unsigned constants were described in Sec. 2.2. Function designators appear in Sec. 4.3, set constructors in Chap. 13, and bound identifiers in Sec. 10.7; variable accesses are described in Chaps. 8, 10, 12, and 14.

Operators are listed below in the order of decreasing precedence:

Boolean negation		Highest precedence
Multiplying operators	*, /, **div, mod,** ∧	
Adding operators	+, −, ∨	
Relational operators	=, ≠, ≤, <, >, ≥	Lowest precedence

Remember that the ISO-*Standard* preferred representation uses different character combinations for ¬, ∧, ∨, ≠, ≤, and ≥ (see Sec. 2.2). Contrary to their use in many programming languages, logical operators in Pascal are at the same level as arithmetic operators, i.e., ∧ with multiplying operators

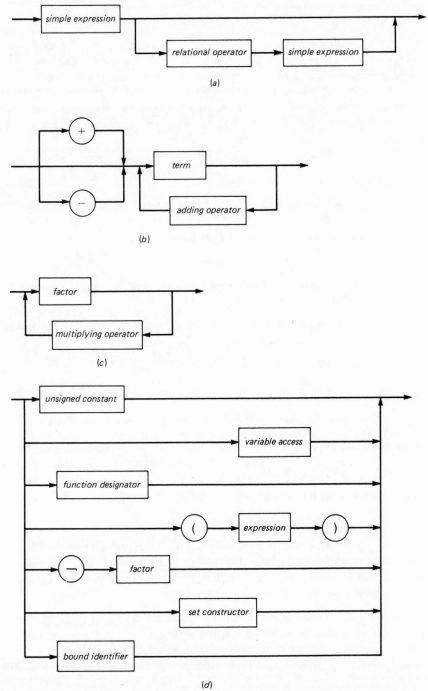

Fig. 4.1 The four precedence levels: (a) expression; (b) simple expression; (c) term; and (d) factor.

and $\vee$ with adding operators. This was done to allow for use of comparison operators with boolean values, especially $=$ for the boolean equivalence. An unfortunate consequence is that parentheses are needed around some comparisons in Pascal, where other languages do not need them. However, since an expression is valid only if every operator has operands that are compatible with the type it requires (see Sec. 3.1), most possible errors are caught by the compiler.

Example 4.1

If a, b, and c are variable identifiers of type *integer* (or subrange thereof):

$a + 1$ is a simple expression (of type *integer*);

$a \leqslant b$ is an expression (of type *Boolean*);

$-b/2 * a$ is a simple expression (of type *real*: see Sec. 4.2), evaluated as $(((-b)/2) * a)$ and not as $(-b)/(2 * a)$;

$(a + b) \vee c$ is an incorrect simple expression (although syntactically valid) because of a type incompatibility;

$(a - b)$ is a factor (of type *integer*).

REMARKS

Every expression becomes a factor when enclosed within parentheses. This allows the programmer to write any expression, however complicated. Thus, the Fortran expression

A .EQ. B .AND. A .GE. C

must be written in Pascal as

$(a = b) \wedge (a \geqslant c)$

Anyway, parentheses cost nothing, and complicated expressions are very infrequent in normal programs, so it is suggested that the programmer use parentheses freely to completely avoid reading ambiguities and potential errors.

The elementary components of an expression are described by the "factor" rule. Possible choices include an unsigned constant, i.e., a constant (according to the rule of Sec. 2.4) without a sign or the symbol **nil**, which denotes a value of any pointer type (see Chap. 14). Another possible choice is a variable access (in which case the value of the denoted variable is used), i.e., a variable identifier (if the expression contains no operator), a simple variable identifier, a bound identifier (Sec. 10.7), or a chain of references denoting a component of a structured variable. The syntax of such a chain appears in Fig. 4.2, but

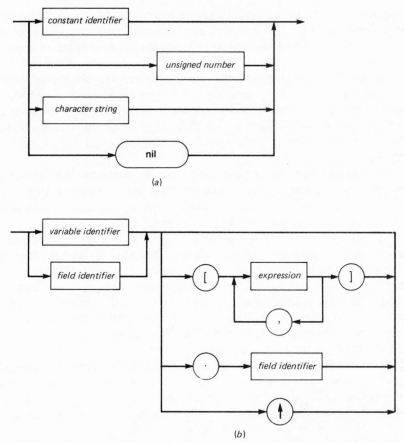

Fig. 4.2 Some elementary components of an expression: (a) unsigned constant and (b) variable access.

the constituting elements of the rule are covered in detail in the chapters corresponding to the designated data structures. Function designators are covered in Sec. 4.3 and set constructors in Chap. 13.

The type of an expression results from the types of its component factors, from the nature of the operators involved (for example, a comparison operator always yields a value of type *Boolean*), and from application of the rules of type compatibility defined in Sec. 3.1. Thus, any factor whose type is a subrange of some host type T is considered to be of type T. The "expansion" of a subrange type to its host type is done automatically (and this implies no work), while the "contraction" back to the subrange type is done just before assignment to a variable of a subrange type (and this implies a run-time check in most cases).

The value delivered by an expression of type *integer* is mathematically exact if the mathematical result is within the subrange $[-maxint, +maxint]$; otherwise, it cannot be computed, and an error is detected. The value delivered by an expression of type *real* is always only approximate. (*Real* operations are exact operations dealing with approximate numbers; i.e., they return approximate results). The precision of *real* computations depends on the particular properties of the computing unit that executes the program and on the particular Pascal implementation, since it can choose to implement real numbers in simple or double precision, if both are available on the computer. The language itself does not provide any way for specifying in programs the precision desired for computation of reals, since such a specification would be too machine-dependent.

Wherever an expression or a factor of type *real* is needed, a value of type *integer* may be given; it is automatically converted. In contrast, there is no automatic means for converting a real value to an integer value, and a transfer function must be explicitly called (see Sec. 4.4).

Operator precedence partly specifies the order of operations; for example, in $a * b + c$, the multiplication is done before the addition. However, the order of evaluation of the *operands* of a binary operator is implementation-dependent: the operands may be evaluated in their textual order, in reverse order, in parallel, or even, in the case of a boolean operator, only one operand may be evaluated. For example, in $a * b + c / d$, the multiplication may be done before the division, or after, or in parallel. This means that no program may rely on this order. In a boolean expression such as $a \wedge b$ (or $a \vee b$), on some implementations only one operand is evaluated if that is enough for giving the resulting value, while on other implementations both operands are systematically evaluated. This rule forbids some compound conditions which are somewhat natural and which work on some implementations, but which fail completely on others (see, for example, Example 12.6).

4.2 ARITHMETIC, LOGICAL, AND RELATIONAL OPERATORS

Arithmetic operators fall into two categories:

- Unary operators + and −;

- Binary operators +, −, *, **div**, **mod**, and /.

The tables on pages 47 and 48 specify their meanings and the types of their operands. Note that integer subrange types do not appear, since a value of such a type is automatically considered to be of type *integer*, as seen in the preceding section. Note also that there is in Pascal no exponentiation operator. This was done for two main reasons: First, the type of an integer raised to an integer power could not be known at compile time, since it should be integer in the case of a positive power, and real otherwise. Second, integer exponentiations are much too easily misused by programmers, while they are not very frequently used for powers greater than 2. For this single case, Pascal provides the predefined function *sqr*; for raising a real x to a real power y, one uses $exp(ln(x)*y)$, as in Example 4.2. The operator / denotes real division, with rounding. Whatever the type of its operands, its result is real; it is an error if the divisor is zero. The operator **div** denotes integer division, with truncation towards zero: i **div** j is the integral part of the quotient $i : j$, i.e., zero if abs(i) < abs (j). The following relation holds:

$$\text{abs}(i) - \text{abs}(j) < \text{abs}((i \text{ div } j) * j) < \text{abs}(i)$$

Both operands must be of type *integer*, and it is an error if the divisor is zero. Although the result is defined even with negative operands, this is done mostly for the sake of completeness, since such a case is somewhat unusual (and its mathematical meaning has two incompatible definitions). The value of i **mod** j, for positive operands, is the rest of the integer division of i by j. More precisely, j must be strictly positive, otherwise it is an error; $i \text{ mod } j = i - k * j$ for k such that $0 < i \text{ mod } j < j$; if $i > 0$, the ordinary relation holds:

$$(i \text{ div } j) * j + i \text{ mod } j = i$$

Note that the three operators $+$, $-$, and $*$ are also defined, with a different meaning, for operands of set types (see Chap. 13).

Boolean operators include $\neg$, $\vee$, and $\wedge$; the first one is unary, the others are binary. Logical operators of equivalence ($\equiv$) and implication ($\supset$) do not exist

Operator	Operation	Operand type	Result type
+	Identity	Integer or real	Same as operand
−	Sign inversion		

Operator	Operation	Type of operands	Result type
+	Addition	Integer or real	Integer if both operands are integer, otherwise real
−	Subtraction		
*	Multiplication		
/	Division	Integer or real	Real
div	Truncated division	Integer	Integer
mod	Modulus		

Operator	Operation	Type of operand(s)	Result type
¬	Negation		
∨ (or)	Logical union	Boolean	Boolean
∧ (and)	Logical intersection		

exist in Pascal. However, since the type *Boolean* is an enumerated type with *false* < *true*, the comparison operator = denotes logical equivalence; similarly, < denotes logical implication. For example, $(a < b) = (c < d)$ is true if both comparisons are true or false at the same time; otherwise it is false. Anyway, these operators are rarely needed in ordinary programs.

Relational operators are displayed in the following table. The four operators =, ≠, ≤, and ≥, as well as the operator **in** (absent from the table), are also defined for operands of set types (see Chap. 13). Operands of relational operators must be of compatible types (see Sec. 3.1), or such that one operand is of type *real* and the other of type *integer* (or subrange thereof). See Sec. 10.5 about string types, Chap. 13 about set types, and Chap. 14 about pointer types.

Note that relational operators cannot be directly combined in the common mathematical sense. To test if the value of an integer x lies between two integer values a and b, one must write the compound expression

$$(a \leqslant x) \wedge (x \leqslant b)$$

since $a \leqslant x \leqslant b$ is illegal. It would be interpreted as $(a \leqslant x) \leqslant b$, and the first expression returns a value of type *Boolean*, which cannot be compared with

Operator	Operation	Types of operands	Result type
=	Equal to	Any simple type, pointer type, string type, or set type	
≠	Not equal to		
<	Less than	Any simple type or string type	
>	Greater than		Boolean
≤	Less than or equal to	Any simple type, string type, or set type	
≥	Greater than or equal to		

the integer b. The problem is the same in Fortran and PL/I (moreover, PL/I would accept A $<=$ X $<=$ B with an absurd meaning). Only Cobol allows the usual notation.

4.3 FUNCTION DESIGNATORS

A factor may be also the value returned by a function. A function designator specifies the activation of the named function. Although the concepts of sub-program and activation are covered in the next chapter, function designators will be presented here. (They already appeared in Sec. 3.2, in the case of the predefined functions *succ*, *pred*, and *ord*.)

A function designator specifies the activation of a function, either pre-defined (like *succ* or *sin*) or declared in the procedure- and function-declaration part of a block. If the function has formal parameters, the function designator must specify a list of actual parameters, which are substituted for the corresponding formal parameters of the function declaration. (See Fig. 4.3.) The correspondence between formal and actual parameters is by posi-

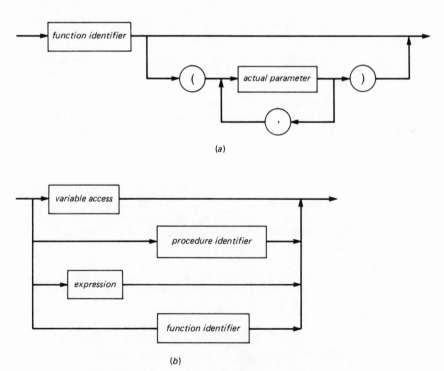

(a)

(b)

Fig. 4.3 (a) Function designator and (b) actual parameters.

tion, as in almost all programming languages. All actual parameters must be present (i.e., no default mechanism exists), and they must be of types corresponding to the specifications of the formal parameters. (This correspondence will be detailed in Sec. 5.4.) Every actual parameter must be evaluated or accessed, then transmitted to the function, but the order in which these operations are made for all parameters is implementation-dependent; i.e., a program must not rely on a particular order. Several examples of function designators appear in the next section, especially in Example 4.2.

4.4 PREDEFINED FUNCTIONS

Predefined functions are supposed to be declared in the program environment. They deal with some type transfers (*trunc, round, ord, chr*) and with usual mathematical functions (*odd, abs, sqr, sqrt, sin, cos, arctan, ln, exp*). Some of these functions could not be written in Pascal without modification, because the type of the value they deliver depends on the type of their actual parameter. Most of these functions could be considered as unary operators not using the operator syntax.

TYPE-TRANSFER FUNCTIONS

trunc (*x*)   returns the integer value obtained by truncating the real value *x* (i.e., the integral part of *x*). It is an error if the result is not of type *integer*, i.e., if it does not belong to the closed subrange [$-maxint..+maxint$].

round(*x*)   returns the integer value obtained by rounding the real value *x*; i.e., *trunc*(*x* + 0.5) if *x* > 0, and *trunc*(*x* − 0.5) if *x* < 0. Examples: *trunc*(2.6) returns 2; *trunc*(−2.6) returns −2; *round*(2.6) returns 3; and *round*(−2.6) returns −3.

ord(*x*)   is defined for *x* of any ordinal type: If *x* is of type *integer*, *ord*(*x*) returns *x*. If *x* is of type *char*, *ord*(*x*) returns the integer corresponding to the rank of *x* in the enumeration of the values of type *char*, the first value having a zero rank. If *x* is of an enumerated type, *ord*(*x*) delivers the integer corresponding to the rank of *x* in the enumeration of the values of this type, the first having a zero rank.

chr(*x*)   returns the value of type *char* whose ordinal number is the integer *x*; it is an error if this character does not exist. The following relation always holds

$$chr(ord(ch)) = ch$$

for any character *ch*.

MATHEMATICAL FUNCTIONS

For all the following functions, the actual parameter may be either *real* or *integer*. The result is of type *real*, except for functions *abs* and *sqr*, in which case the result is of the same type as the actual parameter.

abs(x) returns $|x|$;

sqr(x) returns x^2;

sqrt(x) returns $\sqrt{x}$ (it is an error if $x < 0$);

ln(x) returns $\log_e x$ (it is an error if $x < 0$);

exp(x) returns e^x;

sin(x) returns sin x, with x in radians;

cos(x) returns cos x, with x in radians;

arctan(x) returns the principal value, in radians, of the arctangent of x.

The following predicate (a function with a boolean result) needs an integer parameter:

odd(x) returns *true* if x is odd, *false* otherwise; it is equivalent to the expression *abs*(x) **mod** $2 = 1$.

Example 4.2: Calls of Predefined Functions

{Given the following declarations:}
const *pi* = 3.1415926536;
type *day* = (*mon,tues,wednes,thurs,fri,satur*);
var *ch*: *char*; *i*: *integer*;
   tgx, *x*, *fulldegree*, *y*, *z*: *real*;
   xdegree, *xminute*: *integer*;
begin
  . . .
  {Then, after reading a digit character:}
  read(*ch*);
  {The integer value of the digit just read is computed by:}
  i := *ord*(*ch*) − *ord*(*'0'*);
  . . .
  {ord(succ(wednes)) is an expression with value 3}
  . . .
  read(*x*) {x is an angle in radians};

```
tgx := sin(x)/cos(x) {Compute the value of tangent x.};
{Let xdegree and xminute be the value of x in degrees and minutes:}
fulldegree := x*360/pi;
xdegree := trunc(fulldegree);
xminute := round((fulldegree−xdegree)*60);
write(exp(z * ln(y))) {Write the value of y raised to the power of z.}
  . . .
end.
```

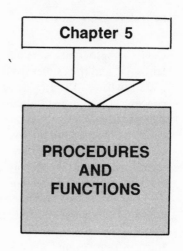

Chapter 5

PROCEDURES AND FUNCTIONS

The subprogram, as a concept, is probably the most powerful and the most productive of all programming concepts. Its full importance was not fully recognized, however, before the revolution in programming philosophy known as *structured programming*. In the first programming languages, a subprogram was considered only a means for abbreviating the program text when some complex action had to be executed in several different places. Writing a subprogram to use it only once was often thought to be a sheer waste of time, and the use of parameters was discouraged because of the complexity and inefficiency they introduced.

The increasing costs of software development and maintenance provoked a shift of emphasis from sheer efficiency to reliability, maintainability, and portability, and subprograms are now considered an important method of structuring programs. The general principles of top-down program design call for breaking the problem to be solved down into several subproblems. If each of these subproblems is solved, then a simple composition of their solutions yields a solution to the main problem. Similarly, each subproblem may be broken down, if necessary, into several sub-subproblems, and so on. A subprogram is then the linguistic feature corresponding to the subproblem.

Readers of this book are assumed to know what a subprogram is, and the only purpose of the preceding remarks is to explain why a language designed in the late sixties, like Pascal, considers subprograms in a manner somewhat different from languages designed 10 or 15 years before. In Fortran, a subprogram, called a subroutine or a function, is mainly a way to reduce the size of compilation units, and not a tool for program structure. The different subprograms that constitute a complete program are all at the same level, no embedding is possible, and the communication between these different parts is made more often by using common areas than by using parameters. In Basic and

Cobol, subprograms were added a long time after the initial definition of the language, and they suffer from numerous and various restrictions, limitations, and drawbacks. PL/I, which partly used ideas taken from Algol 60, gives the concept of a subprogram (called a procedure) much more importance, but it inherits from Fortran a poor design of parameters and difficulty in communication between subprograms.

The idea of a subprogram in Pascal is directly inherited from Algol 60, with improvements in syntax and parameter specification to allow both a more efficient implementation on present-day computers and greater security in use. The rest of the present chapter is divided into four parts. In the first one, we consider the syntax of subprogram declarations and its most important consequences for local names. Parameters are considered in the second part; the third introduces and details the subprogram call, and the last presents the predefined subprograms provided by Pascal.

The name "subprogram" is only a generic term, and it does not appear in Pascal, which makes the distinction between functions, which return a value that replaces their calling expression, and procedures, which normally communicate with their environment only through their parameters. However, procedures and functions bear many properties in common, and the generic term "subprogram" will be used every time something applies to both concepts.

5.1 PROCEDURE AND FUNCTION DECLARATIONS

5.1.1 SYNTAX

A subprogram declaration is made of two related parts: the subprogram heading, which specifies the interface between the subprogram and its environment, and the subprogram block, which describes the inner working of the subprogram. These two parts may be physically separated, in which case the heading is followed by a directive that replaces the subprogram block. This latter part appears somewhere later, preceded by a subprogram identification, which specifies the name of the subprogram thus completed. If the heading and the block appear together, the directive and the subprogram identification may be omitted. This is the most frequent situation in ordinary programs, although a clear separation between the interface with the environment and the inner description of the subprogram may be considered extremely desirable.

The only standard directive is *forward*, which serves exactly the purpose just described, i.e., it specifies that the subprogram heading is predeclared, so that its interface may be fully known and the corresponding block may appear later. Many implementations give supplementary nonstandard directives, used when the block is not a part of the program being compiled. For example, the directive *external* might specify that the block is compiled separately by the Pascal implementation, and should be included in the executable module before execution. The subprogram heading thus allows a specialized linkage editor to check that the separately compiled subprogram has the same specifications. In some situations, a directive *Fortran* could specify that the corresponding block was written in Fortran and probably uses linkage conventions different from those of Pascal. Since the possibility of separate compilation is not defined in standard Pascal, this matter cannot be pursued, and the reader is invited to consult the appropriate documentation about the implementations available.

Formal parameters will be considered in Sec. 5.2. A procedure declaration and a function declaration are very similar (see Fig. 5.1), the only differences being the introductory keyword, the type specification of the function result, and the necessity of assigning a value to this result during function execution. Contrary to Fortran and PL/I, which use a special statement (RETURN expression) for this latter action, the ordinary assignment statement is used in Pascal, with the function identifier as the left part. This special meaning of the function name is valid only within the function block.

Parameterless subprograms may be defined; the parameter list is entirely omitted, along with the corresponding parentheses.

5.1.2 BLOCK STRUCTURE

The body of a subprogram is a block, which was defined in Sec. 2.3, and is made up of several declaration or definition parts, in a fixed order, followed by a compound statement, which is the executable part of the subprogram. Since subprograms are embedded in the block of the program, and since their blocks may contain further subprogram declarations, several blocks may be embedded in a sort of parenthesized structure, known since Algol 60 as a "block structure." Pascal is a block-structured language, like PL/I and unlike Fortran, Basic, and Cobol. In a Fortran subprogram, for example, all names belonging to the subprogram are visible, but the only external names that can be used are those corresponding to other subprograms and to named common blocks. In PL/I or in Pascal, on the contrary, names belonging to an embedding block are visible, if they are not hidden by names of the same spelling declared locally.

A proper description of this somewhat complex notion calls for some definitions:

1. A name is an identifier or a label; identifiers may be used to call constants, types, variables, procedures, functions, record fields, and parameters.

2. Every name in a Pascal program has a defining point, which differs for each category. Labels, constants, types, variables, procedures, and functions are defined in label declarations, constant definitions, type defini-

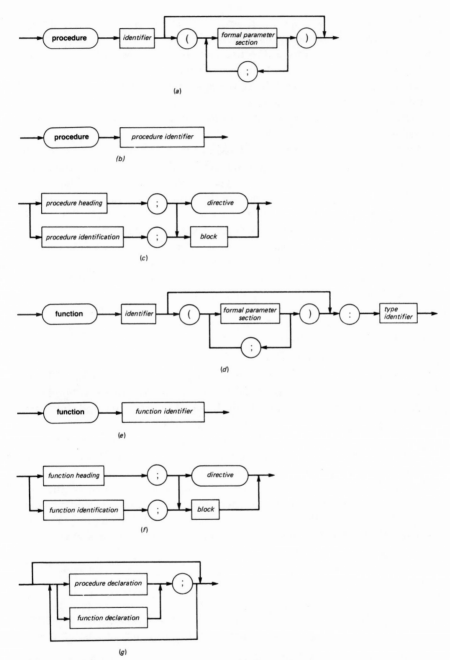

Fig. 5.1 Syntax of procedure and function declaration: (*a*) procedure heading; (*b*) procedure identification; (*c*) procedure declaration; (*d*) function heading; (*e*) function identification; (*f*) function declaration; and (*g*) procedure- and function-declaration part.

56

tions, variable declarations, procedure declarations, and function declarations, respectively. Constants denoting the values of an enumerated type are defined in the corresponding type denoter. Record fields are defined in the type denoter that describes the corresponding record type. Parameters are defined in the corresponding parameter list. Predefined identifiers are (supposedly) defined in the environment of the program.

3. All occurrences of a name that are not its defining point are called *applied occurrences*.

4. That part of the program where a given name is defined is called its *region*; that part of the program where it is visible (i.e., where it can be used) is called its *scope*.

Given these definitions, some simple rules explain the mechanism of a block structure:

1. Every name used in a program must be defined, and every use of a name must occur within the scope of its definition. There is no way to define or declare a name implicitly.

2. A given name must have one and only one defining point in its scope; i.e., it cannot be defined twice, within the same scope, with different meanings (for example, as a constant, then as a function) or even with the same meaning.

3. With only two exceptions, the defining point of a name must precede textually all its applied occurrences. This ensures that the compiler can handle the complete identification process in only one pass of the program. The exceptions deal with variables used as program parameters, which occur in the program heading before they have been defined (see Sec. 2.3), and pointer types (see Sec. 14.2).

4. The region of a name is defined for each name category in the following way: for labels, constants, types, variables, procedures, and functions, it is the block in which the corresponding definition occurs; for constants denoting the values of an enumerated type, it is the most embedded block containing the type denoter; for subprogram parameters, it is the formal parameter list in which they are specified and the corresponding subprogram block; for field identifiers, it is the record-type denoter in which they are specified (field identifiers are also visible in two other very restricted contexts—see Sec. 12.2); for predefined identifiers, it is a fictitious region enclosing the program.

5. The scope of a name is its region, excluding all regions where a name of the same spelling is defined.

6. A variable exists during the complete activation of the block that is its region. Its does not exist when this block is not activated. This is similar to the behavior of AUTOMATIC variables in PL/I and in contrast to the behavior of STATIC variables in that language or to the behavior assumed in most implementations of Fortran. The most important consequence for the programmer is that all variables local to a subprogram have an undefined value when an activation of this subprogram begins. Another important consequence is that the storage space needed by local variables may be reclaimed when the activation of their block terminates.

Some important consequences of these rules must be noted when a block A includes a block B (B is the block of some subprogram declaration occurring in A or is embedded in such a block, at any depth):

1. A name defined in A is visible in B if and only if no variable of the same name is defined in B; it is a *global* name in B.

2. A name defined in B is never visible in A; it is called *local* to B.

3. If an applied occurrence of a name defined in A occurs in B, no name of the same spelling may be defined in B; otherwise, the same name would have two different meanings in the same context, which would be an error. The situation is more complicated in Pascal than in a language like PL/I, for example, since a name may denote not only a variable or a subprogram, but also a constant or a type.

Example 5.1:   Scopes and Regions

```
program P(infile, outfile);
   const a = 5;
   type b = (c, d, e);
   var f: b; g: integer; infile, outfile: file of real;
   procedure P1;
      const h = c;
      var g: b; i: integer;
   begin . . . end {P1};
   procedure P2;
      type a = (h, j, k);
      procedure P3;
         var b, j: a;
      begin . . . end {P3};
   begin . . . end {P2};
begin . . . end {program P}.
```

The static structure of this example may be represented by the schema of Fig. 5.2; arrows delimit the region of each name, and their solid part marks the scope of the name.

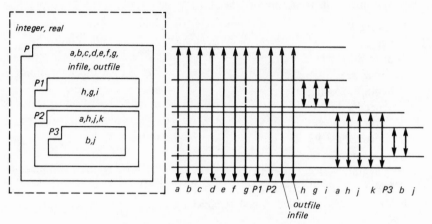

Fig. 5.2   Static structure of Example 5.1.

REMARKS

1. *infile* and *outfile* are used in the program heading before having been defined. They must be defined in the program block, not in an embedded block.

2. *integer* and *real* are defined in a fictitious environment, since they are predefined types. They could be hidden by a name of the same spelling defined in the program, although it would be very bad practice.

3. The integer *g*, declared in *P*, is hidden in *P1* by the variable of the same name of type *b*. The type *b* is visible in *P1* since it is not hidden.

4. In *P1*, the constant *c*, of type *b*, is used in the constant definition of *h*. Consequently, it cannot be redefined in the same block, as a constant or as anything else.

5. The constant *h* in procedure *P1* bears no relation to the constant of the same name in procedure *P2*, since they occur in two disjointed blocks.

6. The variable *j* in procedure *P3* hides the constant *j* of the procedure *P2*. Consequently, the type *a* in procedure *P2*, and its enumerated constants, is partially hidden in procedure *P3*. It could be possible to use *a*, *h*, and *k* in *P3*, but it would also be bad practice, since one value of

the type would be invisible and accessible only by way of an expression such as *succ*(*h*) or *pred*(*k*).

Example 5.2: Span of Life of Variables

```
program P;
  var a: . . .;
  procedure P1;
    var a1: . . .;
  begin . . . end {P1};
  procedure P2;
    var a2: . . .;
    procedure P3;
      var a3: . . .;
    begin . . . P1 . . . end {P2};
  begin . . . P3 . . . end {P2};
begin . . . P1; . . . P2 . . . end {program P}.
```

The dynamic structure of this example may be represented by the schema of Fig. 5.3, in which a box represents an activation of the block of a subprogram and arrows delimit the span of life of each variable.

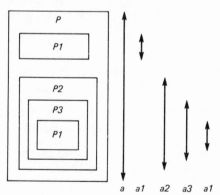

a   a1   a2   a3   a1

Fig. 5.3 Dynamic structure of Example 5.2.

REMARKS

Note that *a1* has two distinct existences, with no relation between them. When the first activation of *P1* terminates, the current value of *a1* is lost. If some intermediary result must be saved between calls of *P1*, a global variable like *a* may be used.

The rules of existence and visibility of names will be illustrated in many subsequent examples of this book. They have been defined in such a way that a subprogram may be inserted in a program regardless of the names it uses internally. With global names, on the contrary, several disjointed subprograms can refer to the same names. However, since these rules are somewhat complicated, they need careful handling. Two perils of global names must be especially noted:

- If the definition of a local name is forgotten in some subprogram, and a like name of the same category is accidentally defined in an embedding subprogram, the error may go unnoticed, and lead to strange behavior.

- A like name in an intermediary embedding subprogram may hide a global name from a subprogram more deeply embedded. Here again, in some rare circumstances, the error may go unnoticed and have strange consequences.

As a general rule, it is advisable in all cases to define names as locally as possible. Thus the two dangers explained above can be avoided, as far as possible, and in the case of variables, the use of storage is optimized, since the space needed by their values is used only during their lifetime, i.e., during the activation of the subprogram that declares them. The counterpart to this possible optimization is that, if the value of a variable must be saved between two activations of the same subprogram, it must be declared globally for this subprogram. Illustrations will be numerous in subsequent examples in this book. Once more, it is important to emphasize that the behavior of variables in Pascal, and especially their span of life, is completely different from that encountered in most Fortran implementations. Note, however, that the Fortran standard does not specify that the value of variables should be saved between two calls of the program to which they belong.

5.1.3 LABELS AND STATEMENTS

Labels constitute a very peculiar thing in Pascal: their name is not an identifier but a small positive integer, they are neither constants nor variables, they must be declared, and their only use is in **goto** statements (see Sec. 2.8). Moreover, in the statement part of the block in which it is declared, a label must prefix one and only one statement. The mandatory declaration of all labels allows one-pass compilation, since the block level at which they prefix a statement is known even in embedded blocks.

We can now give the complete definition of a statement, as illustrated in Fig. 5.4.

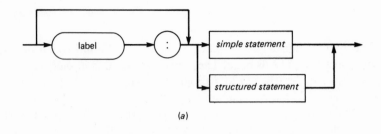

(a)

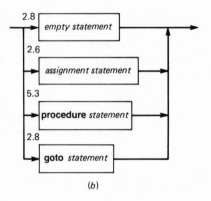

(b)

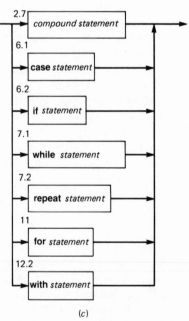

(c)

Fig. 5.4 Syntax diagram for a statement: (a) statement; (b) simple statement; and (c) structured statement. The numbers identify the sections of this book where the corresponding statements are described.

5.2   FORMAL PARAMETERS

The formal parameters of a subprogram, which are the normal means of communication between the body of the subprogram and its environment, are specified in their entirety in Pascal in the heading of the subprogram, which is not the case with many other programming languages. In Fortran and PL/I, the heading simply enumerates the names of the parameters, and their description comes afterward in the body of the subprogram, in a manner identical to that of an ordinary variable declaration. In Pascal, all the necessary information is localized in only one place, which constitutes the interface of the subprogram with its environment. Further evidence of the intermediary role of formal parameter descriptions is given by virtue of the fact that their specifications must be visible from outside, while their names are visible only from inside. The specification of a formal parameter describes its characteristics, i.e., its type if it is an object, or its heading if it is a subprogram. It describes also its transmission mode, which can be chosen from among the five different modes provided by Pascal. The modes serve to describe the way in which the actual parameter is accessed and handled from inside the subprogram. Only the first four (see Fig. 5.5) are described in the present section; the last one will be presented in Sec. 10.7.

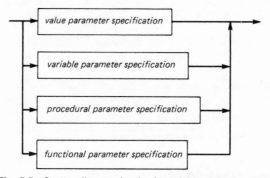

Fig. 5.5   Syntax diagram for the formal parameter section.

First, we consider parameters in connection with subprograms; subprogram calls and actual parameters will be considered in the next section.

5.2.1   VALUE PARAMETERS

Value parameters have no equivalent in many other programming languages, yet they constitute the simplest and safest mode of transmission. Within the subprogram, the value parameter is simply a local variable of the specified type, which is assigned the value of the corresponding actual parameter before execution of the statement part of the subprogram. (See Fig. 5.6.) No other binding with the environment exists during subprogram execution—thus the environment cannot be modified via a value parameter. This mode of transmission, consequently, is properly used for input parameters, i.e., data for the subprogram. Note that the type of value parameters must be named, and consequently defined, in an embedding block.

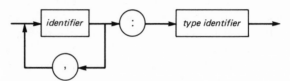

Fig. 5.6 Syntax diagram for a value parameter specification.

Example 5.3:   Value Parameters

function *Celsius* (*temperature*: *degree*): *integer*
{Convert the given temperature from degrees Fahrenheit to degrees Celsius.};
begin {Celsius}
  Celsius := *5* * (*temperature* − *32*) **div** *9*
end {Celsius}

REMARKS

The type *degree*, used in the function heading, must be defined somewhere in the environment of the function, for example, in the block immediately embedding it or in any embedding block. This type is supposed to be some integer subrange—for example, −*50..*+*120* for an ordinary weather thermometer.

5.2.2 VARIABLE PARAMETERS

The specification of variable parameters is identical to that of value parameters, except for the keyword **var**, which occurs in front. (See Fig. 5.7.) Variable parameters are approximately equivalent to the normal transmission mode in Fortran or PL/I, except that the corresponding actual parameter cannot be

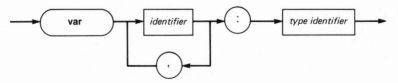

Fig. 5.7 Syntax diagram for a variable parameter specification.

an expression or a constant. Within the subprogram, the formal parameter behaves like an ordinary local variable, but in fact it denotes the corresponding actual parameter. In other programming languages, this is often called *reference* or *address transmission* (or *call by reference*). Variable parameters are such that a subprogram can modify its environment, and consequently they are properly used for output parameters, i.e., results delivered by the subprogram. However, this mode of transmission is not exactly symmetrical to the preceding one, and we shall see in Sec. 10.6 that it may be dangerous if misused.

Example 5.4: Variable Parameters

procedure *Sphere* (*radius*: *real*: **var** *area*, *volume*: *real*)
{Compute the area and volume of a sphere of a given radius.};
    const *pi* = *3.1415926536*;
    var *temp*: *real* {auxiliary variable};
  begin {Sphere}
    temp := *pi* * *sqr*(*radius*);
    area := *4* * *temp* {4 π R^2};
    volume := *4/3* * *radius* * *temp* {4/3 π R^3}
  end {Sphere}

5.2.3 PROCEDURAL AND FUNCTIONAL PARAMETERS

For purposes of the following discussion, we shall call procedural and functional parameters *parametric subprograms*, i.e., subprograms that are parameters of other subprograms (see Fig. 5.8). Fortran and PL/I offer this possibility, but these two languages do not provide it in a completely general and safe way; i.e., no specification of the parametric subprogram allows the compiler to check its correct use. The situation was the same in the original definition of Pascal, and the present syntax was introduced only during the ISO standardization process. As a consequence, several Pascal implementations still accept only the original syntax, in which the parameters accepted by parametric subprograms cannot be specified at all.

The specification of a parametric subprogram has exactly the same form as the declaration of an ordinary subprogram: it specifies the number, mode of transmission, and type or characteristics of the parameters, but it also gives them a name. However, this name has no significance outside the subprogram specification; i.e., it constitutes a sort of mandatory comment. This was done in order to avoid the introduction into the language of yet another syntactic concept, which would have been somewhat complicated.

Parametric subprograms are in themselves an intricate concept, seldom

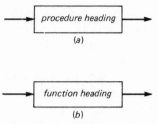

Fig. 5.8 Syntax diagram for parametric subprograms: (a) procedural parameter specification and (b) functional parameter specification.

used. However, when they are needed, no other method can easily replace them, and that is the main reason for introducing them as a general tool of the language. Two situations where a subprogram should have a subprogram as a parameter may be quoted here and illustrated in examples. However, we do not have enough Pascal tools available yet, and the body of the corresponding subprograms will be replaced here by comments.

Example 5.5: Functional Parameter

{The first example is that of a function that computes an approximation of the integral of a given function in a given interval. The function to integrate is passed as a functional parameter.}

function *Integrate* (**function** $f(x: real): real; from, upto: real): real$

{f(x) must be well defined in the interval from $\leqslant x \leqslant$ upto; Integrate returns an

approximation of $\int_{from}^{upto}$ f(x) dx, using some suitable numeric method.};

const *epsilon* = . . . {a suitable absolute precision};

var *result*: *real* {for computing the desired integral};

{Other variables are declared here as needed.}

begin {Integrate}

{For examples of possible methods, see Wirth (1973, pp. 98–102). A value of the function for some argument is computed by value := f(argument)}

Integrate := *result*

end {Integrate};

{The following function is a suitable candidate as an actual parameter for the function Integrate.}

function *Func* $(x: real): real$;

begin {Func}

Func := $1 / sqrt(sqr(a * cos(x)) + sqr(b * sin(x)))$

end {Func};

{A possible call to Integrate would be: writeln(Integrate(Func, 0, pi / 2)).}

REMARKS

1. With the original Pascal definition, f would appear without any parameter within the heading of the function *Integrate*. Here, we know very well that the parametric function must have one real parameter, transmitted by value. Moreover, the compiler can check it.

2. Without parametric subprograms, we would have no simple and satisfactory solution to our problem; i.e., we could not build a function able to integrate any real function with one real argument.

3. The name x, which appears in the heading of f, included in the heading of *Integrate*, bears no relation to any other name. It could be replaced by y or *realargument*, without changing anything in the meaning of this example.

4. Parametric subprograms lead to complicated situations as regards the block structure. When *Integrate* is called with *Func* as a parameter, these two names must be visible, but not necessarily in the same region and scope. For example, *Integrate* may be at the same level as the procedure that calls it, while *Func* may be local to this later procedure. That means that, when *Integrate* calls *Func*, via its formal parameter f, *Func* may be invisible. There is a complete change in the visible landscape when control goes from *Integrate* to *Func*, and again when it comes back to *Integrate*. The two global names a and b, used in *Func* (they must be constants or variables, probably of type *real*), must be visible from *Func*, but there is no visibility condition about them in the body of *Integrate* or of the subprogram that calls it.

Example 5.6: Procedural Parameters

This second example is that of a procedure that applies some given process to every component of a given structured object. The object is passed as a variable parameter and is supposed to have components of a given type T. The process is passed as a procedural parameter.

```
procedure ApplyAProcess
  (procedure Process(var component: T);
  var object: structuredtype);
  {Local definitions and declarations for ApplyAProcess, if any}
begin {ApplyAProcess}
  {Every time a component c of the structured object is isolated, it is processed by the
    statement Process(c).}
  {The procedure terminates when all components have been processed.}
end {ApplyAProcess}
```

REMARK

An actual example of such a situation occurs in Example 15.5.

5.3 SUBPROGRAM CALLS AND ACTUAL PARAMETERS

A function is called by using a function designator, already seen in Sec. 4.3. A procedure is called by using a procedure statement, which is the last simple statement to be described. The syntax (Fig. 5.9) is exactly the same as that of a function designator. Note especially that there is in Pascal no special key-word to denote this statement, contrary to Fortran or PL/I. Any occurrence of a procedure identifier at the beginning of a statement introduces a procedure statement.

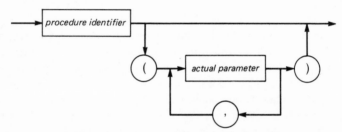

Fig. 5.9 Syntax diagram for a procedure statement.

The procedure statement causes the activation of the statement part of the named procedure, after binding all actual parameters to the corresponding formal parameters. The nature of this binding depends on the mode of parameter transmission, and the correspondence is established by the respective positions of actual and formal parameters in the procedure statement and in the procedure heading. As already noted in Sec. 4.3, this correspondence by position is the rule in almost all programming languages, and with Pascal there is no way one can omit actual parameters or provide more than specified.

The rest of this section explains the rules of type compatibility and correspondence between actual and formal parameters, depending on the transmission mode.

5.3.1 VALUE PARAMETERS

The value transmission of a parameter is exactly equivalent to the assignment symbolized by

formal parameter := actual parameter

This means that the actual parameter may be any expression (this includes a variable or a constant), provided its type is assignment-compatible with the type of the formal parameter specified in the subprogram heading (see Sec. 2.6). For example, if the formal parameter is specified of type *real*, the corresponding parameter may be a real expression, but it may also be an integer one. On the contrary, a real expression is an illegal actual parameter for a formal parameter specified of type *integer*. If the formal parameter is specified of a subrange type, an error will be detected, generally at run time, if the value of the corresponding actual parameter is not within the specified range. Since assignment is allowed for most structured types, value transmission may be used for structured parameters, but the cost of the implied copy is not negligible.

5.3.2 VARIABLE PARAMETERS

Since the formal parameter behaves as a local variable, but in fact denotes the corresponding actual parameter, no simple equivalent to this mechanism may be found elsewhere in the language. The best explanation is probably one that uses the low-level concept of reference or address, and this is an indication that this mode of transmission is both powerful and dangerous, as all low-level features are.

The name of a simple variable is a reference to that part of storage that contains its successive values. While in value transmission only the current value is passed to the subprogram and stored in another variable (the formal parameter), in variable transmission it is this reference itself which is passed. As a consequence, when the formal parameter occurs in a statement within the subprogram, it refers to the storage part associated with the variable that is the corresponding actual parameter.

Since there is no restriction on the possible uses of the formal parameter, the actual parameter must deliver a reference to something valid; i.e., it must be what will be called a *variable access*. This includes variable names and also references to components of structured variables. But it excludes constants or expressions that are not variable accesses.

Moreover, no implicit conversion may be invoked by the variable transmission mode, so the actual parameter must be of exactly the same type as the formal parameter. A real needs a real, an integer needs an integer, and a subrange type needs the same subrange, not just a subrange of the same host type or a subrange which happens to have the same limit values. If several formal parameters are enumerated in a list in the procedure heading, the corresponding actual parameters must all be of the same type.

Variable parameters can be dangerous, especially when they are of a structured type. This will be discussed in Sec. 10.6 and later. However, another danger occurs if the subprogram uses global variables, i.e., variables that are not accessed via parameters but referred to directly within the subprogram. If such a global variable is also passed to the subprogram as an actual variable parameter, it becomes accessible under two different names.

When the subprogram modifies the variable denoted by one of these names, the variable denoted by the other is also modified, since it is the same. This is a very unfortunate situation, where the internal working of a subprogram depends on its environment and the way it is called and cannot be simply described with context-independent antecedents and consequents. The best solution to this problem is to avoid, as far as possible, the modification of global variables, to avoid even their use, to consider them as implicit variable parameters to the subprogram that uses them, and never to use the same variable twice as a variable parameter (implicit or not) in the same subprogram call.

5.3.3 PROCEDURAL AND FUNCTIONAL PARAMETERS

The actual parameter corresponding to a parametric subprogram must be the name of a subprogram of the same sort (procedure or function). The formal parameter denotes the actual parameter during execution of the subprogram that has it as a parameter, but this does not need the notion of reference, and the problems described in the case of variable parameters do not exist. If the parametric subprogram is a functional parameter, the corresponding actual parameter must be the name of a function with the same result type.

Formal and actual parameters must have *congruent* formal parameter lists. Although in most cases parameter lists of parametric subprograms are very simple, the notion of congruent formal parameter lists is very general, as described below.

Two formal parameter lists are congruent if they have the same number of formal parameter sections that match in corresponding positions. To put it plainly, two formal parameter sections match if they are identical, except as regards the parameter identifiers: same number of parameters, same type, same transmission mode. In the case of formal parameter sections that specify parametric subprograms, they must be of the same sort (procedure or function), have the same result type (if they are functions), and have congruent formal parameter lists. Of course, this last part of the rule is seldom used, since it is very difficult to find an example of a parametric subprogram with a parametric subprogram parameter that is not contrived. However, it would be more complicated to forbid such a capability, even if it is never going to be used in actual programs, than to allow it as a natural consequence of allowing parametric subprograms.

One restriction, however, is prescribed in standard Pascal: the actual parameter corresponding to a parametric subprogram must be a name defined within the program; i.e., it cannot be the name of a predefined subprogram. This is because predefined subprograms do not follow, in general, the same rules as ordinary subprograms, as explained in the next section. For example, the predefined function *sin* could not be used as an actual parameter of the function *Integrate* in Example 5.5. Instead, another function must be defined in the program, its body being only a call to *sin* with assignment of the result to the function name.

5.4 PREDEFINED PROCEDURES AND FUNCTIONS

Predefined subprograms are called standard subprograms in many languages, and are called *required subprograms* in the ISO *Standard* on Pascal. Like all other predefined identifiers, which include constants, types, and variables, predefined subprograms are supposed to be defined in an environment enclosing the program. This means that they are global names for the whole program, provided they are not hidden by the definition of identifiers of the same name. All predefined identifiers are enumerated in App. IV. Predefined functions are described in Sec 4.4, in the case of arithmetic and transfer functions, and in Chap. 8 and 9 in the case of the two file predicates. Predefined procedures are described in Chaps. 8 and 9 (input-output procedures), 10 (pack-unpack), and 14 (dynamic allocation procedures). The following lists are given only to provide a unique reference for all predefined subprograms and a first intuitive grasp of their utility.

PREDEFINED FUNCTIONS

Arithmetic

abs(x)	Absolute value of x
sqr(x)	Square of x
sin(x)	Sine of x
cos(x)	Cosine of x
exp(x)	Exponential of $x(e^x)$
ln(x)	Natural logarithm of x
sqrt(x)	Square root of x
arctan(x)	Arctangent of x

Transfer

trunc(x)	Truncation of x
round(x)	Round value of x

Ordinal

ord(x)	Ordinal number of x
chr(x)	Character whose ordinal number is x
succ(x)	Successor of x
pred(x)	Predecessor of x

Predicates

odd(x)	True if x is odd
eof(f)	End of file on f
eoln(f)	End of line on f

PREDEFINED PROCEDURES

File handling

rewrite(f)	Initialize f for generation
reset(f)	Initialize f for inspection
put(f)	Pass to the next component during generation
get(f)	Pass to the next component during inspection
read(f, v1, v2, . . ., vn)	Read values from f
write(f, v1, v2, . . ., vn)	Write values onto f
readln(f, v1, v2, . . ., vn)	Read and pass to the next line
writeln(f, v1, v2, . . ., vn)	Write and pass to the next line
page(f)	Begin a new page

Dynamic allocation

new(p)	Allocate a new dynamic variable
new(p, c1, c2, . . ., cn)	Allocate a new dynamic variable with variants
dispose(p)	Delete a dynamic variable
dispose(p, c1, c2, . . ., cn)	Delete a dynamic variable with variants

Transfer

pack(a, i, z)	Pack a into z beginning at $a[i]$
unpack(z, a, i)	Unpack z into a beginning at $a[i]$

These 17 functions and 13 procedures are the only standard predefined subprograms, i.e., those that are required to be available in any Pascal implementation. Of course, a given Pascal implementation may provide additional predefined identifiers and predefined subprograms.

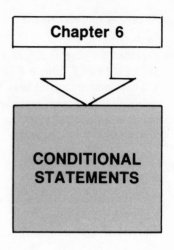

Chapter 6

CONDITIONAL STATEMENTS

The execution of a procedure is accomplished by the execution of a sequence of individual actions. Each action is denoted by a statement, and for every statement in a procedure, three cases may occur: the statement is executed exactly once; it is not executed at all; it is executed several times. Three different classes of statement structures are provided for these three situations: *sequential structures*, already considered in Chap. 2; *conditional structures*, which are the subject of the present chapter; and the *iterative* and *repetitive structures*, which will be considered in Chaps. 7 and 11, respectively.

The conditional statement structures are means for choosing among several different actions. The most general structure is the **case** statement, whose counterparts in other languages are complicated, undisciplined, and restricted: computed and assigned GOTOs in Fortran and Basic, GOTO . . . DEPENDING ON . . . in Cobol, and GOTO with a label variable operand in PL/I.

In some situations, when there are only two different cases to consider, the **if** statement may be useful as a simplification of the **case** statement; it exists in Pascal in roughly the same way as in other programming languages, but Fortran and Basic have no **else** part. However, it is important to note that the **case** statement is more general than the **if** statement, and leads in many situations to simpler and clearer programs, as it will be demonstrated below.

6.1 THE case STATEMENT

To make a choice, one has to distinguish between several possible cases, according to a given criterion; this criterion will be, logically, a value of an *ordinal type*, and especially of an *enumerated type*. The different cases to consider are associated with different values of this type, denoted by constants which label the corresponding statements. If the same statement has to be

73

executed for several different values, those values can be listed in front of the statement (see Example 6.2). If some action needs more than one statement, a compound statement may be used (see Example 6.3). Of course, the order in which the different **cases** appear has no significance, since only one **case** may occur at a time. Similarly, no value may occur more than once in a given **case** statement.

Syntax

The symbol **end** is a sort of superparenthesis, which serves to close the **case** statement. (See Fig. 6.1.) Consequently, a **case** statement may be used anywhere a simple statement is allowed. Note that this is an instance where **end** occurs without a preceding **begin**. Another instance will be described in Chap. 12.

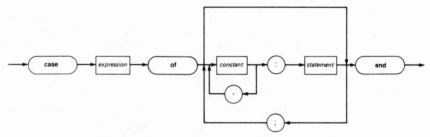

Fig. 6.1 Syntax diagram for a **case** statement.

Semantics

Given the **case** statement:

case *expression* **of**
    value₁: *statement₁*;
    value₂: *statement₂*;
    - - - -
    valueₙ: *statementₙ*
end
if, for all i from 1 to n,
    $\{P \wedge (\text{expression} = \text{value}_i)\}$ *statement*ᵢ $\{Q\}$
then $\{P\}$ **case** statement $\{Q\}$

Thus, if *expression* $= value_i$, *statement*ᵢ is executed, and the **case** statement is terminated. If no such *valueᵢ* exists, it is an error. In the deduction rule, the same Q is used as a consequent for all statements; in fact, and more generally, each *statement$_i$* has a consequent Q_i, and Q is such that each Q_i implies it. The most frequent situation is when Q is simply the union of all Q_i (as in Example 6.1).

Example 6.1

type *color* = (*green, amber, red*);
- - - -
var *trafficlights*: *color*;
- - - -
    case *trafficlights* **of**
      red: *writeln* ('*stop*');
      green: *writeln* ('*go ahead*');
      amber: *writeln* ('*stop if possible, else go ahead*')
    end

Example 6.2

var *hexa: char* {The only possible values are the hexadecimal digits.};
    hexvalue: 0..15 {the integer value of a hexa digit};
- - - -
    case *hexa* **of**
    '*a*', '*b*', '*c*', '*d*', '*e*', '*f*':
      hexvalue := *ord*(*hexa*) − *ord*('*a*') + 10;
    '*0*', '*1*', '*2*', '*3*', '*4*', '*5*', '*6*', '*7*', '*8*', '*9*':
      hexvalue := *ord*(*hexa*) − *ord*('*0*')
    end {Hexvalue is the integer value of the hexa digit.}

Example 6.3

var *day*: (*sun, mon, tues, wednes, thurs, fri, satur*);
    weather: (*snowy, rainy, cloudy, sunny*);
- - - -
    case *day* **of**
      mon, tues, wednes, thurs, fri:
        begin *GoToJob*; *DoTheJob*; *ReturnHome* **end**;
    sun: {Do nothing.};
    satur: **case** *weather* **of**
      sunny: *WashTheCar*;
      cloudy: Jog;
      snowy, rainy: *TryTheTv*
        end
end

REMARKS

1. Although the syntax diagram does not say so, a semicolon is possible before **end**, but has no meaning.

2. A particular statement may be empty if the action to be executed is void, as on Sunday in Example 6.3. This is not the same thing as the omission of the corresponding value in the case labels, since it would be an error if the expression would take this value.

3. Two slight extensions have been proposed for the **case** statement: allow a value range as a case label (in Example 6.2, the two label sequences would become respectively 'a'..'f' and '0'..'9'); include an optional **otherwise** part, for catching all the case values not explicitly enumerated as case labels. These two extensions are recognized by several compilers, but there are different variants for the second one, and the ISO *Standard* does not include them presently.

4. It is somewhat difficult to find a proper layout for complicated **case** statements, as in Example 6.3. Whether case labels should be indented or not, occur on a separate line or not, is really a matter of taste.

More complicated and significant examples of the use of the **case** statement will appear later, especially from Chap. 10 through subsequent chapters.

6.2 THE if STATEMENT

In many circumstances, the choice to make is only between two different situations, generally represented by the value of a boolean expression (a predicate). For example:

```
case itrains {type Boolean} of
    true: StayInBed;
    false: GoToBeach
end
```

Although it is perfectly correct, and acceptably clear, this formulation is too far from ordinary spoken language and from other programming languages. It may be replaced with the equivalent formulation:

```
if itrains then StayInBed else GoToBeach
```

Syntax

The syntax for the **if** statement appears in Fig. 6.2. The **else** part is optional, and may be omitted if no action is to be executed when the (boolean) expres-

Fig. 6.2 Syntax diagram for an **if** statement.

sion is false. Each statement may be replaced with a sequence of statements between a **begin** and an **end** (a compound statement), so **if** statements may be embedded.

> **if** *itrains* **then**
>   **if** *clock* $\leqslant$ *10* **then** *StayInBed*
>   **else** *HaveBreakfast*
> **else if** *distancefrombeach* $<$ *2* {miles} **then** *Walk*
>   **else** *TakeATaxi*

An apparent ambiguity occurs if two **if** statements are embedded, but only one has an **else** part:

> **if** *expression₁* **then if** *expression₂* **then** *statement₁* **else** *statement₂*

The general rule, in such a case, is that each **else** part is coupled with the next left unpaired **then** part. Thus, in the above example, if *expression₁* is false, nothing is executed, and the whole statement is equivalent to:

> **if** *expression₁* **then**
>   **begin if** *expression₂* **then** *statement₁*
>   **else** *statement₂*
>   **end**

Semantics

> If {$P \wedge B$} *statement₁* {Q}
> and {$P \wedge \neg B$} *statement₂* {Q}
> then {P} **if** B **then** *statement₁* **else** *statement₂* {Q}

Similarly,

> if {$P \wedge B$} *statement₁* {Q}
> and $(P \wedge \neg B) \supset Q$
> then {P} **if** B **then** *statement₁* {Q}

Thus, if the boolean expression B is true, *statement₁* is executed; if B is false, *statement₂*, if it exists, is executed.

Example 6.4

var *hexa*: *char*; *hexvalue*: *0..15*; {see Example 6.2}

- - - -

if (*hexa* $\geqslant$ '*a*') $\wedge$ (*hexa* $\leqslant$ '*f*') **then**
  hexvalue := *ord*(*hexa*) − *ord*('*a*') + *10*
else *hexvalue* := *ord*(*hexa*) − *ord*('*0*')
{Note that, in the boolean expression after if, parentheses are mandatory and that 'a' $\leqslant$ hexa $\leqslant$ 'f' would be an illegal expression.}

Example 6.5

procedure *QuadraticEquation*
  (*a*, *b*, *c*: *real* {a $\neq$ 0, ax^2 + bx + c = 0};
  var *r1*, *i1*, *r2*, *i2*: *real* {the roots of the equation represented by a, b, and c—
    r1 and r2 being the real parts and i1 and i2 the corresponding imaginary
    parts}
  );
var *discriminant*: *real*;
begin {QuadraticEquation}
  discriminant := *sqr*(*b*) − *4* ∗ *a* ∗ *c*;
  if *discriminant* $\geqslant$ *0* **then**
  begin {Compute the two real roots; for avoiding cancellation errors when b^2 is much
    larger than 4ac, first compute the larger root.}
    if *b* > *0* **then**
    r1 := −(*b* + *sqrt*(*discriminant*)) / (*2* ∗ *a*)
    else *r1* := (*sqrt*(*discriminant*) − *b*) / (*2* ∗ *a*);
    if *r1* = *0* **then** *r2* := *0* {for avoiding a division by zero}
    else {Use the relation x1 ∗ x2 = c / a.}
      r2 := *c* / (*a* ∗ *r1*);
    i1 := *0*; *i2* := *0* {no imaginary part}
  end {real roots; (x − r1) ∗ (x − r2) = 0}
  else {complex roots}
  begin
    r1 := −*b* / (*2* ∗ *a*); *r2* := *1*;
    i1 := *sqrt*(−*discriminant*) / (*2* ∗ *a*); *i2* := −*i1*
  end {complex roots}
end {QuadraticEquation}

REMARKS

1. Contrary to PL/I, for example, a semicolon before an **else** is always an error, since **else** cannot begin a statement: it is only a part of the composite statement structure, like **if** and **then**. Remember that in Pascal the semicolon is a statement separator and not a terminator.

2. A comparison between Examples 6.2 and 6.4 shows that, even when there are only two situations, the **if** statement is not necessarily better than the **case** statement. In this particular example, it is definitely worse, since, contrary to the **case** statement, it cannot catch the illegal values of *hexa*, for example, a blank or a punctuation mark. [Admittedly, however, it would be better yet to catch the illegal values explicitly, for example, with the use of a set of characters (see Chap. 13). The important point is that the **case** statement explicitly states all the legal situations, while the **if** statement does not.] More generally, a **case** statement is simpler, safer, more understandable, and more efficient than an **if** statement in all situations where there are several different cases that are mutually exclusive, with equivalent probabilities of being chosen. Although very complicated embedded **if** statements are legally acceptable, they are better avoided, generally in favor of a unique **case** statement.

3. Note, in Example 6.5, the careful way in which the roots are computed to avoid cancellation errors. Note also, in this first nontrivial program, how minimal assertions appear in critical places, for convincing the reader of the validity of the procedure.

EXERCISES

6.1 Find a Minimum

Given a scalar type t, write a function with the following heading:

function *Minimum* $(a,b: t) : t$

which yields the minimum value in the couple (a,b).

6.2 Print a Title

The various possible personal titles are enumerated in this order: Lady, Madam, Mistress, Miss, Sir, Professor, and Mister and codified with letters *L, D, T, M, S, P,* and *R*. Write a procedure with the following heading:

procedure *PrintTitle* (*title: char*)

which prints the title corresponding to the code. Parameter *title* is guaranteed to have only a legal value.

6.3 Analyze a Character

All possible characters are partitioned in the following sets: letters, digits, brackets (parentheses, square brackets, curly brackets, and angle brackets), terminators (dollar sign, number sign, exclamation mark, and interrogation mark), blanks (the blank space), and separators (all other characters). Given the following type definition:

tyupe *class* = (*letter, digit, bracket, terminator, separator, blank*)

write the function

function *Analyze* (*c*: *char*): *class*

which yields the class of the given character *c*.

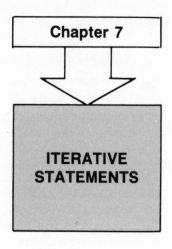

Chapter 7

ITERATIVE STATEMENTS

The statement structures described in the preceding chapters provide no means for repetition of an action (except by actually writing the corresponding statement several times or by using the powerful but difficult tool given by the recursive call of a procedure, a topic that will be deferred until Chap. 15). Consequently, the statement structures that allow repetition of an action add a necessary and extremely important dimension to the Pascal language.

Three different structures are given: the **while** statement, the **repeat** statement, and the **for** statement. The first two are means for building iterative statements and are used when the number of executions is not known in advance, but when the statement must be repeated until some condition is satisfied. Iterative statements are generally used when the repeated execution of actions is a way to progress towards a given goal.

In contrast, the **for** statement is a way to build repetitive statements and is used when the number of repetitions is known in advance. Repetitive statements are generally used when the same action must be done for every object in a predetermined set.

Fortran and Basic have no counterpart for the **while** and **repeat** statements of Pascal. Cobol gives the PERFORM verb with its UNTIL option, but the statement to be repeated must appear elsewhere. Only PL/I has an equivalent feature with its DO WHILE (condition).

Since repetitive statements are more complicated than iterative statements and generally may be synthesized with the use of the latter, their description will be deferred until Chap. 11.

7.1 THE while STATEMENT

For this iterative statement structure, two different things must be specified: the statement to be repeated and the condition (a predicate, i.e., a boolean expression) which must be satisfied before any execution of the statement.

Syntax

This statement structure is not fully parenthesized, since no symbol marks its end (see Fig. 7.1). Consequently, if the action to be repeated needs more than one statement, a compound statement must be used. However, the **while** statement itself is syntactically equivalent to a simple statement and can be used everywhere a simple statement is allowed. This last remark is true for every statement structure in Pascal, and it will not be repeated hereafter.

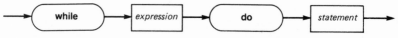

Fig. 7.1 Syntax diagram for a **while** statement.

Semantics

Given the **while** statement:

> **while** *expression* **do** *statement*
> if {P ∧ expression} *statement* {P}
> then {P} **while** *statement* {P ∧ ¬expression}

Note that this deduction rule does not explicitly specify that the statement must be repeated.

The execution of this statement structure works as follows:

- The expression is first evaluated.

- If its value is false, then the **while** statement is terminated and the deduction rule is satisfied.

- If its value is true, the statement is executed (thus maintaining true the assertion *P*), and control returns to the expression.

Thus, if the expression is false before the execution of the **while** statement, nothing is executed.

The deduction rule of the **while** statement is extremely simple and makes clearly visible both *P*, the condition which is maintained by the statement (the invariant of the loop), and *expression*, the negation of which must be achieved by the statement (the goal of the loop).

Example 7.1:   Integer Division

type *natural* $= 0..maxint$;
procedure *IntegerDivision*
    $(a,b : natural$ {dividend and divisor; a $\geqslant$ 0, b $>$ 0};
    var $q,r : natural$ {quotient and rest; a = b $\times$ q + r; 0 $\leqslant$ r $<$ b}
    );
begin {IntegerDivision}
    $r := a; q := 0$;
    while $r \geqslant b$ **do**
        begin {a = b $\times$ q + r; 0 $\leqslant$ r}
            $r := r - b; q := q + 1$
        end
    {a = b $\times$ q + r; 0 $\leqslant$ r $<$ b}
end {IntegerDivision}

REMARKS

1. The invariant of the loop is noted as an assertion right at the beginning of the statement, near the **while** expression. These two conditions together form the best explanation of the working of the loop, and we will not write any iterative statement without explicitly noting its invariant, either formally, like here, or in plain English, as in Example 7.3.

2. If $a < b$, the loop is not executed at all, giving a quotient of zero and a remainder of b. This property of the **while** statement is absolutely necessary in this case.

3. Since reasonable people may disagree on what should be the result of an integer division with negative operands, we prefer to restrict our procedure to natural numbers. The definition of the corresponding type is a simple and secure way to ensure that a and b will never be negative.

4. Of course, this procedure is not necessary, since Pascal has the **div** operator, which is also defined for negative operands.

Example 7.2:   Linear Search

type *sequence* $= \ldots$
    {An unspecified type, which describes a sequence of objects of a given simple type T, with the following operators (procedures):

            • procedure Initialize (var s : sequence) prepares s for examination;

            • function EndOfSequence (var s : sequence): Boolean is true if there exists no more component of s, false if there remains at least one component;

- function Next (var s : sequence): T gives as a result the next component of s, if it exists.};

procedure *Search*

(**var** *s* : *sequence* {the sequence to be examined};

x : *T* {the value to be searched in s};

var *i* : *integer* {the rank of the first object in s that is equal to x, if there exists one};

var *found* : *Boolean* {true if there exists at least one object in s equal to x, false otherwise}

);

begin {Search}

Initialize(*s*); *i* := 0; *found* := *false*;

while ¬(*EndOfSequence*(*s*) ∨ *found*) **do**

begin {i is the rank of the next component of s;

s₁, s₂, . . . , sᵢ₋₁ all are different from x}

i := *i* + *1*;

if *x* = *Next*(*s*) **then** *found* := *true*

end

{either found ∧ x = ith component of s

or ¬found ∧ no component of s equals x}

end {Search}

REMARK

The **while** condition used in this example is somewhat complicated, mainly because the loop must end in two different situations: when *x* is found or when the sequence is exhausted. In Example 7.6, we shall see that the sensible use of an enumerated type yields a more readable and more efficient loop.

Example 7.3: Binary Search

type *table* = . . .

{An unspecified type, which describes a set of numbered objects of a given simple type T, with the following operators:

- function LowerBound (var tb : table): integer gives the lowest object number in tb;

- function UpperBound (var tb : table): integer gives the highest object number in tb;

- function Component (var tb : table; i : integer): T gives the value of the ith component of tb (the object that is numbered i).};

procedure *BinarySearch*

    (**var** *tb* : *table* {the table to be examined, which must be sorted, i.e., Component(tb,j) $\leq$ Component(tb,k) if j < k};

    x : *T* {the value to be searched in tb};

    var *i* : *integer* {if found is true, Component(tb,i) = x};

    var *found* : *Boolean* {true if at least one component of tb equals x, false otherwise}

    );

    var *left*,*right* : *integer* {the bounds of the subtable to be examined};

begin {BinarySearch}

    left := *LowerBound*(*tb*); *right* := *UpperBound*(*tb*);

    found := *false*;

    while ¬*found* ∧ (*left* $\leq$ *right*) **do**

    begin {x does not appear in tb before left or after right.}

        i := (*left* + *right*) **div** 2 {middle component};

        if *Component*(*tb*,*i*) = *x* **then** *found* := *true*

        else if *Component*(*tb*,*i*) < *x* **then**

            {x cannot appear before i, since tb is sorted.}

            left := *i* + *1*

        else {Component(tb,i) > x ; x cannot appear after i.}

            right := *i* − *1*

    end {while ¬found ∧ (left $\leq$ right)}

end {BinarySearch}

REMARKS

1. Many variants of this well-known algorithm exist. The present one makes the minimum number of comparisons but has a complicated **while** condition, for the same reasons as in Example 7.2. Example 7.4 shows another variant, with a simpler condition.

2. The **while** loop is sufficiently long that it makes useful the repetition of its heading as a comment at its end. Some compilers or paragraphers do this automatically.

Example 7.4:   Binary Search (Variant)

type *table* = . . . {as in Example 7.3};

procedure *BinarySearchVariant* {same parameters as BinarySearch}

    (**var** *tb* : *table*; *x* : *T*; **var** *i* : *integer*; **var** *found* : *Boolean*);

    var *left*,*right* : *integer*;

begin {BinarySearchVariant}

    left := *LowerBound*(*tb*); *right* := *UpperBound*(*tb*);

while *left* ≤ *right* **do**
  begin {x does not appear in tb before left or after right.}
    i := (*left* + *right*) **div** *2*;
    if *Component*(*tb,i*) ≤ *x* **then** {x does not appear before i.}
      left := *i* + *1*;
    if *Component*(*tb,i*) ≥ *x* **then** {x does not appear after i.}
      right := *i* − *1*
  end {while left ≤ right};
  found := *x* = *Component*(*tb,i*)
end {BinarySearchVariant}

REMARKS

This procedure needs a nonempty table; otherwise, the reference to *Component*(*tb,i*) in the last statement is illegal.

7.2 THE repeat STATEMENT

In some situations, the repeated statement must be executed at least once. If that occurs because the **while** condition is guaranteed to be true at the beginning of the **while** statement, this statement structure is sufficient, although somewhat overdone. In other cases, however, a statement structure which examines the value of the condition after executing the statement is simpler and more readable.

Syntax

Since the action to be repeated is parenthesized between the symbols **repeat** and **until,** no **begin-end** pair is necessary if that action needs more than one statement. See Fig. 7.2.

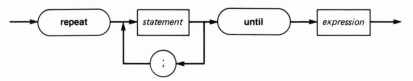

Fig. 7.2 Syntax diagram for a **repeat** statement.

Semantics

Given the **repeat** statement:

  repeat *statement* **until** *expression*
if {P} *statement* {Q}

and $\{Q \wedge \neg\text{expression}\}$ *statement* $\{Q\}$
then $\{P\}$ **repeat** *statement* $\{Q \wedge \text{expression}\}$

As for the **while** statement, this deduction rule does not explicitly specify that the statement must be repeated. The execution of this statement structure works as follows :

• First, the statement is executed, yielding assertion Q.

• The expression is then evaluated; if its value is false, control returns to the execution of the statement.

• If the expression is true, the **repeat** statement is terminated, and the deduction rule is satisfied.

The deduction rule is slightly more complicated than the rule of the **while** statement, because it must express the fact that the statement is executed at least once. Since the expression is true when the **repeat** statement terminates, it can be said to be its termination condition, while Q is its invariant. Contrary to the **while** statement, the invariant of a **repeat** statement is generally not its antecedent.

Example 7.5:   Linear Search

{In Examples 7.2, 7.3, and 7.4, the sequence or table to be examined probably can be guaranteed to be nonempty, so a repeat statement is acceptable. Here follows a variant of Example 7.2.}
type *sequence* $= \ldots$ {as in Example 7.2};
procedure *Search WithRepeat* {same parameters as Search}
   (**var** s : *sequence*; x : T; **var** i : *integer*; **var** *found* : *Boolean*);
begin {SearchWithRepeat}
   Initialize(s); $i := 0$; *found* $:=$ false;
   repeat
      {i is the rank of the next component of s;
      $s_1, s_2, \ldots, s_{i-1}$ all are different from x.}
      $i := i + 1$;
      if $x = Next(s)$ **then** *found* $:=$ *true*
   until *EndOfSequence*$(s) \vee$ *found*
end {SearchWithRepeat}

REMARKS

1. The invariant of the **repeat** loop is true from the beginning of its execution; in other words, it is identical to its antecedent. This proves that a **while** loop would have been equivalent.

2. We note again that the termination condition is somewhat complicated and that the use of a three-way indicator instead of a boolean indicator would yield a simpler and more efficient loop, as we shall see in Example 7.6.

Example 7.6: Maximum Sales

{The sales records of some shops are given as sequences of information, coded with integer numbers, one sequence per year. The sequence for one year has the structure shown in Fig. 7.3. Month is an integer between 0 and 12, 0 marking the end of the sequence; an item is coded with an integer between 1000 and 99999; items are in ascending order for each month; qty is the quantity of this item that was sold during this month, and tnvr is the corresponding turnover. The following procedure, given some item and some year, determines the month with the maximum sales and the corresponding turnover. A procedure PrepareSalesRecord is supposed to be available for preparing to read the sequence corresponding to a given year.}

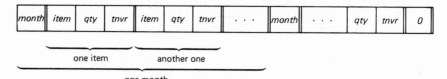

Fig. 7.3 Sequence structure for Example 7.6.

type *amonth* = *0..12*; *year* = *1970..2000*;
   itemnumber = *1000..99999*;
procedure *MaxSales*
   (*y* : *year* {the year to examine};
   item : *itemnumber* {the item of interest};
   var *qty,tnvr* : *integer* {maximum qty and corresponding tnvr};
   var *themonth* : *amonth* {corresponding month}
   );
const *endofsequence* = *0*;
   minimtemcode = *1000* {for distinguishing an item from a month};
   var *month* : *amonth*;
   curqty, curtnvr : *integer* {current maximum qty and tnvr};
   n : *integer*;
   searchstatus : (*searching,found,absent*);
   procedure *SkipEndOfMonth*;
     {The global variable n is the last value read, either a month or an item. After execution of this procedure, the sequence is positioned on the first item of the next month, the number of which is in n.}
     var *qty, tnvr* : *integer* {for ignored values};

begin {SkipEndOfMonth}
   while $n \geq minimtemcode$ **do**
      {We are not at the beginning of the next month.}
      $read(qty,tnvr,n)$
end {SkipEndOfMonth};
begin {MaxSales}
   $PrepareSalesRecord(y)$;
   $curqty := 0$; $read(month)$;
   while $month \neq endofsequence$ **do**
   begin {processing of one month}
      $searchstatus := searching$ {item not yet found};
      $read(n)$ {current item};
      repeat {Search the desired item.}
         if $(n < item) \wedge (n \geqslant minimtemcode)$ **then** {Continue.}
            $read(qty,tnvr,n)$
         else if $n = item$ **then** $searchstatus := found$
         else $searchstatus := absent$
      until $searchstatus \neq searching$;
      case $searchstatus$ **of**
      $found$:
         begin $read(qty,tnvr)$ {corresponding parameters};
            if $qty > curqty$ **then** {bigger sale this month}
            begin
               $curqty := qty$; $curtnvr := tnvr$;
               $themonth := month$
            end ;
            $read(n)$; $SkipEndOfMonth$
         end {found};
      $absent$: $SkipEndOfMonth$
      end {case searchstatus};
      {The last value read is n, which is not an item number.}
      $month := n$
   end {processing of one month};
   $qty := curqty$; $tnvr := curtnvr$ {Pass the results.}
end {MaxSales}

REMARKS

1. Like most other procedures (or complete programs) in this book, this one
   is an example, but not necessarily a model. Of course, many other solutions to the given problem exist; moreover, this solution does not pretend
   to be perfect. Its main defect is that it is not fault-tolerant, i.e., it simply
   gives wrong results when given bad data, instead of giving some error

message. For example, if the desired item does not appear in the given sequence at all, *qty* = 0, but *tnvr* and *themonth* are simply garbage. A less important remark is that the local variables *curqty* and *curtnvr* are not necessary and could be replaced everywhere by *qty* and *tnvr*.

2. The **while** loop in the auxiliary procedure *SkipEndOfMonth* could not be replaced by a **repeat** loop, since it is possible that we are already at the end of a month when this procedure is called.

3. Note the use of the (anonymous) enumerated type for variable *searchstatus*. The termination condition for the **repeat** loop is now very simple, because we have no longer to consider two different cases for termination; they are separated after the end of the loop. One of the main advantages of this solution is its clarity, which makes comments almost useless.

EXERCISES

7.1 Cash Turnover

A cash register produces on a punched tape a copy of all sums entered on its keyboard (integer numbers of cents). The tape begins with the cash number. The procedure to write must compute the global turnover of a cash register, given its tape. Use the type *sequence* and its associated operators, as described in Example 7.2.

7.2 Dice Game

Two players throw a die at the same time. The player with the best score marks one point. The game stops when one player has a total of 11 points. Write a program that simulates this game, using the predefined integer function *random*(*n*), which delivers a pseudorandom number between *1* and its argument *n*.

7.3 Function Root

A root of the equation $f(x) = 0$ may be computed using the method of Heron of Alexandria (wrongly attributed to Newton), which computes the sequence given by the recurrence relation :

$$x_{i+1} = x_i - \frac{f(x_i)}{f'(x_i)}$$

This sequence converges toward a root if the initial value x_0 is an acceptable approximation. Write a procedure which uses this method, checking the convergence by counting the iterations and stopping them after a given limit, if the desired precision is not obtained before.

procedure *HeronRoot*

(*xzero* : *real* {initial approximation of the root};

function f(x : *real*) : *real* {the function itself};

function fprime(x : *real*) : *real* {its derivative};

epsilon : *real* {the desired relative precision};

var *convergence* : *Boolean* {true if the desired precision was obtained before the limit number of iterations};

var *solution* : *real* {the desired root}

);

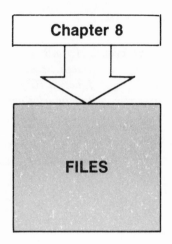

Chapter 8

FILES

All the data types that were presented in Chap. 3 and that have been used so far are *simple* or *scalar types*—i.e., an object of such a type is atomic; it cannot be separated into different components. Of course, this is true only if one does not try to go down to the representation level of these objects—for example, an integer number is atomic, but its decimal representation is not, since it is a sequence of decimal digits.

It is clearly necessary to introduce another category of objects, containing several components, which will be called *structured objects*. This notion exists in almost all other programming languages, but Pascal was the first language to embed it in the more general concept of a type. Thus, a structured object is in Pascal an object of a *structured type*. It is, in fact, a collection of objects that can be considered and handled as a whole or individually, depending upon the circumstances.

There are an infinite number of possible structures for objects, differing in the nature of the components; in restrictions in size, access, updating, and other operations on the structured object or its components; in relative efficiency of these operations; and so on. Moreover, some abstract structured types, such as a sequence, a stack, or a binary tree, may be implemented in many widely different ways, each having different advantages and weaknesses. Consequently, Pascal, as most other programming languages, does not provide these abstract structures, but only a few *structuring methods,* which can be used for implementing these abstractions in different ways.

In Chaps. 8, 10, and 12 to 14, we shall consider the five structuring methods provided by Pascal. Some have counterparts in other languages, some do not, and comparisons will be made with Fortran, Cobol, Basic, and PL/I. Since a component of a structured object very often may be itself structured, these five different structuring methods will give the programmer the potential to define an infinite variety of structured types.

For each structuring method, we shall describe first an abstract structured data type, with its desired general properties. The associated structuring method provided by Pascal will show how, if some restrictions to these properties are accepted, a very efficient implementation can be built in the language. If the restrictions are not acceptable in some situations, other structuring methods very often may be used, and they will be briefly discussed in the text or in the examples.

The description of a structured type must specify the structuring method that is used, as well as the type (or types) of the components. The structuring methods of Pascal are called the **file**, the **array**, the **record**, the **set**, and the *pointer*. They are, respectively, implementations of the abstract mathematical concepts of a sequence, a mapping, a cartesian product, a set, and a recursive object. That does not mean, as will be shown many times, that the only way to implement a sequence, for example, is by a file or to implement a mapping is by an array.

8.1 SEQUENCES

The sequence is one of the simplest abstract structures. It is simply a succession of objects that must be all of the same type, so that the type of any component may be known without knowing its position. For defining its properties, we introduce a very limited set of operators, being careful to use *a notation which is not Pascal,* to avoid confusion between abstract and actual structuring methods. Moreover, we do not try to give a complete formalization of these concepts, since it would be too much for the present text and the normal programmer, and such formalization can be found in other books [see especially Chap. 2 of Dahl, Dijkstra, and Hoare (1972) and Alagič and Arbib (1978)].

Given a sequence type S, of components of type T, we make $S < >$ the empty sequence and $S < t >$ (t is of type T) the sequence that contains only t. We set $\&$ as the concatenation operator, which takes two sequences of the same type as operands and delivers a result which is a sequence of the same type, made with the components of the first sequence, in the same order, followed by the components of the second sequence, again in the same order.

The different objects of type S may all be built with the two following rules:

1. $S < >$ is an object of type S.

2. If s is of type S and t is of type T, then $s \& S < t >$ is of type S.

The operators that complete the definition of the abstract structure called a sequence are the following:

- *firstof* s gives the first component of s, if it exists; *firstof* $(S < t > \& s)$ is t.

- *restof s* gives the sequence *s* with its first component deleted (if *s* contains at least one component); *restof* $(S < t > \&s)$ is *s*.

- *lastof s* gives the last component of *s*, if it exists; *lastof* $(s\&S < t >)$ is *t*.

A given sequence of type *S* is made up, at any given time, of three different parts: its *left part*, its *right part* and its *access mode*. The left part and the right part are both sequences, which may be empty. The access mode may have two values, *generation* and *inspection*. The sequence itself is the concatenation of its left part and its right part, in that order. At any given time, the only component of the sequence that can be accessed is the first component of its right part. Whether this particular component can be examined or modified depends upon the value of the access mode.

Given only the preceding properties, several different implementations are conceivable; they differ in the set of properties that are considered important and must be efficiently handled, and those which are considered less important or even superfluous, and which may be handled inefficiently or are completely forbidden. For example, if the handling of entire sequences and access to individual components are considered important, an implementation with an **array** structure (see Chap. 10) is possible, but concatenation will be very difficult, and the number of components of any sequence will be severely limited. If we want to handle sequences of widely varying lengths, while being able to access components with reasonable efficiency, we can use pointers (see Chap. 14) for implementing a *list*, but the total size of the sequence will be limited. If we want to set no practical limit to the length of a sequence, we must store it outside the main memory of the computer, but generation and inspection operators will be severely restricted. This last possibility is the chosen implementation in Pascal and is called the *sequential file.*

8.2 SEQUENTIAL FILES

Since all files in Pascal are sequential, the adjective "sequential" will be omitted in this discussion. However, it is clearly a limitation of the language, in the present state, to provide no means for accessing nonsequential files (which, incidentally, are not used for sequences but for some sorts of mapping; see Chap. 10). Several Pascal implementations provide nonstandard extensions in this area.

The Pascal file is, at the same time, an implementation of the abstract notion of a sequence and an abstraction of an actual peripheral input-output device, the magnetic tape. As such, the file concept provides a set of operators which respects both the properties of the sequence and the restrictions imposed by the magnetic tape. Its principal characteristics are that the concatenation will not be directly provided, that the selective updating of a given component will be forbidden, and that it will be impossible to freely mix generation and examination of a given file. This is because the file is *sequential;* i.e., one cannot access a component without having previously accessed all its predecessors in sequence.

At any given time, only one file component is immediately accessible, the one that corresponds to the *current position* of the file. File operations allow us to modify this current position, either for accessing the next component or for accessing the first component of the entire file. For accessing the current component, Pascal provides the concept of a *buffer variable,* which may be considered as the name of this distinguished component.

A file type has the syntactic form shown in Fig. 8.1. The component type is any simple or structured type, with the important restriction that it must not contain any file type, directly or indirectly. This restriction is imposed for reasons of implementation, since the file concept must be an efficient abstraction of the various sequential peripheral input-output devices: magnetic tapes, card readers and punches, printers, and interactive terminals. However, the Pascal definition does not place any restriction on the use of files as components of other structured objects or on the declaration of file variables in procedures embedded in the main program. Note that many implementations restrict file variables to simple variables declared in the main program, to ensure that they have distinct and visible names and that they exist from the beginning of execution to the end. This important restriction, though common, is nonstandard, and it has regretable consequences in applications of the file concept. The following examples will not take it into consideration (see Examples 8.5 and 8.7).

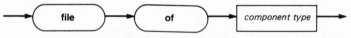

Fig. 8.1 Syntax diagram for a file type.

Given a file variable, i.e., a denotation of a file (not necessarily a simple variable), the associated buffer variable is implicitly declared and is denoted as shown in Fig. 8.2. This buffer variable may be used exactly as any other variable, and is of the type of the file components. The only restriction is that it is illegal to modify the current position of a given file while referencing its buffer variable. This occurs in three different situations:

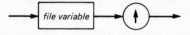

Fig. 8.2 Syntax diagram for a buffer variable.

1. If the buffer variable is used as an actual variable parameter of a procedure which modifies the current position of the file, either directly or indirectly

2. If the buffer variable is used as an element of the record variable list of a **with** statement (see Chap. 12) which does this modification

3. If the buffer variable appears in the left-hand side of an assignment statement which does this modification (by calling a function having a side effect)

These situations are sufficiently complicated to be rather unlikely, so most compilers do not even check for this error.

In other programming languages, files do not constitute structured objects, but are entities external to the program and accessible only via some specialized statements. The notion itself is absent in "standard" Basic and is represented in Fortran only by the concept of an input-output unit, referenced with a number and with no precise component associated with it. In PL/I, it is the "file name" which represents this notion, but the implicit philosophy is the same as in Fortran. Only Cobol provides something similar to Pascal, with the file descriptions in the DATA DIVISION. However, it is more restrictive than Pascal, since components of files are always structured as records. For the possibly baffled Cobol programmer, let us note that the record concept exists in Pascal (see Chap. 12) and that, although not especially linked to the file concept, it allows the definition and handling of files with record components, which are those most frequently used.

None of the four languages we use for comparison provides the concept of a buffer variable.

8.3 OPERATIONS ON FILES

File types are the only ones that do not allow global manipulation, since they describe objects external to the memory of the computer. Assignment and comparison of files are impossible using the assignment statement and comparison operators. They must be done explicitly, componentwise (see Examples 8.1 and 8.2). Consequently, all files operations are provided in Pascal with several (predefined) standard procedures and one (predefined) standard function. In the description which follows, each standard procedure or function is described both formally, with deduction rules which use the abstract sequence operations of Sec. 8.1, and informally in plain English.

After its declaration, as with any other variable, a file variable is undefined. In the rest of the present section, we assume the declaration

var f:**file of** T

and we denote f_0 the state of f before the operation and f_1 its state after the operation. It will always be an error if none of the antecedents of an operation is valid before its execution.

$eof(f)$ is a boolean standard function which yields *true* if *right-part f* is empty (we are at end of file) and *false* if *right-part f* is not empty. It is an error if f is undefined when $eof(f)$ is called. This predicate will allow the inspection of a complete file. It is also defined, for completeness, when the file is being generated (and always *true*), but this is not very useful.

8.3.1 INITIALIZATIONS

Two operations are provided for initializing file variables, depending upon the desired setting of the access mode: *rewrite*(f) prepares f for generation (i.e., writing), discarding its possible preceding value; *reset*(f) prepares f for inspection (i.e., reading) of its value, which is generated earlier. Both operations place the current position at the beginning of the file.

$\{\quad\}$*rewrite* (f) $\{$left-part f_1 = right-part f_1 = F< > $\land$access-mode f_1 = generation $\land f_1 \uparrow$ is undefined$\}$

Since *right-part* f_1 is empty, $eof(f)$ is true as a consequence of *rewrite*(f).

Case 1

$\{$left-part f_0 and right-part f_0 are not undefined and not both empty$\}$
reset(f)
$\{$left-part f_1 = F< >
$\land$ right-part f_1 = left-part f_0 & right-part f_0
$\land$ access-mode f_1 = inspection
$\land$ $f_1 \uparrow$ = firstof right-part f_1 $\}$

Case 2

$\{$left-part f_0 = right-part f_0 = F< >$\}$
reset(f)
$\{$left-part f_1 = right-part f_1 = F< >
$\land$ access-mode f_1 = inspection
$\land$ $f_1 \uparrow$ is undefined$\}$

Case 2 is only for completeness, in the case of inspection of an empty file. After *reset(f)*, $f\uparrow$ refers to the first component of f, if it exists; *reset*(f) is the only operation that can make $eof(f)$ false if it was true.

The operations *reset* and *rewrite* correspond to what are ordinarily called *open operations,* for input and for output, respectively. Explicit open statements are present in Cobol and PL/I. However, Pascal does not provide the symmetric *close operation,* and one may consider that *reset* (or *rewrite*), before opening a file, first closes it if it was already open. The only difficulty is that the status of the physical file, at the end of existence of its corresponding file variable, is not defined in the language. For a temporary file, local to a procedure, one may assume that it is deleted or discarded; for a file variable known to the environment (see Sec. 8.4), this status is entirely determined by choices made in the implementation.

8.3.2 INPUT AND OUTPUT

Two operations are provided for modifying the current position of a given file, one when the access mode is *generation* and the other when it is *inspection.* In the first case, the buffer variable must have been assigned some suitable value, and this object is concatenated to the end of the file. In the second case, the next component of the file (if it exists) becomes accessible via the buffer variable.

$\{$access-mode f_0 = generation
$\wedge$ left-part f_0 is not undefined
$\wedge$ right-part f_0 = F $<>$
$\wedge$ $f_0 \uparrow$ is not undefined$\}$

put(f)

$\{$access-mode f_1 = generation
$\wedge$ left-part f_1 = left-part f_0 & F $<f_0 \uparrow>$
$\wedge$ right-part f_1 = F $<>$
$\wedge$ $f_1 \uparrow$ is undefined$\}$

Thus *eof(f)* is invariably *true* during the complete file generation.

Case 1

$\{$access-mode f_0 = inspection
$\wedge$ left-part f_0 and right-part f_0 are not undefined
$\wedge$ right-part f_0 is not empty
$\wedge$ restof right-part f_0 is not empty$\}$

get(f)

$\{$access-mode f_1 = inspection
$\wedge$ left-part f_1 = left-part f_0 & firstof right-part f_0
$\wedge$ right-part f_1 = restof right-part f_0
$\wedge$ $f_1 \uparrow$ = firstof f_1 $\}$

Case 2

$\{$Same assertions, but restof right-part f_0 = F $<>$ $\}$
get(f)
$\{$Same assertions, but right-part f_1 = F $<>$ and $f_1 \uparrow$ is undefined$\}$

Thus, the effect of *get*(*f*) is not defined if *eof*(*f*) is true before its execution; i.e., that situation is an error. Moreover, *put*(*f*) is valid only during generation, and *get*(*f*) during inspection. This means that the four operations just defined cannot be mixed in any order. Figure 8.3 shows the only possible sequences. The two unlabeled exits of this graph correspond to files which are either saved or deleted, depending upon the context (and possibly upon operating system commands).

Example 8.1: Copy a File

type *fileofT* = **file of** *T;*
    {T is any type not containing a file, either directly or indirectly.};
procedure *CopyFile* (**var** *infile, outfile*: *fileofT*)
    {Infile is copied onto outfile.};
begin{ *CopyFile* }
    reset(*infile*); *rewrite*(*outfile*);
    while ¬*eof*(*infile*) **do**
    begin {Copy one component.}
        outfile ↑ := *infile* ↑;
        put(*outfile*); *get*(*infile*)
    end
end {CopyFile}

REMARKS

1. This procedure is valid even if *infile* is empty, because of the **while** loop. If it could be guaranteed that *infile* is nonempty, a **repeat** loop could be used instead. The program scheme given in this procedure is extremely general, and it will be used in every similar situation of file inspection.

2. Since assignment of files is forbidden, a file cannot be passed as an actual value parameter; the value transmission implies a hidden assignment of

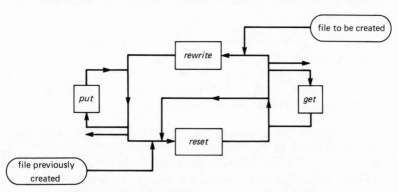

Fig. 8.3 Possible sequences of input-output operations.

the actual parameter to the corresponding formal parameter, as seen in Chap. 5. All file parameters will be variable parameters.

Example 8.2: Compare Two Files

type *fileofT* = **file of** *T*;
> {T is any type not containing a file, either directly or indirectly. Objects of type T may be compared, using the given boolean function Equals (a, b:T). Of course, if T is a simple type, Equals (a,b) may be replaced by a=b.}

procedure *CompareFiles*(**var** *file1, file2: fileofT*; **var** *equal: Boolean*)
> {Equal is true if and only if file1 is equal to file2; i.e., they have the same number of components, and the ith component of file1 is equal to the ith component of file2, when i takes all the values from 1 to the length of the two files.};

  var *searching: Boolean*;
  begin {CompareFiles}
    reset(file1); reset(file2); searching := true;
    while *searching* **do** {left-part file₁ = left-part file2}
      if *eof(file1)* **then**
        begin *searching := false; equal:= eof(file2)* **end**
      else if *eof(file2)* **then**
        begin *searching := false; equal := false* **end**
      else if ¬*Equals(file1↑, file2↑)* **then**
        begin *searching := false; equal:= false* **end**
      else
        begin *get(file1); get(file2)* **end**
  end {CompareFiles}

REMARKS

1. Although the statement controlled by the **while** loop is somewhat complicated, it constitutes a single statement, and no **begin-end** pair is necessary.

2. This procedure is a very crude one, since it stops at the first discrepancy between the two files, and answers only "no" or "yes," without ever pointing to the faulty component. A procedure for comparing similar files and pointing to the differences is much more complicated and will be proposed as an exercise in Chap. 9.

3. The use of the two boolean indicators in this procedure results from its specifications, since the condition for terminating the loop is not the same as the result of the procedure. A three-value indicator, as in Example 7.6, would simplify the loop by distinguishing the three different situations: files equal so far, end of at least one file, and corresponding components

differ. However, a further examination of the situation at the end of the loop would be necessary, and the procedure itself would be more complicated.

8.3.3 ABBREVIATIONS

The four preceding procedures, combined with the function *eof,* are perfectly sufficient for all input-output on ordinary files (i.e., files which are not intended for communication between programs and humans; these latter will be considered in the following chapter). However, abbreviations are provided for operations which appear frequently. The notation

$$read(f, v_1, v_2, \ldots, v_n)$$

where $v_1, v_2, \ldots, v_n$ are variables (either simple variables or components of structured variables), is equivalent to

begin $read(f, v_1)$; $read(f, v_2)$; $\ldots$; $read(f, v_n)$ **end**

and $read(f, v)$ is equivalent to

begin $v := f\uparrow$; $get(f)$ **end**

Similarly,

$$write(f, e_1, e_2, \ldots, e_n)$$

where $e_1, e_2, \ldots, e_n$ are expressions, is equivalent to

begin $write\ (f, e_1)$; $write\ (f, e_2)$; $\ldots$; $write\ (f, e_n)$ **end**

and $write\ (f,e)$ is equivalent to

begin $f\uparrow := e$; $put(f)$ **end**

Note the complete symmetry between these two notations, and especially the fact that $get(f)$ follows $v := f\uparrow$. This occurs because, as soon as f is initialized for inspection by $reset(f)$, its first component is accessible via the buffer variable $f\uparrow$.

Standard predefined procedures *write* and *read* are provided for convenience, but they could involve some overhead in many situations, and programmers should not forget *get* and *put*, even if they have no counterpart in most other programming languages.

Example 8.3: Copy a File

```
type fileofT = file of T;
procedure CopyFileVariant (var infile, outfile : fileofT)
   {a variant of CopyFile (Example 8.1), using read and write};
   var buffer : T;
```

```
begin {CopyFileVariant}
  reset (infile); rewrite(outfile);
  while ¬eof(infile) do
  begin {Copy one component.}
    read(infile, buffer);
    write(outfile, buffer)
  end
end {CopyFileVariant}
```

REMARKS

This procedure is slightly less efficient than *CopyFile* (Example 8.1) because of the two implied assignments, one from *infile* ↑ to *buffer* and the second from *buffer* to *outfile* ↑. If *T* is a complicated and bulky type, the corresponding overhead is not negligible.

8.4 FILES AND THE PROGRAM ENVIRONMENT

The concept of a file in Pascal is completely independent of its implementation on any given input-output peripheral device. For example, the procedure of Example 8.1 could be used for copying a magnetic tape onto a disk data set, a floppy disk onto a card punch, or any other combination, provided the first device is suitable for input, the second one for output, and both for recording objects of type *T*. No provision is given in Pascal for defining in a program the physical and logical characteristics of the actual files or data sets with which the abstract files used in the program are associated. The reason is that these characteristics, and the ways to define them, are heavily dependent upon the peculiarities of the various devices and the idiosyncrasies of the host operating system.

The *Standard* definition of Pascal makes the (implicit) assumption that files may be separated into two categories: *internal files,* which are only means for storing intermediate data which do not fit in the main memory, but which have no existence outside the program; and *external files,* which exist before the program (they will be inspected) or after (they are generated for subsequent usages). For the first category of files, the programmer does not care much about their precise physical organization, and any not-too-unsympathetic host operating system should accept these temporary files very easily. External files, however, have been prepared or will be processed by other programs, and there must be some means for describing any relevant detail about their material support, their physical organization, their location or identification, and so on. The interface between the system-independent Pascal program and its host operating system is provided, in this case, by the names of the file variables, and the *Standard* definition specifies that they should appear in the program heading (see Chap. 2). A Pascal program may thus be considered as a sort of procedure, called by the operating system, whose parameters are the external files it inspects or generates.

An important remark must be made: since the correspondence between the abstract Pascal files, internal to the program, and the external physical files, supported by various peripheral devices, is done only in the program heading, it is entirely static; i.e., a given Pascal file cannot be successively associated with different physical files during the same program execution. Consequently, it is impossible to write in standard Pascal a program which would, for example, process different files whose names would be given by an interactive user.

To avoid system dependencies or implementation restrictions, the *Standard* definition does not specify how a Pascal program is called, how the correspondence between actual files and formal file parameters is established, and so on. In all the examples of complete programs that appear in the rest of this book, all external file names will appear as program parameters, and there will be no other such parameters, since their existence and meaning are entirely implementation-dependent.

Example 8.4: Compare Two Files of Integers

program *CompareFilesOfIntegers*(*sourcefile, probablecopy*)
{This program compares two files, using the procedure define in Example 8.2.};
type *fileofT* = **file of** *integer*;
var *sourcefile, probablecopy*: *fileofT*; *answer*: *Boolean*;
procedure *CompareFiles* {See Example 8.2, in which Equal is replaced by =.} . . . ;
begin {CompareFilesOfIntegers}
CompareFiles(*sourcefile, probablecopy, answer*);
if *answer* **then** *writeln*('*The two files are identical*')
else *writeln*('*Something is wrong*')
end {CompareFilesOfIntegers}.

REMARKS

As will be explained in Chap. 9, the heading of this program is not complete, since it must mention *output*, the implicit name of the file upon which the final message will be written.

8.5 MORE COMPLEX EXAMPLES

Example 8.5: Prepare a File for Concatenation

type *fileofT* = *file of T*;
procedure *PrepareForConcatenation*(**var** *f*: *fileofT*)
{Since inspection and generation cannot be freely mixed in a given file and since there is no close procedure and no inquiry function giving the access mode of a

file, appending a copy of one file at the end of another one (i.e., concatenating the two files) cannot be done without making some assumptions about the initial state of the first file. This procedure avoids the problem and leaves its file parameter in a state suitable for concatenation at its end.};

var *Localcopy*: *fileofT*;

procedure *CopyFile* {See Example 8.1.} . . . ;

begin {PrepareForConcatenation}

    CopyFile(*f*, *Localcopy*);

    CopyFile(*Localcopy*, *f*);

    {Left-part f^1 = Left-part f^0 & right-part f^0

    right-part f^1 = fileofT $< >$

    access-mode f^1 = generation}

end {PrepareForConcatenation}

REMARKS

The price to pay for being completely general is heavy, since the given file must be copied twice. The file concept in Pascal is not well suited for some operations, including concatenation. Similarly, it would be very expensive to try to modify one component of a given file, since it would require making two copies of the file: the first one, without any change, onto a temporary file; the second one back to the original file, changing the component on the fly when it appears in the sequence. The normal method for sequential files is to group the modifications in a batch and use a sequential update procedure (see Examples 9.5 and 12.7).

Example 8.6: Merge Two Files

type *fileofT* = **file of** *T*

    {Objects of type T are supposed to be comparable, by the way of a given boolean function LessThan(a, b): T, probably using some key present in every object. Of course, if T is a simple type, LessThan(a, b) may be replaced with a < b};

procedure *MergeFiles*(**var** *infile1*, *infile2*, *outfile*: *fileofT*)

    {Files infile1 and infile2 are supposed to be sorted according to function LessThan. This procedure merges infile1 and infile2, producing outfile, which contains all components of the two input files, also sorted.};

begin {MergeFiles}

    reset(*infile1*); *reset*(*infile2*);

    rewrite(*outfile*);

    while ¬(*eof*(*infile1*) ∨ *eof*(*infile2*)) **do**

    {outfile is sorted; outfile↑ < infile1↑ and outfile↑ < infile2↑}

    if *LessThan*(*infile1*↑, *infile2*↑) **then**

    begin {outfile↑ < infile1↑ < infile2↑}

        write(*outfile*, *infile1* ↑); *get*(*infile1*)

    end

```
    else {outfile↑ < infile2↑ < infile1↑}
    begin
      write(outfile, infile2↑); get(infile2)
    end;
    {At most, one of the two input files is not terminated.}
    while ¬eof(infile1) do
    begin write(outfile, infile1↑); get(infile1) end;
    while ¬eof(infile2) do
    begin write(outfile, infile2↑); get(infile2) end
  end {MergeFiles}
```

REMARKS

1. It is perfectly legal to mix the use of different input-output procedures, *put* and *get* on one side, *write* and *read* on the other. Here, *get* is systematically used for input and *write* for output. This avoids the use of explicit temporary variables for storing file components, and the buffer variables are used as means for doing the "look-ahead" necessary for comparing the current components of each file.

2. Of the two **while** loops at the end of the procedure, only one (at most) is executed, since the main **while** loop terminates when at least one of the two input files is exhausted. The order in which the last two loops are written is therefore irrelevant.

Example 8.7:   Sort a File

```
type fileofT = file of T;
procedure NaturalMergeSort (var f: fileofT)
  {This procedure sorts file f using the method known as "natural merge sort." See Wirth
      (1976).};
  var nor: integer {number of runs merged};
    eor: Boolean {end-of-run flag};
    a, b: fileofT {temporary files}
  procedure CopyRecord(var infile, outfile: fileofT)
    {Copy one component from infile to outfile, and detect ends-of-run on infile.};
    var buffer: T;
  begin {CopyRecord}
    read(infile, buffer); write(outfile, buffer);
    if eof(infile) then eor := true
    else eor := LessThan(infile↑, buffer)
  end {CopyRecord};
  procedure CopyRun(var infile, outfile: fileofT)
    {Copy one run from infile to outfile.};
  begin {CopyRun}
```

```
      repeat CopyRecord(infile, outfile)
      until eor
   end {CopyRun};
   procedure Distribute
      {Initial run from f to a and b};
   begin {Distribute}
      repeat CopyRun(f, a);
         if ¬eof (f) then CopyRun(f, b)
      until eof(f)
   end {Distribute};
   procedure MergeRun {from a and b to f};
   begin {MergeRun}
      repeat {Merge one run.}
         if LessThan(a↑, b↑) then
            begin CopyRecord(a, f);
               if eor then CopyRun(b, f)
            end else
            begin CopyRecord(b, f);
               if eor then CopyRun(a, f)
            end
      until eor
   end {MergeRun};
   procedure MergeFiles {a and b onto f};
   begin {MergeFiles}
      repeat MergeRun; nor := nor + 1
      until eof(a) ∨ eof(b);
      while ¬eof(a) do
         begin CopyRun(a, f); nor := nor + 1 end;
      while ¬eof(b) do
         begin CopyRun(b, f); nor := nor + 1 end
   end {MergeFiles};
begin {NaturalMergeSort}
   repeat {one distribute and merge pass}
      reset(f); rewrite(a); rewrite(b);
      Distribute {runs from f to a and b};
      reset(a); reset(b); rewrite(f);
      nor := 0; MergeFiles {a and b onto f}
   until nor = 1 {only one run on f, which is thus sorted}
end {NaturalMergeSort}
```

REMARKS

1. The overall structure of this procedure is the result of its development by stepwise refinement. Of course, calls to procedures *Distribute*, *MergeRun*, and *MergeFiles*, which appear only once, could be replaced

by their expansion in-line. This would make the whole process slightly more efficient. Note, however, that the call to a parameterless procedure is normally extremely cheap in Pascal implementations.

2. This procedure uses only two auxiliary files, but is less efficient than a procedure using the same algorithm with three auxiliary files; this would allow us to perform merging and distribution of the new (longer) runs at the same time, in a more symmetric way. The resulting procedure appears in Alagič and Arbib (1978).

3. In real life, file *f* would normally not be sorted on itself, since its initial contents would be destroyed. With magnetic tapes, for example, the initial tape would be dismounted immediately after the first distribution pass and replaced with a blank one, which would receive the sorted result. However, such tape manipulation cannot be expressed in Pascal without the aid of some implementation-defined procedure. This is often done by adding nonstandard optional parameters to the standard procedures *reset* and *rewrite*, or by adding a predefined procedure for explicitly closing files.

4. The procedure *CopyRecord* could be made slightly more efficient by avoiding the auxiliary variable "buffer" (see Remarks after Example 8.3). However, some care would be necessary, because the value of the file buffer of an output file is considered to be undefined after a call to *put*. The following body for *CopyRecord* is consequently less readable than that which appears in the example:

```
begin {CopyRecord (variant)}
    outfile ↑ := infile ↑; get(infile);
    if eof (infile) then eor := true
    else eor := LessThan(infile ↑, outfile ↑);
    put(outfile)
end {CopyRecord}
```

EXERCISES

8.1 File List

A file of some business concern is made up of a series of sequences of five integers: an item code, a unit price, a quantity in stock, a month, and a year, respectively. These last two values denote the most recent date the unit price was updated. The procedure to write must produce a listing of all item codes for items whose unit price has not been updated since some date, given as parameter:

```
type fileofinteger = file of integer;
procedure Listing(var f: fileofinteger; month, year: integer);
```

8.2 Selective File Update

The file described in Exercise 8.1 must be updated by raising all items not updated since a given date (*month*, *year*), by a given rate *r1* if their unit price is less than *p*, and by *r2* otherwise:

procedure *Inflation* (**var**: *oldfile*, *newfile*: *fileofinteger*;
                                actualmonth, *actualyear*: *integer*;
                                month, *year*: *integer*;
                                r1, *r2*: *real* {percentage};
                                p: *integer*
                                );

8.3 Discard and Discount

In the same concern as in Exercise 8.1, it is decided to discontinue all items which are considered too expensive or of which there is a minimum quantity, since these items needlessly tie up capital. The procedure to write must create a new file, taking into account all these parameters: an item is to be discarded if its price is greater than *maxprice* or if its quantity in stock is less than *minqty*. The procedure must also list the references (code, quantity, and price) of all items to be discarded. An identical discount is allowed on all discarded items: the rate is *r1* percent if their global cost is less than *p1* (cents), *r2* percent if their global cost is between *p1* and *p2*, and *r3* percent otherwise:

procedure *Discontinue* (**var**: *oldfile*, *newfile*: *fileofinteger*;
                                maxprice, *minqty*: *integer*;
                                r1, *r2*, *r3*: *real*;
                                p1, *p2*: *integer*
                                );

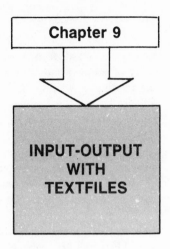

Chapter 9

INPUT-OUTPUT WITH TEXTFILES

9.1 READABLE INPUT-OUTPUT

The files that were considered in Chap. 8 allow the transmission (input or output) of one of their components at a time, without any change of representation. All of their components are of the same type, generally a structured one. They are very well suited for the storage and communication of very large amounts of repetitive information, precisely the sort of thing which is evoked by the usual connotation of the word "file." However, they are not serviceable as means for communicating between the program and its human users; i.e., they are not readable by humans. Any information intended for such a use must be coded with printable characters.

A very important category of file, consequently, is one whose components are characters, but that alone is not sufficient for two reasons. The first reason is that it would be extremely cumbersome to have to program the necessary conversions of any object being input or output, from its external representation as a string of characters to its internal representation, or vice versa. The second reason is that data which are produced or which must be read by humans are not simply sequences of characters; they are structured in *lines*, and this structure has to be recognized on input and built on output. A file declared as a **file of** *char* would not be sufficient for such a purpose, and a specialized predefined type is provided in Pascal. Its name is *text,* and files of this type are named *textfiles*.

Many programming languages make a distinction between *record input-output* and *stream input-output*. In the first case, file components are *records*; i.e., they each contain several subcomponents, not necessarily of the same type, but all records of one file have the same structure (with the possibility of some variant subpart). No change of representation is implied during reading or writing. This concept is equivalent to the general concept of a file in Pascal, this language being more general in the sense that file components may be of any type, record types being only a particular case (see Chap. 12).

With stream input-output, in contrast, files are considered as character sequences, with some way to control their separation into lines, and some change of representation is implied during every *read* or *write* operation. This concept is equivalent to the notion of a textfile in Pascal.

The distinction between record and stream input-output is particularly clear in PL/I, and is dealt with by two different sets of statements: READ and WRITE in the first case, GET and PUT in the second one. It exists also in Fortran, where stream input-output (the most common) uses formats, while record input-output does not (although the concept of a record is not clearly defined). In Basic, the notion of a file is completely missing, and all input-output operations are stream. In Cobol, the only concept analogous to stream input-output is the verb pair ACCEPT/DISPLAY, which is of very limited use. All files are made up of records, but some read-write operations may imply some change of representation.

In the special case of stream input-output, a further distinction appears in PL/I and is also present in some versions of Fortran. It deals with the way in which the external appearance of data is specified in the program. There are three different transmission modes in PL/I, with three corresponding variants in the associated GET or PUT statements: formatted transmission (GET EDIT or PUT EDIT), where a *format* specifies the exact and precise representation of values on the external medium; list transmission (GET LIST or PUT LIST), where this representation is determined by the data on input and by default options on output; named transmission (GET DATA or PUT DATA), where, in addition to the list transmission, each datum is preceded by the name of the variable to which it will be (on input) or has been (on output) assigned.

Standard Fortran provides only formatted input-output, which is very often extremely cumbersome and error-prone on input. Some versions provide a sort of named transmission with the NAMELIST statement. Basic provides only unformatted transmission, and Cobol transmission is equivalent to formatted transmission in most respects.

In Pascal, unformatted transmission is the only type of input. On output, a combination of formatted and unformatted transmission is available, but in a much simpler way than in other programming languages, since the format depends mainly on the type of the transmitted objects, and consequently does not need to be respecified in the input-output statements. Examples will show

how the effect of all transmission modes may be achieved, generally in a very simple and flexible way.

9.2 TEXTFILES

The type *text,* predefined in Pascal, is not equivalent to the type **file of** *char:* the components of a textfile are characters, but the textfile is further structured in *lines.* A line is a sequence of characters, possibly empty, terminated by a special component, the *end-of-line.* This component is indistinguishable from the space character, except for the four predefined procedures *reset*, *writeln, readln*, and *page* and for the predefined function *eoln*. That means that it is not possible to detect or to write an end-of-line with the ordinary predefined procedures *get* (or *read*) and *put* (or *write*). Note that nothing is specified about the underlying representation of lines: on some implementations, there is a particular character at the end of every line; on other implementations, there may be several characters, or a character count at the beginning of each line, or any other feature. The important point is that these differences of implementation are transparent for the user.

A textfile is a (possibly empty) sequence of lines. During generation, the last line may be incomplete, if its end-of-line has not yet been generated. All predefined functions and procedures that handle files apply to a textfile as if it were a **file of** *char,* but in that case the end-of-line is invisible on input and cannot be generated on output.

The predefined function *eoln* (*e*nd *o*f *l*ine) is used for detecting the end-of-line during input. If *tf* is a textfile, *eoln*(*tf*) is true if and only if the current position of *tf* is at an end-of-line. When *eoln*(*tf*) is *true, tf*↑ contains a space character. This may be expressed with the following deduction rule:

if *access-mode* tf = generation,

then *firstof right-part* tf = end-of-line ⟹ *eoln*(*tf*) ∧ *tf*↑ = ɓ

Example 9.1:   Count Lines in a Textfile

procedure *CountLines*(**var** *tf*: *text*; **var** *number*: *integer*)
    {This procedure counts the number of lines in textfile tf.};
    begin {CountLines}
        reset(*tf*); *number* := 0;
        while ¬*eof*(*tf*) **do**
        begin {Number counts the number of lines in left-part tf.}
            while ¬*eoln*(*tf*) **do** *get*(*tf*) {Advance one character.};
            {One more line has been inspected.}

```
        number := number + 1;
        get(tf) {Pass the end-of-line.}
      end {while ¬eof(tf)}
    end {CountLines}
```

REMARKS

1. This procedure could have been defined as a function, yielding as its result the number of lines of its textfile parameter. This would be poor programming, because of the very important and expensive side effect it would have. We could reset *tf* at the end of the procedure, thus almost eliminating the side effect, but the cost will remain. We will generally refrain from defining any function doing input or output.

2. As can be observed in this example, *eof(tf)* may only be *true* just after *reset(tf)* (the textfile is empty), or just after a *get(tf)* called when *eoln(tf)* was *true*. Note particularly that *eof(tf)* may not be *true* when *eoln(tf)* is *true*. This is a consequence of the fact that all lines that constitute a textfile being inspected are complete, including the last one. Any implementation in which this assertion is false is not standard Pascal.

Textfiles are often used for interactive communication between a program and a user. The interactive terminal conceptually constitutes a couple of files with the same support, one for input and one for output. A careful reading of the assertions given about procedures *reset* and *get* is necessary in such a case. The ISO *Standard* explicitly states that the consequents of these two procedures are not to be satisfied immediately after the procedure call, but immediately before any subsequent reference to the file or its buffer variable. Thus, the physical reading of the next character will not be done when *reset(tf)* or *get(tf)* is called, but only when *tf↑* is referred to, or when *get(tf)* is called another time.

This is necessary for proper behavior of interactive input-output. For example, when resetting the input file associated with the terminal, the program must not ask for some data without printing some explanatory message. If the consequent of *get* had to be satisfied immediately after its call, there would be an annoying discrepancy between input and output on the terminal, and the user would have to key something before knowing what is needed. Unfortunately, this is what is done on some Pascal implementations which make no distinction between ordinary files and interactive ones.

On most operating systems, any program may access two textfiles of special significance, generally called *standard files*. The standard input file has generally the same support as the text of the program, and it is that part of the input deck or stream which immediately follows the text of the program, perhaps with some job-control commands interspersed. The standard output file is that upon which the output of the compiler is listed, along with any messages delivered by the operating system.

Two predefined names are provided in Pascal for these privileged textfiles, the simplest possible names: *input* and *output*. These names are standard because the corresponding files generally exhibit a particuliar behavior: *input* may only be inspected, and *output* may only be generated; neither of them may be reread or rewritten.

For mainly historical reasons, these two files are treated in Pascal in a very peculiar way, which is expressed in the following rules:

1. They are considered to be defined in every program which uses them; consequently, they must not be declared.

2. Like any other file external to the program, they must be listed in the program heading of any program using them.

3. If *input* is used, a call to *reset* (*input*) is implicitly made just before the beginning of the program. Similarly, if *output* is used, a call to *rewrite* (*output*) is also implicitly made just before the beginning.

4. The effect of an explicit call to *reset* or *rewrite* for these predefined textfiles is implementation-defined (and generally forbidden).

5. If the first (or only) parameter of the predefined procedures or functions *read*, *readln*, *eof*, and *eoln* is omitted (as well as the corresponding parameter delimiter), the predefined file *input* is implied. Similary, if the first (or only) parameter of the predefined procedures *write* and *writeln* is omitted, the predefined file *output* is implied.

Rules 1 to 3 cannot be ignored. Rule 4 implies that any program intended to be implementation-independent must refrain from using *reset* and *rewrite* for predefined textfiles. Rule 5, in contrast, gives only a possible abbreviation, and may be entirely ignored. We will do that most often, since this abbreviation adds no generality or power to the language, and on the contrary may yield less clear programs.

Some Pascal implementations may add further nonstandard restrictions on the use of predefined textfiles. In some cases, *output* must appear in the program heading even if it is not be used within the program. A careful study of the documentation associated with the implementation is thus highly recommended.

9.3 INPUT FROM TEXTFILES

The predefined procedure *read*, presented in Chap. 8 as a means of simple abbreviation, is extended to textfiles, where it takes a special meaning as a way for reading more than one file component (one character) at a time and for interpreting the representation of numerical data. The syntax of the parameter list of *read* may be described by the diagram shown in Fig. 9.1.

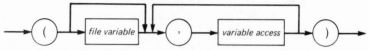

Fig. 9.1 Syntax diagram for the parameter list of *read*.

If the file variable is omitted, it is implied to be *input*. A variable access is either the name of a simple variable or a reference to a simple component of a variable of a structured type. A call to *read* with several variable accesses is equivalent to as many calls with only one variable access and the same file parameter. All these rules are true for any file parameters and not only for textfiles, as we have seen in Chap. 8.

For ordinary file parameters, the variable accesses must have the same type as the components of the file, or an assignment-compatible type, since

$read(f, v)$

is equivalent to

begin $v := f\uparrow$; $get(f)$ **end**

In the case of textfile parameters, however, three different types are permitted for the variable access v:

1. If v is of type *char*, or a subrange of *char*, we are in the same situation as before, the only difference between a textfile and a **file of** *char* being that $eoln(f)$ may be modified as a side effect.

2. If v is of type *integer*, or a subrange of *integer*, the call $read(f,v)$ reads from f a sequence of characters which must form a (possibly signed) integer constant, according to the syntax given in Chap. 2. Preceding space characters (and consequently ends-of-line) are skipped. The reading stops when the current character (the value of which is in $f\uparrow$) cannot be a part of an integer. In other words, $read(f, v)$ successively reads spaces (possibly none), an optional sign, and decimal digits, until it finds some character which is not a digit. Four different errors may occur during this reading: (*a*) an end-of-file occurs on f before any digit has

been read; (*b*) no digit has been read when an illegal character stops reading; (*c*) the resulting integer is not within the implementation-defined limits; (*d*) the resulting integer is not assignment-compatible with *v*. As always in Pascal, all these errors are terminal ones, and the program aborts.

3. If *v* is of type *real*, all proceeds as in case 2, but the character sequence which is read must represent a (possibly signed) number, i.e., either an integer constant or a real constant, and error (*d*) cannot occur.

Another predefined procedure, *readln*, is available only for textfiles. A call to *readln* with several variable access parameters is equivalent to a call to *read* with the same parameters, followed by a call to *readln* with no variable access parameter. Since the textfile parameter may be omitted, *readln* may be called without any parameter, and this is equivalent to the call:

readln (*input*)

The call *readln* (*f*) has simply the effect of skipping any trailing characters in the current line, and of positioning *f* at the beginning of the next line, if it exists. (Note that if the next line is empty, its beginning is also its end, *f*↑ is a space, and *eoln*(*f*) is *true*). Thus, *readln*(*f*) is equivalent to:

```
begin
   while ¬eoln (f) do get (f);
   get (f) {Pass the end-of-line.}
end
```

The preceding discussion of input from textfiles seems simple, but some hidden details must be explained, and some pitfalls pointed out. The main characteristic of text input in Pascal is probably the total lack of any format describing the expected data. Thus, the character reading and decoding is directed both by the expected data type (the type of the parameters of the procedure *read*) and by the appearance of the data themselves. Numerical data must be separated by some nonnumerical characters, and two situations may occur. If several numbers are read in sequence, they can be separated only by spaces and/or ends-of-line; a space sequence terminates the preceding number and is skipped when the following one is read. If only one number is read, the character that terminates it is available in the file buffer, and may be inspected as a character, whatever it is.

The line length does not appear in the preceding discussion and in fact has no significance. When reading on the standard file *input*, one cannot assume that lines have equal lengths, and in fact, most Pascal implementations trim the input lines, leaving only their significant part and removing all trailing spaces. After reading one or several numbers, the status of *eoln* is consequently difficult to predict, since it may depend upon the presence or absence of trailing spaces. The simple following loop is not guaranteed to work properly:

while ¬*eoln*(*input*) **do**
   begin *read*(*input, n*); *write*(*output, n*) **end**

Since *eoln*(*input*) has no special reason to be *true* immediately after *read* (*input, n*), the termination condition may not be achieved before the end-of-file, which causes an error.

One useful recommendation, consequently, is not to test *eoln* when using the extended forms of *read*. Similarly, *eof* may not be used, since it is *true* only immediately after *eoln*, and *eoln* is not necessarily *true* immediately after *read*. In fact, if *eof* occurs when *read* is searching for numerical digits, a terminal error occurs. The call to *read* where several numerical data are used at the same time is especially dangerous; if *eof* occurs before all the requested numbers are read, the program aborts. For reading and copying several numbers, separated by spaces, until the end-of-file, the following loop must be used:

while ¬*eof*(*input*) **do**
   if *input* ↑ = '*b̸*' **then** *get*(*input*)
   else begin *read*(*input, n*); *write*(*output, n*) **end**

Yet another reason limits the usefulness of the extended forms of *read* to the few situations where the exact format of the input data may be guaranteed: if the number to be read contains any error—for example, a keypunch error or a missing separator—the program cannot regain control, and aborts. This is not acceptable in many situations—for example, when reading data keyed in by an interactive user. In such a case, the program must define its own *read* procedure, with some built-in way for recovering from input data errors (see Example 9.2). Some implementations add nonstandard features for runtime recovery.

Finally, it must be remarked that Pascal contains no tools for reading values of enumerated types or character strings. In particular, a boolean cannot be directly read. The main reason why input-output of enumerated types has been discarded is that the corresponding identifiers are purely local to the program, and have no significance outside it. Moreover, the handling of bad input data would be much too crude. For character strings, the concept in itself is not Pascal, and a simple *read* procedure for the equivalent data type (see Chap. 10) is very simple to write.

Example 9.2:   Read Integers in a Textfile

procedure *ReadInteger*

   (**var** *tf*: *text* {the input textfile};

   var *result*: *integer* {the number read on tf};

   var *error*: *Boolean* {true if an incorrect number was read};

   length: *integer* {number of characters to read; zero if free format}

   );

   const *blank* = ' ';

     radix = *10* {Decimal numbers are read.};

   var *endoffield*, *sign*, *digitsread*: *Boolean* {flags};

     nch: *integer* {number of characters read so far};

   procedure *NextChar*;

     {Passes to the next character if possible; sets error, nch, and endoffield}

     begin {NextChar}

       if *eof*(*tf*) ∨ *endoffield* **then** *error* := *true*

       else begin *nch* := *nch* + *1*; *get*(*tf*);

         if *nch* = *length* **then** *endoffield* := *true*

       end

     end {NextChar};

   begin {ReadInteger}

     error := *false*; *endoffield* := *false*; *nch* := *0*;

     result := *0*;

     while (*tf*↑ = *blank*) ∧ ¬*error* **do**

       {Skip Leading blanks.}

       NextChar;

     if ¬*error* **then**

     begin *sign* := *false*; {Process the optional sign.}

       if *tf*↑ = '+' **then** *NextChar*

       else if *tf*↑ = '−' **then**

         begin *sign* := *true*; *NextChar* **end**;

       if ¬*error* **then**

       begin {Process the number itself.}

         digitsread := *false*;

         while (*tf*↑ >= '*0*') ∧ (*tf*↑ <= '*9*')

           ∧¬(*error* ∨ *endoffield*) **do**

         begin *digitsread* := *true*;

           result := *radix* ∗ *result* + *ord*(*tf*↑) − *ord*('*0*');

           NextChar

         end;

         if ¬*digitsread* ∨ (*length* ≠ *0*)

           ∧ ¬*endoffield* **then**

> *error* := *true*
> **else if** *sign* **then** *result* := − *result*
> **end** {processing the number itself}
> **end** {processing after skipping leading blanks}
> **end** {ReadInteger}

REMARKS

1. This procedure is somewhat complicated, because it must read numbers in free or fixed format, and also because it will not give run-time errors in the presence of bad data. Unfortunately, it cannot be fault-tolerant in the presence of bad programming, since the program will abort all the same if this procedure is called when *tf* is not being inspected. This is because the access mode of a file is not accessible within the program.

2. Of course, in the presence of bad data, when the procedure sets error to *true*, it is the responsibility of the calling program to handle the situation, for example, by skipping illegal characters until the procedure can be recalled.

9.4   OUTPUT WITH TEXTFILES

As with the predefined procedure *read*, its counterpart, the predefined procedure *write*, is extended to textfiles, for permitting more than one value to be written at a time, for coding with characters the values to be written, and for describing some characteristics of the codification. The syntax diagram of the parameter list of *write* (as applied to textfiles) is shown in Fig. 9.2.

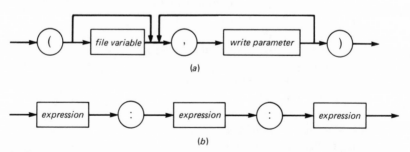

Fig. 9.2   Syntax diagram of the parameter list of *write:* (*a*) *write* parameter list and (*b*) *write* parameter.

If the file variable is omitted, *output* is implied. A call to *write* with several *write* parameters is equivalent to as many calls with only one *write* parameter and the same file parameter. One important difference from what was discussed in Chap. 8 is the special form of the *write* parameter, which, when applied to textfiles, may have the three following forms:

expression
expression : *total-width*
expression : *total-width* : *fraction-digits*

expression gives the value to be written onto the textfile; *total-width* and *fraction-digits* are integer expressions which determine the precise output format of the value, in the following way:

1. *total-width* and *fraction-digits* must be greater than zero, if they are present.

2. *total-width* is the minimum number of characters to be written; if *expression* needs more than this number for its representation, the smallest consistent width is chosen; if fewer characters are needed, blanks are added before the representation, which is always right-adjusted.

3. If *total-width* is not specified, a default value is chosen, depending both on the type of the expression and on the implementation.

4. *fraction-digits* is applicable only when the expression is of type *real.*

Five different types are permitted for the *expression*, each with different rules for building its representation:

9.4.1 CHARACTER OUTPUT

The default value of *total-width* is 1. Consequently, (*total-width* − *1*) blanks (possibly none) are written, followed by the character value of the expression.

9.4.2 INTEGER OUTPUT

The default value of *total-width* is implementation-defined and generally gives the width necessary for writing the greatest possible integer. If necessary, blanks are added on the left; i.e., the decimal representation of the integer is right-adjusted. Negative values are preceded by a minus sign.

9.4.3 REAL OUTPUT

Two different representations are provided for real values: floating-point representation if *fraction-digits* is not specified or fixed-point representation if it is specified. This corresponds, respectively, to formats E and F of Fortran or PL/I.

In floating-point representation, the characters written are, successively:

- Blanks, as necessary, to attain *total-width* characters for the complete representation

- A minus sign if the number is negative, otherwise a blank

- The leading digit of the decimal representation of the real number

- A decimal point

- The fractional digits: one digit only if *total-width* is too small, otherwise (*total-width* − *exponent-digits* − 5) digits, where *exponent-digits* is the (implementation-defined) number of digits in the exponent (generally 2 or 3)

- The exponent character ("e" or "E", as defined by the implementation)

- The sign of the exponent

- The *exponent-digits* digits of the exponent, with leading zeros if necessary

In fixed-point representation, the characters written are, successively:

- Blanks as necessary to attain *total-width* characters for the complete representation

- A minus sign if the number is negative

- The integer part of the decimal representation of the real number

- A decimal point

- The first *fraction-digits* digits of the fractional part

9.4.4 BOOLEAN OUTPUT

If *expression* is of type *Boolean*, then the statement

write (*tf*, *expression* : *tw*)

is equivalent to:

if *expression* **then** write (*tf*, 'true' : *tw*)
else write (*tf*, 'false' : *tw*)

The character string that is written uses lowercase or uppercase characters, as defined by the implementation. The default value of *total-width* is also implementation-defined.

9.4.5 STRING OUTPUT

Character strings will be described in Chap. 10, but the behavior of *write* is described here for completeness. If *total-width* is greater than the length of the string, the value of the string is right-adjusted and preceded by blanks. If it is less than the length of the string, only the first *total-width* characters of the string are written. This is the only case where the width is not extended to accommodate the complete value. The default value for *total-width* is the length of the string.

The predefined procedure *writeln* is available only for textfiles. A call to *writeln* with several *write* parameters is equivalent to a call to *write* with the same parameters, followed by a call to *writeln* with no *write* parameters. Like *readln*, *writeln* may be called with no parameter, and thus operates on the standard file *output*. The call *writeln* (*tf*) has the sole effect of appending an end-of-line to the textfile *tf*, thus terminating the current line.

The predefined procedure *page* has only one parameter of type *text*. It has an implementation-defined effect, with the net result that when the file is subsequently printed on any suitable device, a new page is begun. If the current line is not complete, an implicit *writeln* on the file is called by *page*. Since the effect of *page* is supposed to be implementation-defined, one cannot predict what will happen if the textfile is subsequently inspected; some invisible characters may appear, nothing may happen at all, or an error may occur.

When the predefined procedure *reset* is called for a textfile currently in generation mode, an end-of-line is appended to the file if its last line is not completed. This is necessary for ensuring that all textfiles being inspected contain only complete lines. For a textfile intended to be printed after termination of the program, the situation is similar, and a final *writeln* is not necessary before program termination.

The preceding description of the predefined procedures for text output conforms exactly to the ISO *Standard*. However, some older Pascal implementations contain some deviations in this respect: no implicit *writeln* for generated textfiles at program termination; special interpretation of the first character of each printed line, which controls the printer device and remains invisible (as in Fortran); no definition for the predefined procedure *page*. One can only expect that these deviations will be eventually removed.

For a programmer accustomed to the complexities of text output in Fortran or PL/I, the possibilities offered by Pascal generally seem overly simple, and probably not powerful enough for normal applications. In fact, they suffice for describing any complicated output format, differing from the preceding two languages only in that what is built into Fortran and PL/I must be programmed in Pascal. This is done very easily because one does not have to build a complete line before writing it; instead, the line may be built progressively, component by component. Examples of elaborate output editing will appear in subsequent chapters.

9.5 COMPLETE EXAMPLES OF TEXT INPUT-OUTPUT

Example 9.3: Textfile Copy

```
procedure CopyText (var infile, outfile : text)
{Copy infile onto outfile, preserving its line structure.};
begin {CopyText}
  reset(infile); rewrite(outfile);
  while ¬eof(infile) do
  begin {We are at the beginning of a line.}
    while ¬eoln(infile) do
    begin {Process one ordinary character.}
      outfile↑ := infile↑;
      get(infile); put(outfile)
    end {of a (possibly empty) line};
    writeln(outfile); readln(infile)
  end {of infile}
end {CopyText}
```

REMARKS

1. Procedure *CopyFile*, which appears in Example 8.1, would not work properly on textfiles; since the end-of-line is invisible for *get* (and impossible to write for *put*), it would not be copied on the output textfile.

2. Used with the predefined file variables *input* and *output* as actual parameters, *CopyText* would copy the standard *input* data file onto the standard *output* result file only if the particular implementation accepts *reset(input)* and *rewrite(output)* as nonoperations. Some implementations might consider these calls errors, and others might interpret them in other ways.

Example 9.4: Textfile Copy with Line Control

```
procedure CopyPages (var infile, outfile: text)
{Outfile is expected to be subsequently printed, so page headings are numbered};
const pagelength = . . . {number of lines in a page};
  pagelengthplus1 = . . . {pagelength + 1};
var linecount: 1..pagelengthplus1;
  pagecount: 0..maxint;
```

```
begin {CopyPages}
  reset(infile); rewrite(outfile);
  pagecount := 0;
  linecount := pagelength {for forcing an initial page skip};
  while ¬eof(infile) do
  begin {We are at the beginning of a line.}
    linecount := linecount + 1 {Count the line to print.};
    if linecount > pagelength then
    begin {We are at the beginning of a page.}
      page(outfile);
      pagecount := pagecount + 1;
      writeln(outfile, 'page ', pagecount: 1)
          {minimal width for pagecount, which will
           be printed left-adjusted};
      writeln(output); writeln(output)
      {Print two empty lines.};
      linecount := 1
    end {page heading};
    while ¬eoln(infile) do
    begin {Process one ordinary character.}
      read(infile, outfile↑) {a variant of Example 9.3};
      out(outfile)
    end {of a line};
    writeln(outfile); readln(infile);
  end {of infile}
end {CopyPages}
```

REMARKS

A comparison between Examples 9.3 and 9.4 shows that, by adding suitable actions to the algorithmic scheme illustrated in the first example, it is very easy to program any transformation on textfiles. This scheme is illustrated below in an abstract form:

```
while ¬eof(infile) do
begin < action at line begin >;
  while ¬eoln(infile) do
  begin < action on a character >;
    get(infile)
  end {of line};
  < action at line end >;
  readln(infile)
end {of infile}
```

Example 9.5: Sequential Update of a Textfile

program *TextFileUpdate(input, output, infile, outfile)*

{This program updates the textfile infile, according to commands on input, to yield outfile; information and error messages appear on output. Four update commands, of the form <letter> <spaces> <integer> <end-of-line>, are recognized:

C n copies lines from infile to outfile until line n on infile;

D n deletes lines from infile (does not copy them) until line n;

I n copies n lines from input (immediatly following the command) onto outfile;

E (without parameter) terminates processing by copying all residual lines from infile to outfile.};

type *errornumber = 1..5*;
var *infile, outfile: text*;
   command: char;
   operand, linenumber, counter: 0..maxint;
   normalend, errorencountered: Boolean;
procedure *CopyLine* (**var** *sourcefile: text*)
   {Destination is always outfile.};
begin {CopyLine}
   while ¬*eoln(sourcefile)* **do**
   begin *outfile↑ := sourcefile↑*;
     get (sourcefile); put(outfile)
   end {of line};
   readln (sourcefile); writeln(outfile)
end {CopyLine};
procedure *ErrorMessage(error: errornumber)*;
begin {ErrorMessage}
   writeln(output); writeln('output');
   case *error* **of**
      1: writeln(output, 'operand < linenumber');
      2: writeln(output, 'premature end of file');
      3: writeln(output, 'premature end of input');
      4: writeln(output, 'illegal command');
      5: writeln(output, 'command E missing')
   end;
   errorencountered := true
   end {ErrorMessage};
begin {program TextFileUpdate}
   reset(infile); rewrite(outfile); linenumber := 1;
   normalend := false; errorencountered := false;
   while ¬*(eof(input)* ∨ *normalend)* **do**

```
begin {Process a command.}
    read (input, command); write (output, command);
    if (command = 'I') ∨ (command = 'C')
      ∨ (command = 'D') then
    begin {ordinary command}
      readln (input, operand);
      writeln (output, ", operand: 1);
      case command of
        'C', 'D':
          begin {Copy or delete until line 'operand'.}
            if operand < linenumber then
              ErrorMessage (1)
            else
            begin
              while ¬eof (infile)
                ∧ (linenumber < operand) do
              begin {Process one infile line.}
                if command = 'C' then
                  CopyLine (infile)
                else readln (infile);
                linenumber := linenumber + 1
              end {of copy or delete};
              if linenumber < operand then
                ErrorMessage (2)
            end {no error 1}
          end {'C' or 'D' command};
        'I':
          begin {Insert 'operand' lines from input.}
            counter := 0;
            while ¬eof (input) ∧ (counter < operand) do
            begin {Copy one line from input.}
              CopyLine (input); counter := counter + 1
            end {of insert};
            if counter < operand then
              ErrorMessage (3)
          end {'I' command}
    end {command with operand}
  end else if command = 'E' then
    begin {end of update}
      while ¬eof (infile) do CopyLine (infile);
      normalend := true; readln (input);
      writeln (output)
    end else
      begin ErrorMessage (4); readln (input) end
```

```
    end {of processing all commands};
    if ¬normalend then ErrorMessage(5);
    if errorencountered then
      writeln(output, '***Error(s) in the preceding update***')
  end {TextFileUpdate}.
```

REMARKS

1. The main difficulty in the preceding program is the proper handling of ends-of-line on *input* and *output*.
2. This program is not perfectly fault-tolerant, since any illegal character after a command will result in its abortion. To avoid this, the call to *read* at the beginning of processing an ordinary command should be replaced by a call to a slighly modified version of procedure *ReadInteger* (Example 9.2). This procedure should also intercept negative operands.
3. If the predefined files *input* and *output* were linked to an interactive terminal, it would probably be useless to print an echo of what is read, since this would be done by the terminal or the operating system.

EXERCISES

9.1 Record Reader

A textfile contains records with the following format:

ca	ƀ	code	ƀ	identification	ƀ	price	ƀ	tax	eoln
1	1	5	1	20	1	6	1	4	1

this corresponds to the Fortran format:

I1,1X,I5,1X,20A1,1X,F6.2,1X,F4.2

or to the Cobol data description:

```
01 TEXTFILE-RECORD
  02 CA PICTURE 9.
  02 FILLER PICTURE X.
  02 COD PICTURE 9(5).*
  02 FILLER PICTURE X.
  02 IDENTIFICATION PICTURE A(20).
  02 FILLER PICTURE X.
```

*Since *CODE* is a keyword in Cobol, we truncate it here.

02 PRICE PICTURE 9(4)V99.
02 FILLER PICTURE X.
02 TAX PICTURE 9(2)V99.

Write a Pascal procedure for reading such a record, with the following heading:

procedure *ReadARecord* (**var** *ca*: *integer*; **var** *code: codetype*; **var** *identification*: *string20*; **var** *price*, *tax*: *real*)

Type *codetype* is an integer subrange. The structured type *string20* is provided with three operators:

- *Initialize* (**var** *s* : *string20*) prepares for an assignment to *s*;

- *Append* (**var** *s* : *string20; c* : *char*) appends *c* to *s*;

- *Close* (**var** *s* : *string20*) terminates what was initialized by the first operator.

9.2   Record Reader II

Same exercise as 9.1, with the same record but without spaces separators. This corresponds to the Fortran format:

I1,I5,20A1,F6.2,F4.2

or to the Cobol data description without any filler.

9.3   Design Format

Given the three integer parameters a, b, and c, which represent lengths measured as numbers of characters, and a framing character m, the procedure to write must print the following design:

9.4 Report Generator

Write a set of procedures for generating reports in the format shown in Fig. 9.3. Hint: Use the following procedure headings:

procedure *LineOfStars* (*totallength* : *length*)
procedure *ReportHeading* (*heading* : *string20*; *usedwidth*; *string20length*; *reportlength* : *length*)
procedure *ColumnHeading* (*heading* : *string20*; *usedwidth*; *string20length*; *columnlength* : *length*)
procedure *PrintReal* (*no* : *real*; *fractionlength* : *integer*; *columnlength* : *length*)
procedure *PrintInteger* (*no* : *integer*; *columnlength* : *length*)
procedure *EndOfColumn*

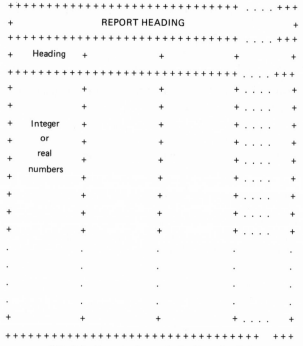

Fig. 9.3 Format of reports for Exercise 9.4.

9.5 File Comparison

The files to compare are textfiles, with lines of variable length, generated by a text editor. Every line contains a line number (an integer generated by the editor) followed with some text (keyed in by the user). The reference textfile has its lines numbered in a strictly ascending sequence, beginning at 1. The textfile to verify is also numbered in ascending sequence, but with possible holes because of lines deletion, or lines with a null number because of line insertions. If a line is only modified but not inserted or deleted, its number is not affected.

The procedure to write has three parameters: the reference textfile, the textfile to verify, and a new reference textfile, which is generated by renumbering the second one. It prints a succession of messages for displaying differences between the two input files:

1. Modifications in a particular line: the reference line and the line to verify are printed, from the first discrepancy to the end.

2. Insertion or suppression of a line: the line inserted or suppressed is printed.

Line numbers are read using the call *read* (f, *lineno*), and are written with the call *write* (f, *lineno* : 5, '$\not b$').

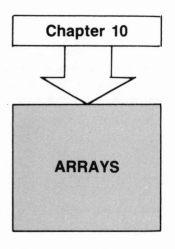

Chapter 10

ARRAYS

The array is the most frequently encountered data structure, even the only one in some languages—for example, Fortran, Algol 60, Basic, and APL. This does not necessarily mean that it is the most important one, or the simplest, or the most general. Moreover, its definition and its usage are frequently unduly restricted; thus it may be interesting and useful to first examine the underlying abstract structure of which the array is only a particular realization.

10.1 MAPPINGS

In a sequential structure, only one component of the structured object is accessible at any given time. To access a particular component, one must have previously accessed all its predecessors. Other properties and behaviors may be found in completely different data structures, whose access mode is *direct* or *random*, instead of sequential. The mapping is such a direct structure.

A *mapping* establishes a correspondence between values in a given domain and values in a given range. The source domain is the *index type*, and the object range is the *component type*. In other words, given a value of the index type, the mapping delivers a value of the component type. This is different from a function, in the sense that a mapping is not a piece of program which computes the component, but a *structure* which *contains* it.

Given a mapping type M, from an index type I to a component type C, we denote $M < c^+ >$ (c is of type C), the mapping that yields c for every index value, i.e., the mapping whose components are all equal to c. We denote $M < m ; i : c >$ (m, i, and c are of types M, I, and C, respectively), the mapping that is identical to m, except the component with index i, which is c. The different objects of type M may all be built with the two following rules:

1. If c is of type C, then $M <c^+>$ is of type M.

2. If m is of type M, i of type I, and c of type C, then $M <m ; i : c>$ is of type M.

We call the notation $M < m ; i : c >$ a *selective modification* of the mapping m: the component with index i is modified and takes the value c. The meaning of this notation in combination is specified by the following rule.

3. If m is of type M, i and i' of type I, and c and c' of type C, then $M <M <m ; i : c> ; i' : c'>$ has the following meaning: if $i = i'$, it is $M <m ; i' : c'>$; otherwise, it is $M <M <m ; i' : c'> ; i : c>$. A possible abbreviation for this notation is $M <m ; i : c, i' : c'>$.

Finally, we define the *component selection*, which yields a component, given an index, and which is established by the denotation of the mapping, followed by the index between square brackets. The two following rules define the component selection:

4. If i is of type I and c of type C, then $M <c^+>[i]$ is c (because all components of $M <c^+>$ are c).

5. If m is of type M, i and i' of type I, and c of type C, then $M < m ;$ $i : c > [i']$ has the following meaning: if $i = i'$, it is c (this precise component was just selectively modified); otherwise, it is $m[i']$.

The preceding rules suffice for defining a very abstract data structure, which is almost impossible to use without further operations, but which does not imply any particular implementation. Note, for example, that we did not restrict the index type, which may be any finite type (but all types are necessarily finite if they have to be represented on a computer). On the other hand, the notation for selective modification suggests that, given a particular mapping, to modify one of its components necessitates the construction of another mapping, which is a copy of the first one, except for the relevant component.

In exactly the same way as for the abstract sequence, different implementations may be provided for a mapping, depending upon the restrictions that are considered acceptable and the operations that must be done efficiently. For example, if the number of components has to be extremely large, an implementation on an external device is necessary, and the random access makes necessary the use of a so-called *random-access device* like a disk, a diskette, or a drum. If the range of the index type, which determines the maximum number of components, is much larger than the actual number of significant or useful components, the resulting structure is often called an *associative table,* if implemented in memory, or an *indexed file,* if implemented on back storage.

If there are exactly as many components as there are distinct values in the index type, the resulting structure is a *direct file* on back storage or an *array* in main memory. This last possibility is the chosen implementation in Pascal, as well as in most other programming languages, for example, Fortran and PL/I. However, the structure that is called an array in Basic, or even in APL, is more a table than an array, since the component corresponding to a given index value generally does not exist if it is never referenced.

10.2 SOME GENERALITIES CONCERNING ARRAYS

An array is a set of components of the same type, each accessible separately. The number of components is fixed at the definition of the array type and is determined by the cardinality of the index type. This restricts index types to ordinal types: integer or character subranges or enumerated types (including *Boolean*). In contrast, the component type has no reason to be restricted, and it may be any simple or structured type.

Where a mathematician would define a mapping in the form *mapping : domain → range*, an array type in Pascal has the syntax shown in Fig. 10.1, where the index type is any ordinal type and the component type is any type denoter. The possibility of enumerating several index types, separated by commas, will be examined in Sec. 10.3. The square brackets that appear in the type description are redundant, but they remind us of the notation for array indexing.

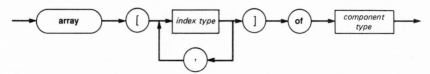

Fig. 10.1 Syntax diagram for an array type.

For abstract mappings, we defined notations for object construction and for selective modification. For actual arrays, this would be undesirable, since it would imply the construction or copy of a new object each time one of its components must be modified. In fact, the Pascal array is a *storage structure,* and the selection of one of its components (by indexing) is a way to access an element of this structure. Instead of the operations defined for the mappings, the Pascal array is endowed with the following operations, very similar to those which are found in other languages:

- *Assignment:* Like every object except files (which are not internal to the main memory), an array may be assigned to an array variable of the same type. Of course, for very large arrays, this assignment may be costly.

- *Indexing:* A component of an array may be selected using the notation shown in Fig. 10.2, where the array variable is any variable access of an array type, and the index expression is assignment-compatible with the index type of this array type. Here again, the possibility of enumerating several index expressions will be considered in Sec. 10.3. The indexed variable is of the component type of the array, and it constitutes a variable access.

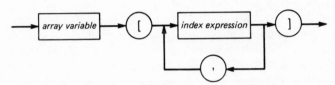

Fig. 10.2 Syntax diagram for an indexed variable.

Thus, there is no notation for array construction or selective modification. The latter operation is achieved by assignment to the indexed variable, and the former by repeated selective modifications of all components of the array. Immediately after its declaration, the value of an array is undefined and remains so until all its components have been assigned.

Example 10.1: Array Declarations and Indexings

type *daynumber* = *28..31*;
    month = (*Jan, Feb, Mar, Apr, May, Jun, Jul, Aug, Sep, Oct, Nov, Dec*);
    year = **array** [*month*] **of** *daynumber;*
    color = (*blue, red, green, yellow*);
var *x*: **array** [*−4..20*] **of** *real*;
    y: **array** [*color*] **of** *color;*
    z: **array** [*char*] **of** *month;*
    i, j: integer;
{x has 25 components of type real, with indices −4, −3, . . ., 0, 1, . . ., 20; y has four components of type color, with indices blue, red, green, yellow; the number of components of z is the number of characters in the implementation defined set, with all available characters as indices, for example, 'a', '4', ';', . . .

x[10] is of type real, as well as x[i + j];

y[red] and y[y[red]] are of type color;

z['+'] is of type month, and x[ord(z[input↑])] is of type real.}

REMARKS

1. In Pascal, an array is not a type of its own; rather it is a type constructor, which allows the definition of an infinite variety of array types. It may be explicitly named, e.g., *year* in this example, or anonymous, e.g., the types of variables *x*, *y*, and *z*.

2. In contrast to Fortran, Basic, PL/I and Cobol, the index type of an array is not restricted to an integer subrange, and its lower bound is not restricted to 1.

3. The number of components of an array is fixed by the cardinality of its index type. Since types can only be statically defined, this number of components is fixed at program construction and cannot vary during execution. The notion of a *dynamic array*, which exists in PL/I, does not appear in Pascal.

4. To use the type *integer* as an index type is legal, but generally impossible, since the size of the resulting array would be probably too large. Using the type *real* would be illegal, since it is not an ordinal type, and one could not determine the number of distinct values in any real subrange.

Example 10.2: Binary Search

type *table* = **array** [*lowerbound..upperbound*] **of** *T*
{Lowerbound and upperbound are two integer constants; T is some simple type.};
procedure *BinarySearch*
    (**var** *tb* : **table** {the sorted table to be examined};
    x : *T* {the value to be searched in tb};
    var *i* : *integer* {if found, is true, tb[i] = x.};
    var *found* : *Boolean* {true if at least one component of tb equals x, false otherwise}
    );
    var *left, right: integer;*
begin {Binary Search; see Example 7.4.}
    left := *lowerbound* ; *right* := *upperbound;*
    while *left* ≤ *right* **do**
    begin {x does not appear in tb before left or after right.}
      i : = (*left* + *right*) **div** 2;
      if *tb*[*i*] ≤ *x* **then** *left* := *i*+1;
      if *tb*[*i*] ≥ *x* **then** *right* := *i*−1
    end {while left ≤ right};
    found:= *x* = *tb*[*i*]
end {BinnarySearch}

REMARKS

1. The index type of *table* cannot be any ordinal type because of the necessary calculations. $i+1$ and $i-1$ could be replaced by *succ(i)* and *pred(i)*, but the expression (*left* + *right*) **div** 2 cannot be generalized for an enumerated type. However, for the type *char* (or a subrange thereof), the expression $chr((ord(left) + ord(right))$ **div** $2)$ could be used; therefore, the binary search may be used for an array indexed with characters.

2. The index bounds are fixed in the type definition; consequently, this procedure cannot handle an array with different bounds, nor even an array with the same bounds but declared with a different type. We shall see in Sec. 10.7 how this restriction may be relaxed.

Example 10.3: Frequency Count of Letters

```
program FrequencyCount(input, output)
   {The textfile input is read and copied on output, followed by a frequency count of
      all lowercase letters which appear in it.};
type natural = 0..maxint;
var count: array['a'..'z'] of natural;
   ch: char;
function IsALetter(ch: char): Boolean
   {Since the underlying character set is unknown, one cannot guarantee that all
      characters between 'a' and 'z' are letters; this function works for all currently
      used character sets, especially ISO (ASCII) and EBCDIC.};
begin {IsALetter}
   IsALetter :=
      ('a' ≤ ch) ∧ (ch ≤ 'i') ∨
      ('j' ≤ ch) ∧ (ch ≤ 'r') ∨
      ('s' ≤ ch) ∧ (ch ≤ 'z')
end {IsALetter};
begin {FrequencyCount}
   ch := 'a';
   while ch ≤ 'z' do {Initialize count.}
   begin count[ch] := 0; ch := succ(ch) end;
   while ¬eof(input) do
   begin
      while ¬eoln(input) do
      begin read(input, ch); write(output, ch);
         if IsALetter(ch) then
            count[ch] := count[ch] + 1
      end;
      writeln(output); readln(input)
   end {while ¬eof(input)};
```

```
page(output); writeln(output, 'Letter Frequency');
writeln(output); ch := 'a';
while ch ⩽ 'z' do
begin
   if IsALetter(ch) then
      writeln(output, ch: 4, count[ch]: 9);
   ch := succ(ch)
   end
end {FrequencyCount}.
```

10.3 MULTIDIMENSIONED ARRAYS

All the arrays that appear in the preceding examples have components of simple types. This is not necessary, since the component type of an array may be any structured type, too. Thus, a programmer can define arrays of files, of records (see Chap. 12), of sets (Chap. 13), or of pointers (Chap. 14) and also arrays of arrays, commonly called *multidimensioned arrays*. The type *matrix* defined as follows:

> **type** *matrix* = **array** $[m..n]$ **of array** $[p..q]$ **of** *real*

has $ord(n) - ord(m) + 1$ components, with indices $m, succ(m), ..., n$, which are arrays of $ord(q) - ord(p) + 1$ components of type *real* and with indices $p, succ(p), ..., q$. If *mat* is a variable of type *matrix*, *mat*[i] is of type **array** $[p..q]$ **of** *real*, and *mat*[i][j] is of type *real*.

For simplicity and for similarity with other languages, Pascal provides abbreviated notations for arrays of arrays. In a type description,]**of array**[may be replaced by a comma in the variable access, and][may be replaced by a comma again. This means that the following type definition is exactly equivalent to the preceding one:

> **type** *matrix* = **array** $[m..n, p..q]$ **of** *real*

and that *mat*[i] [j] is exactly equivalent to *mat*[i,j] in all situations. Moreover, type *matrix* could be defined in yet another way:

> **type** *vector* = **array** $[p..q]$ **of** *real*;
> *matrix* = **array** $[m..n]$ **of** *vector*

which is once again exactly equivalent to the two preceding definitions. Whatever the exact form of the definition of its type, *mat* is always an array of arrays, the variable access *mat*[i] is legal, and it denotes an array of reals that is in a sense a subarray or a row of *mat*. Of course, these abbreviations can be extended to any number of dimensions.

Example 10.4:   Matrix Product

type *matrix* = **array** [*1..n, 1..n*] **of** *real* {square matrix};
procedure *SquareMatrixProduct(a,b: matrix*; **var** *c: matrix*)
    {Compute c = a × b.};
    var *i, j, k:0..n;*
        sum : real;
    begin {SquareMatrixProduct}
    i := 0;
        while *i* < *n* **do**
        begin *i := i+1; j := 0;*
            while *j* < *n* **do**
            begin *j := j + 1; k := 0; sum := 0;*
                while *k* < *n* **do** {sum = $\sum\limits_{m=1}^{k} a_{im}\, b_{mj}$}
                    begin *k := k + 1;*
                    *sum := sum + a [i,k] * b [k,j]*
                    end {Loop on k; sum = $\sum\limits_{m=1}^{n} a_{im}\, b_{mj}$};
                c[i,j] := sum
            end {loop on j}
        end {loop on i; $c_{ij} = \sum\limits_{k=1}^{n} a_{ik}\, b_{kj}$}
    end {SquareMatrixProduct}

REMARKS

For several different reasons (listed below), this procedure is very crude, and subsequent versions will add to it the possibilities it presently lacks.

1. The loops are cumbersome to write and need for the three variables *i, j,* and *k* a subrange starting from 0 instead of 1; this will be replaced by the **for** statement in Chap. 11.

2. Matrices *a* and *b*, being value parameters, are in fact variables local to the procedure and need much storage and copies of the formal parameters at procedure call. This cost can be avoided by using variable parameters, with some care (see Sec. 10.6).

3. The size of the matrices to multiply is fixed in the type definition, and this procedure cannot handle real matrices of a different size, or even square real matrices of the same size but declared with another type (an identical type with a different name, for example, or an anonymous identical type); this limitation can be overcome by using *conformant-array parameters* (see Sec. 10.7).

More significant examples using multidimensioned or complicated arrays will appear in subsequent sections and chapters.

10.4 PACKED ARRAYS

The representation of any data structure on a given computer is necessarily a compromise between time efficiency and space efficiency. This compromise is especially critical when the components of the data structure do not fit well on the storage units of the computer. For example, there is no perfect representation for an array of booleans on a computer with 32-bit storage units; if the array is stored one word per boolean component, the access and modification operations are simple and efficient, but 31 bits are wasted for every bit used; if 32 boolean components are packed in a word, storage is better used, but every access and modification operation requires some complicated action using masks and shifts. Ideally, a compiler could automatically choose the best representation, depending upon the size of the array and its frequency of use. In many situations, the programmer may know what factor—size or speed—should be given the advantage, and inform the compiler accordingly.

Every data-structure definition of Pascal (either in a type definition or within a variable declaration) may be prefixed with the keyword **packed**. This informs the compiler that, if possible, it should give advantage to size considerations, even if this causes operations on components of the structure to be less efficient in time as well as in space. In the absence of this prefix, the default compromise is to give the advantage to speed.

It is important to note that the Pascal programmer has no means to specify the exact representation of structured objects. In fact, it depends upon the host computer and the particular implementation; moreover, the compiler has complete liberty to flatly ignore the prefix **packed**; this should not affect the meaning of the program. Some compilers may try to actually pack only components of some types and not of other types. A packed array of reals probably has exactly the same representation as an unpacked one.

Another important point is that the situations where the prefix **packed** is really useful are very few, and fall in two categories: the first case is when the array must be considered as a character string, and it will be discussed in Sec. 10.5; the second case is when we have a large array (or data structure) of small components. To pack a small array could have a completely negative effect, even in space, since the additional code necessary for accessing packed components may very well exceed the storage saved by packing.

Every structured type may be specified as packed, according to the syntax shown in Fig. 10.3. Record types and set types will be considered in subsequent chapters (12 and 13, respectively). For file types, packing may be specified, but it has generally no effect at all, since its meaning is somewhat difficult to interpret. However, on a 16-bit computer, using the ISO character code, a **file of** *char* could use one word per character and a **packed file of** *char* could pack two characters per word, but this would make sense only if the notion of a word would make sense on peripheral devices.

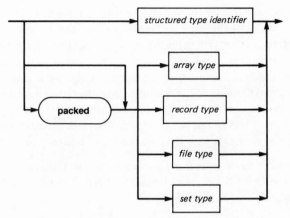

Fig. 10.3 Syntax diagram for a structured type.

Although the packing specification generally does not affect the semantics of the program, only its performance, some important details must be considered.

1. For a multidimensional array, packing may be done at different levels. Given two ordinal (subrange) types *rowtype* and *columntype,* four different situations may occur:

   a. **array** [*rowtype*] **of array** [*columntype*] **of** *componenttype*
      {This is equivalent to array [rowtype, columntype] of componenttype.}

   b. **packed array** [*rowtype*] **of array** [*columntype*] **of** *componenttype*
      {This makes sense, probably, only if each row needs much less space than a 'word' on the host computer.}

   c. **array** [*rowtype*] **of packed array** [*columntype*] **of** *componenttype*

   d. **packed array** [*rowtype*] **of packed array** [*columntype*] **of** *componenttype*
      {This is equivalent to packed array [rowtype, columntype] of componenttype; i.e., packing is transitive in the abbreviated form.}

   Case *c* is generally the only one that makes sense, especially because most compilers normally do not try to pack components larger than a "word."

2. Packing is one of the characteristics of a type, and rules of type compatibility consequently include it. An unpacked type and its packed version are not compatible in assignments or in parameter transmission. Anyway, a packed type cannot be defined by packing another type, i.e.,

   packedT = **packed** *T* is illegal.

3. The actual parameter corresponding to a variable formal parameter cannot be a component of a packed structure, because this would need, for the body of the subprogram, a knowledge of the packing characteristics of this packed structure. However, in every other circumstance, a component of a packed structure has no special behavior and may well correspond to a value formal parameter, for example. Moreover, the various parameters of all predefined subprograms are not described as variable parameters, so this special rule does not hold. In particular, it is legal to read components of a packed structure with the predefined procedures *read* and *readln*.

4. For transferring values from packed arrays to unpacked ones, and vice versa, two predefined procedures are given. Let us have the following declarations, or their equivalent:

> **var** *unpackedvar* : **array** [*indextype1*] **of** *T;*
>
> *packedvar* : **packed array** [*indextype2*] **of** *T*;

and let *low* and *high* be the smallest and largest values of the type *indextype2;* then if *expr* is an expression which is assignment-compatible with *indextype1*, the statement

> pack (unpackedvar, expr, packedvar)

is equivalent to

```
begin temp1 := expr ; temp2 := pred(low);
  while temp2 < high do
    begin temp2 := succ(temp2);
      packedvar [temp2] := unpackedvar [temp1];
      if temp2 ≠ high then temp1 := succ(temp1)
    end
end
```

where *temp1* and *temp2* are two auxiliary variables which do not appear elsewhere in the program. Similarly, the statement

> unpack (packedvar, unpackedvar, expr)

is equivalent to

```
begin temp1 := expr ; temp2 := pred(low);
  while temp2 < high do
    begin temp2 := succ(temp2);
      unpackedvar[temp1] := packedvar[temp2];
      if temp2 ≠ high then temp1 := succ(temp1)
    end
end
```

These two procedures, therefore, realize a partial copy according to the unpacked array, but a complete copy according to the packed array. This lack of symmetry may be somewhat misleading. Types *indextype1* and *indextype2* need not be related in any way, but all references to *unpackedvar* [*temp1*] must be legal; i.e., there must exist in *indextype1* a number of values, from *expr* upwards, which is at least equal to the cardinality of *indextype2*.

10.5 STRINGS

A character string was defined in Chap. 2 as a constant that represents a sequence of characters. The only use of the string that has been made so far is to print these constants. But we now have all the elements needed for completing the description of character strings.

A character string with only one element is a constant of type *char*, but a character string with more than one element is a constant of a particular *string type*, with the same number of components. A string type is a type having the description **packed array** [*1..length*] of *char*, or its equivalent, *length* being some *integer* constant greater than 1. Note the two restrictions in this description: a string type is always packed, and the lower bound is always 1. Note also that a packed array of character subrange components is not a string.

With character string constants and string type variables, it is possible to handle strings almost in the same way as values of simple types, but with the additional properties that result from the accessibility of individual characters and with the restriction that a string cannot be returned by a function (since it is not actually a simple type).

All comparison operators are defined between strings of compatible types (although they are not defined for ordinary arrays). Two strings are equal if they have the same length (otherwise they could not be compared) and equal components in each corresponding position. They are not equal if at least one component pair does not match. Operators $<$, $\leqslant$, $\geqslant$, and $>$ denote lexicographic ordering: given two comparable (i.e., compatible) strings *s1* and *s2*, *s1* $<$ *s2* if and only if there is some index *p* between *1* and *length,* such that for all *i* from *1* to *p* $-$ *1*, *s1*[*i*] $=$ *s2*[*i*], and *s1*[*p*] $<$ *s2*[*p*]. Operators $\leqslant$, $\geqslant$, and $>$ may be defined in a similar way. This means that the implicit order of the underlying character set is determinant. For example, the position of the blank space in this order may imply that '*abb̸*' is greater than '*abc*', instead of the ordinary ordering in dictionaries. For avoiding this problem, a frequent solution is to replace all trailing spaces with *chr(0)*, a character which is not a letter in any common character code.

One more capability exists especially for strings: the possibility of writing them directly in textfiles (see Example 9.5). However, strings cannot be directly read with the predefined procedure *read*, the main reason being that it is extremely simple to program the reading, and more flexible, too, since there can be several ways of handling the length of what is read in relation to ends-of-line.

Although strings in Pascal are sufficient for some applications, they do not provide all that could be wished for. By comparison with PL/I, or with specialized string-processing languages, they lack flexibility and generality, especially because a given string has a fixed length that cannot change in any way. Consequently, no concatenation operator is defined, a given string can be assigned only to a string of the same length (although several nonstandard implementations are more permissive), and their use as subprogram parameters is limited (except with the feature described in Sec. 10.7). We shall see in Chap. 14 an example of a package of type definitions and procedure declarations which could be used for a more general and complete notion of a string.

Example 10.5: Concordance of a Text

```
program TextConcordance(input, output);
   {This program reads a text on input and establishes a simplified concordance of it, i.e.,
      an alphabetic dictionary of all the words that appear in this text. A word is
      defined to be a sequence of letters without any other character inter-
      spersed.}
   const wordlength = 20 {maximum useful length of words};
      dictlength = 1000 {maximum length of the dictionary};
   type wordtype = packed array[1..wordlength] of char {a string};
   var dictionary: array[1..dictlength] of wordtype;
      word: wordtype {the current word};
      dictsize, index: 0..dictlength {two indices in dictionary};
   function IsALetter(ch: char): Boolean; . . .{see Example 10.3};
   procedure ReadAWord
      {The next input character is a letter. Read the coresponding word in the global
         variable word.};
      var wordread: array[1..wordlength] of char {unpacked};
         k: 0..wordlength;
      begin {ReadAWord}
         k := 0;
         repeat {IsALetter(input↑)}
            if k < wordlength then
            begin k := k + 1;
               wordread[k] := input↑
            end;
            get(input)
         until ¬IsALetter(input↑);
         {The word is read.}
```

```
while k < wordlength do {Complete it with blanks.}
begin k := k + 1;
  wordread[k] := ' '
end;
pack(wordread, 1, word)
  {hopefully better than a direct reading}
end {ReadAWord};
procedure SearchAndEnter
  {The word is inserted in the dictionary if it is not already here and if there is at least
    one cell. The dictionary is already sorted.};
  var left, middle, right: 0..dictlength;
begin {SearchAndEnter}
  if dictsize = 0 then {dictionary empty, insert the word}
  begin dictionary[1] := word; dictsize := 1 end
  else
  begin {general case}
    left := 1; right := dictsize;
    while left ≤ right do {binary search}
    begin
      middle := (left + right) div 2;
      if dictionary[middle] ≤ word then
        left := middle + 1;
      if dictionary[middle] ≥ word then
        right := middle - 1
    end;
    if dictionary[middle] ≠ word then
      {Insert it if possible.}
    if dictsize < dictlength then {It fits.}
    begin dictsize := dictsize + 1; right := dictsize;
      if dictionary[middle] < word then
        {but dictionary[middle + 1] > word}
        middle := middle + 1;
      while right > middle do {Shift words.}
      begin dictionary[right] := dictionary[right - 1];
        right := right - 1
      end;
      dictionary[middle] := word
    end
  end {general case}
end {SearchAndEnter};
begin {program TextConcordance}
  dictsize := 0;
  repeat {¬eof(input)}
    if IsALetter(input↑) then {beginning of a word}
```

begin *ReadA Word*
 { ¬IsALetter(input↑) } ;
 SearchAndEnter
end
else *get(input)* {Pass the nonletter char.}
until *eof(input)*;
page(output);
writeln(output, 'Concordance'); writeln(output);
index := 0;
repeat
 index := index + 1; writeln(output, dictionary[index])
until *index = dictsize*
end {TextConcordance}.

REMARKS

1. This program does not give an actual text concordance, only an index of the words. It would be useful to add either a list of the line numbers where a given word appears, or these lines themselves, rotated so that the word considered always appears centered in the output line. The first solution is generally called a *cross-reference index,* especially when the text analyzed is a computer program, and a program doing that work will appear in Chap. 14. The second solution is a true concordance, useful in text and vocabulary analysis, and it needs, for example, the use of an external file which is sorted before being printed.

2. The procedure *SearchAndEnter* uses a binary search and insertion, which is not the most efficient possible solution, since the repeated insertions make it necessary that many previously encountered words be moved, which is rather costly. "Hashing" would be more efficient, and a solution will appear in the concordance example of Chap. 14.

10.6 ARRAYS AS SUBPROGRAM PARAMETERS

The use of arrays as subprogram parameters raises two important problems which will be considered one after the other. The first one is the transmission mode, which was considered only briefly in Chap. 5. If an array parameter is passed by value, it means that the formal parameter is a variable local to the subprogram initialized with the actual parameter. Since this parameter is used as an input parameter, this creates no semantic problems, but efficiency must be seriously considered: the local array needs storage inside the procedure, and the initial copy costs time. The same remark was noted for Example 10.4 (Matrix Product), and it is true that this example was unduly inefficient in this respect.

To avoid these two inconveniences, it seems advisable to use variable instead of value parameters. The cost of double storage and copies is avoided, but at the expense of an important insecurity: since the formal array is not local to the subprogram, its actual counterpart may be modified inadvertently. Moreover, serious problems arise if the same array occurs several times as a variable parameter in the same subprogram call.

Consider, for example, the procedure *SquareMatrixProduct* of Example 10.4. Given the arrays *ma*, *mb*, and *mc* of type *matrix*, the call *SquareMatrixProduct(ma, mb, mc)* yields in *mc* the matrix product of *ma* and *mb*, and these two matrices are unchanged, whether they are value parameters (as in the example) or variable ones. On the contrary, the call *SquareMatrixProduct(ma, mb, ma)* may cause havoc in the case of variable parameters, since the formal parameters *a* and *c* are substituted with the same actual parameter, *ma*. When $c[i,j]$ is assigned, it is in fact *ma* that is modified, and it is the modified value that will be used in a subsequent pass in the loop. The result is almost impossible to predict, but surely it is not the matrix product of the initial values of *ma* and *mb*.

A similar problem may occur when a variable parameter is not a complete array, but a component of an array (or of any structured type). The reference to the component is computed before entering the subprogram, and the array may be almost forgotten. Consider a procedure *ExtendedProduct* (var *a* : *matrix*; var *b* : *real*), which multiplies every component of *a* by *b* (of course, in this somewhat contrived example, there is no need for *b* to be a variable parameter). The call *ExtendedProduct* (*ma*, *x*) modifies *ma* in the expected way, but that is not the case for the call *ExtendedProduct(ma, ma[i,j])*. As soon as the particular component *ma*[i,j] is modified inside the procedure, the formal parameter *b* is also modified, and the rest of the procedure uses another value for its work.

These perils of variable parameters are serious; fortunately, they occur only in one particular situation: when the same array (or, more generally, a structured variable) appears two or more times in a subprogram call as an actual parameter or as a part of an actual parameter, corresponding to a variable formal parameter. This situation must be avoided in every circumstance, not just in the most complicated one, when the array does not even appear as an explicit parameter and is used and modified inside the subprogram as a global variable.

10.7 CONFORMANT-ARRAY PARAMETERS

The second problem raised by array parameters was evoked in connection with Example 10.2, and a solution was promised. The problem is as old as Pascal, and the solution presented here is the one defined in the ISO *Standard* as the best available compromise between the simplicity and rigor of the initial language and the requirements of actual programming.

If we have to write, for example, a binary search procedure, or a sorting procedure, or a matrix product procedure, and if we add nothing to the preceding description of Pascal, we must freeze the exact length of the array parameters when writing the procedure itself. If a binary search procedure handles arrays whose index type is the subrange $m..n$, it cannot handle arrays with other index types, since this type is an integral part of the array type itself. This difficulty may be partly avoided if we have several arrays of the same total length, with differing lengths used, but that is not a general solution.

Consequently, the ISO *Standard* introduces (only for level-1 implementations) the concept of a conformant-array parameter, which is yet another sort of parameter, distinct from value, variable, procedure, and function parameters. In the subprogram heading, conformant-array parameters appear as value or variable parameters, but their type name is replaced with a conformant-array schema, which is much more similar to an array-type definition, as shown in Fig. 10.4. The diagram does not make clear that, if **packed** appears in the specification, there cannot be more than one specified conformant dimension (the last one specified). Moreover, an abbreviation similar to the one explained in Sec. 10.3 is available, but with less generality if **packed** is specified.

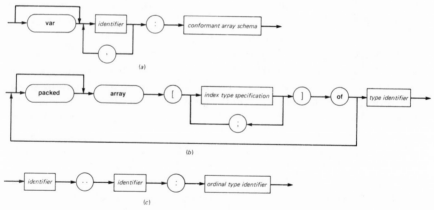

Fig. 10.4 Syntax diagram for the conformant-array parameter: (*a*) conformant-array parameter specification; (*b*) conformant-array schema; and (*c*) index type specification.

Example 10.6: Conformant-Array Parameter Specifications

type *natural* = *0..maxint*;
  table = **array** [*1..100*] **of** *real;*
  string = **packed array** [*1..stringlength*] **of** *char*;
  . . .
{Here follow examples of conformant array parameters:
  var a : array [i..j : natural] of real;
  b : packed array [s1..s2 : natural] of char;

```
c : array [m..n : char] of string;
var d : array [m1..n1 : char] of packed array [m2..n2 : natural] of char;
var e : array [flow..fhigh : integer ; slow..shigh : integer] of real;
This last specification is exactly equivalent to the following one:
var e : array [flow..fhigh : integer] of array [slow..shigh : integer] of real;}
```

Within the subprogram, in the heading of which it is specified, a conformant-array formal parameter is an array whose index type is not entirely known at compile time, in a way similar to Fortran or PL/I. However, the important differences are that the host type of the index type is known and that the exact bounds of the subrange of this host type are known at run time; they may differ from one call of the subprogram to the other. The two identifiers that appear between square brackets in the conformant-array parameter specification are called *bound identifiers*; they may be used somewhat like constants within the procedure, i.e., used in expressions, but not assigned. However, they are not actual constants, and they cannot be used in type definitions, because it would violate one of the main assumptions made for any Pascal type; namely, the size of any object of this type can always be known at compile time. Within the subprogram body, the bound identifiers denote the bound values of the index type of the corresponding actual parameter.

Regarding type compatibility, a conformant-array formal parameter has a type distinct from any other type, since even if its component type is fixed and known at compile time, its index type may differ from call to call. Consequently, it cannot, as a whole, be used in assignment statements unless another conformant-array formal parameter occurs in the same identifier list in the parameter specifications. In fact, a conformant-array formal parameter is very difficult to use as a whole, and its normal usage is componentwise.

At subprogram call, the actual parameter that conforms to the conformant-array formal parameter is a variable access—in case of a variable parameter —or an expression reducing to a variable access or a string in case of a value parameter; the actual parameter denotes an array of a suitable type: the component type must be the same as in the specification, and the index type must be compatible, with bounds within the specified subrange. Packing or nonpacking must be exactly as specified. If several formal parameters appear in the same identifier list of a conformant-array parameter specification, the corresponding actual parameters must be all of the same type, as in the ordinary situation for variable parameters. This is especially necessary in the present situation, because only one pair of bound identifiers is available.

In the case of a value parameter, an anonymous variable of the suitable type is created before the procedure call; this variable is assigned the value of the actual parameter, and the reference to this anonymous variable is communicated to the procedure. This achieves an effect equivalent to an ordinary parameter transmission by value; i.e., an attempt to modify the formal parameter within the procedure is permitted, but it has no effect on the actual parameter. A value conformant array cannot be used as an actual parameter corresponding to another value conformant array; i.e., a value cannot be transmitted again as a value. If this situation were allowed, the size of the anonymous variable to be created before the second transmission cannot be computed. However, it can be transmitted as a variable, since this involves no anonymous variable.

If the conformant-array formal parameter is specified as a packed array of characters, with an integer (or subrange thereof) index type, the corresponding actual parameter may be a character string. Of course, the lower bound of the specified index type must be less than or equal to 1. Within the subprogram, the formal parameter cannot be considered a string type variable, since its lower bound is not known at compile time. Consequently, the special properties of string types (as comparison operands and as an argument for procedure *write*) do not apply. Comparisons and writings, if necessary, must be explicitly programmed.

In the rule about parameter list congruity, which appeared in Sec. 5.3, no mention was made of conformant-array parameters, since this fifth mode of parameter transmission was not known. Two formal parameter sections match in a fifth case, when they are both conformant-array parameter specifications, with the same number of parameters and with equivalent conformant-array schemas. Two such schemas are equivalent if, after removing the possible abbreviations of multidimensioned schemas, they are identical: same index types and component types, same packing or unpacking. Of course, this rule is presented here mainly for completeness, since parametric subprograms with conformant-array parameters are extremely strange things, very uncommon in ordinary programs.

The conformant-array feature is not equivalent to what is often called *dynamic arrays;* in Pascal, all types are completely described at compile time so that the compiler can fully compute the storage needed for any type. A brief comparison may be made with other programming languages. With a compiler complying at level 0 (no conformant arrays), Pascal has the same capabilities as Cobol, regarding array bounds. With a compiler complying at level 1, it has the same capabilities as Fortran or PL/I. The possibility of declaring arrays whose bounds are computed at run time, allowed in Algol 60 and 68, and in APL, does not exist in Pascal and is incompatible with one of the basic design choices of the language.

The conformant array is probably the most complicated feature we have to explain, and examples are clearly necessary. The following are generalizations of examples which appear earlier in a limited form. Other uses of the feature will be made in subsequent chapters.

Example 10.7:   Binary Search (Improved)

type T =.. {some simple type, if comparison operators are to be used, or some type upon which comparison functions are defined};
procedure *BinarySearch*
   (**var** *tb:* **array** [*lowerbound..upperbound : integer*] **of** T {the sorted table to be examined};
   x : T {the value to be searched in tb};
   var *i : integer* {if found is true, tb[i] = x};
   var*found : Boolean* {true if at least one component of tb equals x, false otherwise}
   );
   . . . {The body is exactly identical to Example 10.2, if T is a simple type. If a comparison predicate must be used, the suitable modifications are very easy.}
     . . .
{This procedure may be called with a first actual parameter which is any array of T whose index type is an integer subrange.}

Example 10.8:   Matrix Product (Improved)

procedure *MatrixProduct*
   (**var** *a* : **array** [*fla..fua : integer ; sla..sua : integer*] **of** *real;*
   var *b* : **array** [*flb..fub : integer ; slb..sub : integer*] **of** *real*;
   var *c* : **array** [*flc..fuc : integer ; slc..suc : integer*] **of** *real*
)
{This procedure computes the matrix product of a and b into c. Parameters a and b are variable parameters, for avoiding the cost of copies. The validity condition upon identifier bounds cannot be expressed directly as a type restriction, which could be checked by the compiler. A run-time check must be programmed within the procedure, and a global error procedure may be called if the necessary relations on index bounds do not hold.};
   var *fa, fb, fc, sa, sb, sc : integer*;
   sum : real;
begin {MatrixProduct}
   if(*sua* − *sla* ≠ *flb* − *fub*) {second dim. of a ≠ first dim. of b}
   ∧ (*fua* − *fla* ≠ *fuc* − *flc*) {first dim. of a ≠ first dim. of c}
   ∧ (*sub* − *slb* ≠ *suc* − *slc*) {second dim. of b ≠ second dim. of c}
   then *error* **else**
   begin {Each array has its own set of indices.}
   fa := fla ; fc := flc;
   repeat {loop on first dimension of c and a}
      sb := slb ; sc := slc;
      repeat {loop on second dimension of c and b}
         sa := sla ; fb := flb ; sum := 0;

```
repeat {loop on second dimension of a and first of b}
  sum := sum + a[fa,sa] * b[fb, sb];
  sa := sa + 1 ; fb := fb + 1
until sa > sua;
c[fc, sc] := sum;
sc := sc + 1 ; sb := sb + 1
until sc > suc;
fc := fc + 1 ; fa := fa + 1
until fc > fuc
end
end {MatrixProduct}
```

REMARKS

Twelve distinct bound identifiers and six distinct indices make this procedure exceedingly complicated, although extremely general. Such a generality is not afforded in normal situations, and a simpler procedure will appear in Chap. 11.

Example 10.9:   Error Messages

```
procedure ErrorMessage
  (message : packed array [lb..ub : natural] of char;
  severity, linenumber : integer
  )
  {This procedure, or a similar one, may be used for producing error messages in some
    text-processing program, such as a compiler, a macroprocessor, or more
    simply, a file update program like Example 9.5.};
  var i : natural;
  begin {Error Message}
    writeln(output);
    write(output, '****', severity : 2, ' ');
    i := lb;
    repeat write(output, message [i]) ; i := i + 1
    until i > ub;
    writeln(output, ' in line ', linenumber : 1)
  end {ErrorMessage}
```

REMARKS

This procedure may be called with a variable of a string type as its first actual parameter (if the message includes some variable data, for example) or with a character string constant. This is much more practical than the solution used in Example 9.5. However, within the procedure, the formal parameter may not be considered as a string type variable; consequently, its writing must be explicitly programmed, and it cannot be compared with another string, even of the same type.

EXERCISES

10.1 Sequence

In Example 7.2, a type *sequence* was used for describing a sequence of objects of some simple type *T*, with the following operators:

procedure *Initialize*(**var** *s*: *sequence*) {Prepare s for examination.};
function *EndOfSequence*(**var** *s*: *sequence*): *Boolean* {True if there are no more components of s, false otherwise};
function *Next*(**var** *s*: *sequence*): *T* {yields the next component of s, if it exists};

Assuming that a sequence cannot contain more than 50 objects of type *T*, build the type *sequence* using an array, and write the three preceding operators.

10.2 Table Processing

A fixed-length table *tb*, with *tblength* components, contains entries made of a characteristic key (a character string) and some information of type *T*. For improving access to this table, it has been decided to order the entries according to the length of the keys used: the key of *tb*[*1*] has the shortest length and that of *tb*[*length*] the longest. This establishes a partial order. If *i* and *j* give the indices of the first entries whose key lengths are *ilength* and *ilength* + *1*, respectively, then the search of the index *k* for an entry whose key is known (and of length *ilength*) is made by a linear search between *tb*[*i*] and *tb*[*j* − *1*].

Build the necessary data structures for such a processing, and write the function

function *Search*(*key*: *keytype*; **var** *k*: *index*): *Boolean*

where *keytype* = **packed array**[*1..keylength*] **of** *char* and *index* = *1*.. *tblength*. This function returns *true* if an entry with the given key exists (*k* is its index), and false otherwise. If a key is made of *n* < *keylength* nonblank characters, then *n* is the length used.

Write a procedure which builds the necessary data structures from the textfile that contains *tblength* entries, ordered as in the table (by increasing length of the keys used).

10.3   Merge

Write the following procedure:

procedure *Merge*
   (**var** *from 1*: **array**[*f1l*..*f1u*: *integer*] **of** *integer*;
   var *from2*: **array**[*f2l*..*f2u*: *integer*] **of** *integer*;
   var *into*: **array**[*il*..*iu*: *integer*] **of** *integer*)

which merges *from1* and *from2*, sorted in ascending order, and produces *into*, also sorted.

10.4   Translation of Morse Messages

Write the following procedure:

procedure *MorseTranslation* (**var** *inMorse*, *inEnglish*: *text*)

which produces a message in English as the translation of a message coded in Morse. The Morse dictionary is available on the textfile *Morsecode*, with the following layout: each item of Morse code, terminated by a space, is followed with its corresponding character, and each pair (Morse code, character) is separated with a space; all codes are ordered according to their increasing length, and there are 39 different codes.

In the message that appears on file *inMorse*, one blank delimits two items of Morse code in the same word, and two or more blanks delimit two words. The message is ended with the special code *EndOfMessage* ('.-.-.'). The longest code is of length 8. If an illegal code appears in the message, it is translated as a question mark.

Hint: Use Exercice 10.2 for organizing the dictionary.

10.5   The Longest Word

The TV game show "The Longest Word" asks players to build, in a finite time, the longest possible word using a set of letters [*letnumber* (=8)], randomly chosen. This word must appear in a given reference dictionary. Using a table which contains all words in the dictionary of length < *letnumber*, organized as in Exercise 10.2, write the following procedure:

procedure *LongestWord* (*setofletters*: *word*; **var** *thelongest*: *word*)

with *word* = **packed array**[*1*..*letnumber*] **of** *char*.

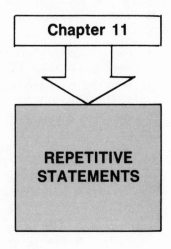

Chapter 11

REPETITIVE STATEMENTS

Frequently the same action (either simple or compound) has to be done for every element of a particular set of objects (especially for every component of an array) or for every value in a discrete subrange. In many cases, moreover, the *order* in which these elements are handled, and the *means* by which the next element is selected, are irrelevant. The two iterative statements introduced in Chap. 7 are not completely adequate. They do not emphasize the important fact that the same job is done for all objects of some group; they give too much importance to the order in which these objects are processed; and they are not completely applicable in some unusual circumstances.

For example, if some action $A(x)$ must be applied to all components of some array a of type **array**[$m .. n$] **of** T, an auxiliary variable i must be declared, of type $m..succ(n)$ (which is not a legal construction in Pascal), and the construct

$$i := m; \textbf{repeat } A(a[i]); i := succ(i) \textbf{ until } i > n$$

must be used. Note that i must be declared on a range with one element more that the index type of a. In some situations, this would be impossible—for example, if this index type is a complete enumerated type, as in the following example:

type *color* = (*purple, blue, green, yellow, orange, red*);
var *table* = **array**[*color*] **of** *sometype*;
  index: *color;*
begin {. . .}

  {We want to call action A for all components of the array table. We cannot initialize
    the index to a value preceding purple which does not exist, so we have to
    make a special case for the first array component.}

index := *purple*; *A*(*table*[*index*]);
while *index* < *red* **do**
begin *index* := *succ*(*index*);
  A(*table*[*index*])
end {Index is now red.}

A new statement structure is therefore very useful for expressing these repetitive statements. It is the **for** statement, which appears in almost all programming languages and which is the only way of expressing repetitions in most of them, especially in Fortran and Basic. In Basic, the corresponding construct begins with the statement FOR < variable > = < expression > TO < expression > STEP < expression > and ends with the statement NEXT < variable >. In Fortran, it is the statement DO < label > < variable > = < expression >, < expression >, < expression >, and the controlled statements end at the statement with the corresponding label (very often a CONTINUE). In Cobol, it is the VARYING . . . FROM . . . BY . . . UNTIL . . . form of the general PERFORM verb. In PL/I, it is a variant of the DO statement, of the form DO < variable > = < expression > BY < expression > TO < expression >, with the possibility of omitting some parts, adding a condition, and enumerating several such specifications. By comparison with all these languages, the **for** statement of Pascal is both simpler and more general, but slightly less powerful, since the step of the progression cannot be chosen.

Syntax

The syntax of the **for** statement appears in Fig. 11.1. Since there is no metaparenthesis for closing this statement structure, a compound statement is required if the controlled action is composite. The control variable must be a simple variable of an ordinal type, which is declared locally in the block in which the statement structure appears. The two expressions must be assignment-compatible with the type of the control variable. The controlled statement must not assign a value to the control variable, either directly or indirectly (for example, by calling a procedure). All these restrictions are enforced in order to allow an efficient implementation of the control structure and to ensure that the apparent meaning of the construct is its actual meaning.

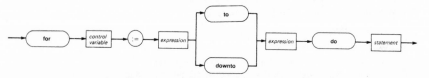

Fig. 11.1 Syntax diagram for a **for** statement.

Semantics

Given the **for** statement:

for *variable* := *expression1* **to** *expression2* **do** *statement*(*variable*)
if {(variable = expression1) ∧ P} *statement*(*variable*) {Q(expression1)}
and {Q(pred(x))} *statement*(*variable*) {Q(x)}
    for all *x* such that *expression1* < *x* ≤ *expression2*
then {(expression1 ≤ expression2) ∧ P} **for** *statement* {Q(expression2)}
and {(expression1 > expression2) ∧ P} **for** *statement* {P}

A similar deduction rule may be obtained by substituting **downto**, *succ*, >, ≥, and <, respectively, for **to**, *pred*, <, ≤, and > in the above.

These two rules are very complicated indeed, and a simpler explanation of the **for** statement may be given by an equivalent program schema. The **for** statement

for *v* := *e1* **to** *e2* **do** *body*

is equivalent to

```
begin
  temp1 := e1; temp2 := e2;
  if temp1 ≤ temp2 then
  begin v := temp1;
    body;
    while v ≠ temp2 do
    begin v := succ(v);
      body
    end
  end
end
```

A similar program schema may be obtained by substituting **downto**, ≥, and *pred*, respectively, for **to**, ≤, and *succ* in the above. In both cases, *temp1* and *temp2* are two auxiliary variables, of a suitable type, which do not appear elsewhere in the program.

The important consequences of the preceding semantic descriptions are the following:

* The bound expressions of the interval that the control variable traverses are evaluated before entering the loop; to change any values involved in these expressions during the loop has no effect on the number of repetitions.

* If the interval is void (*expression1* > *expression2* in the **to** case, or *expression1* < *expression2* in the **downto** case), the body is not executed at all,

in contrast to Fortran, for example, where the body of a DO loop is always executed at least once.

- The step of the progression cannot be chosen: for an integer control variable, it is either 1 or −1; this is a consequence of the fact that the control variable may be also of a character or enumerated type, a very useful feature as we shall see later.

- The number of repetitions of the body of a **for** statement can always be computed before entering the loop; this is in sharp contrast to the two iterative statements (**while** and **repeat**), in which the termination of the loop is controlled within the repeated statement and is not really guaranteed if the logic of the statement is erroneous.

- The program schema is only a way for describing the semantics of the **for** statement, and it does not imply that it must be implemented in such a way. In fact, this schema does not exhibit one important additional restriction—the value of the control variable is supposed to be undefined at the end of the loop, not forcing any implementation method. Therefore, it would be an error to use *v* at the end of the preceding **for** statement without any intervening assignment.

Example 11.1: Matrix Product (Final Version)

procedure *MatrixProduct*
    (**var** *a*: **array**[*fla*..*fua*: *integer*; *sla*..*sua*: *integer*] **of** *real*;
    var *b*: **array**[*flb*..*fub*: *integer*; *slb*..*sub*: *integer*] **of** *real*;
    var *c*: **array**[*flc*..*fuc*: *integer*; *slc*..*suc*: *integer*] **of** *real*
)
    {This procedure computes the matrix product of a[m × p] and b[p × n] into
        c[m × n]. All indices run from 1. If the actual parameters do not have
        suitable index types, the global procedure Error is called, and c is
        unchanged.};
    var *m*, *n*, *p*, *i*, *j*, *k*: *1*..*maxint*;
    sum: *real*;
begin {MatrixProduct}
    if (*fla* ≠ *1*) ∨ (*sla* ≠ *1*) ∨ (*flb* ≠ *1*) ∨ (*slb* ≠ *1*) ∨ (*flc* ≠ *1*)
      ∨ (*sua* ≠ *fub*) ∨ (*fua* ≠ *fuc*) ∨ (*sub* ≠ *suc*)
    then *Error* **else**
    begin *m* := *fua*; *n* := *sua*; *p* := *sub*;
      for *i* := *1* **to** *m* **do**
        for *j* := *1* **to** *n* **do**
        begin *sum* := *0*;
          for *k* := *1* **to** *p* **do**
            sum := *sum* + *a*[*i*,*k*] * *b*[*k*,*j*];

$$c[i,j] := sum$$
     end
  end
end {MatrixProduct}

REMARKS

1. No assertion is provided to give the correctness of the preceding procedure. In fact, although its deduction rule is complicated, the **for** statement is so natural in such a case that no comment at all is really necessary.

2. This procedure is a typical application of the **for** statement: the repeated action must be done once for every value in the interval, which itself is fixed before entering the loop; moreover, the order in which the repetitions are done is irrelevant, and **downto** variants could be used for the three embedded **for** statements. The **for** statement is extremely useful for such situations, but it should never be used in other circumstances. The fact that in Fortran or Basic all built-in loops imply the variation of some integer variable may completely hide simple and natural algorithms that do not exhibit such a property.

Example 11.2:   Digram Frequency

program *Digram* (*input, output*)
  {The textfile input is read and copied on output, followed by a frequency count of all the digrams (consecutive pairs of letters) that occur in it. This may be especially useful in cryptography.};
  type *natural* = *0..maxint*; *letter* = '*a*'..'*z*';
  var *count*: **array**[*letter, letter*] **of** *natural*;
  first, second: *letter* {indices for the array count};
  ch: *char* {the current character};
  function *IsAletter*(*ch*: *char*): *Boolean*; . . . {see Example 10.3};
begin {program Digram}
  for *first* := '*a*' **to** '*z*' **do**
    for *second* := '*a*' **to** '*z*' **do** {Initialize count.}
      count[*first, second*] := *0*;
  while ¬*eof*(*input*) **do** {again the same old schema}
  begin
    while ¬*eoln*(*input*) **do** {Process a line.}
    begin *read*(*input, ch*); *write*(*output, ch*);.
      if *IsALetter*(*ch*) **then**
        if *IsALetter*(*input*↑) **then** {We found a letter diagram.}
          count[*ch, input*↑] := *count*[*ch, input*↑] + *1*

```
    end {of a line};
    writeln (output); readln (input)
  end {while ¬eof(input)};
  page (output); writeln (output, 'Digram frequency');
  writeln (output);
  for first := 'a' to 'z' do
  begin {Process one series of diagrams.}
    for second := 'a' to 'z' do
      if count [first, second] ≠ 0 then
        write (output, first, second, count [first, second]);
    writeln (output) {one blank line as a separation}
  end {loop on first}
end {Digram}
```

REMARKS

1. Once more, we encounter the problem of the lack of standardization of character sets. With the ISO code, the array count has exactly 26 × 26 = 676 components, and the function *IsALetter* may be simpler than that of Example 10.3. With the EBCDIC code, however, there are 924 more components, which are completely useless, since the cardinality of the subrange 'a'..'z' is 40 in such a code (40 × 40 − 676 = 924). In different circumstances, it could be useful to define a mapping between letters and integers from 1 to 26, and to compute this mapping with an **array**['a'.. 'z'] **of** *0..26*, yielding *0* for all nonletter characters. Function *IsALetter* would therefore disappear.

2. We avoided the use of *IsALetter* in the final double loop of the program because digrams that include a nonletter are not counted at all and consequently their count remains zero. If we had to write all letter digrams, even those that do not appear in the text (for example 'tq' or 'zb' in a text written in natural language), that trick would not work.

3. Of course, the most interesting point in the preceding program is that character values may be used in a **for** statement as well as in array indices. Note also the way by which input↑ is used as a "look-ahead" character.

Example 11.3: Shell Sort

procedure *ShellSort* (**var** *table*: **array**[*lower..upper*: *integer*] **of** *T*)
{This procedure sorts the array table, using Shell's algorithm. T is some type, upon which the predicate LessThan is defined: function LessThan(x, y: T): Boolean yields true if x precedes y in some order relation. In the table, components with negative indices are reserved as "sentinels"; the actual lower bound is always 1; with the four passes used in the present procedure, the

lower bound must be -8 or less. Shell's algorithm is not the best one, and
a much better algorithm will be used in Chap. 15. See Wirth (1976).};

```
const maxorder = 4 {number of different increments};
var item: T;
    order: 1..maxorder;
    increment: array[1..maxorder] of integer;
    i, j, step, sentinel: integer;
begin {ShellSort}
    increment[1] := 9; increment[2] := 5;
    increment[3] := 3; increment[4] := 1;
    for order := 1 to maxorder do {Use degressive increments.}
    begin step := increment[order]; sentinel := -step
        {min(sentinel) = -9};
        for i := step + 1 to upper do
        begin item := table[i]; j := i - step;
            if sentinel = 0 then sentinel := -step;
            sentinel := sentinel + 1 {min(sentinel) = -8};
            table[sentinel] := item {lower must be ≤ -8}
            {The sentinel is placed.};
            while LessThan(item, table[j]) do
            begin {insertion}
                table[j + step] := table[j];
                j := j - step
            end;
            table[j + step] := item
        end {loop on i}
    end {loop on order}
end {ShellSort}
```

EXERCISES

11.1 Evaluation of a Polynom

Given a polynom of degree n

$$P = a_n x^n + a_{n-1} X^{n-1} + \cdots + a_1 x + a_0$$

write the function

function *PolynomValue*(**var** *a*: **array**[*lb..ub*: *integer*] **of** *real*; *x*: *real*):
real

which computes the value of P in x, using the table a of coefficients. Hint: Use
the well-known Horner's schema.

11.2 Text Concordance (Continued)

In Example 10.5, several iterative statements could be replaced by repetitive statements. Rewrite this program, using **for** statements where possible, and modifying the printing of results so that the words appear in several parallel columns. Each column is of width *wordlength*, and separated from its neighbor columns by two blank spaces. A constant *linelength* gives the maximum length of an output line.

11.3 Mister Mind

The following game is a simplified version of the well-known Master Mind. Two players have *nbpins* pins each, in two identical sets. Pins are of various colors, and there are *maxcolor* colors. The first player, say A, places *maxpin* pins in a frame hidden from the second player, say B. The goal for B is to infer the color and position of the pins in A's frame. He proceeds in successive guesses, by setting some pins in his frame, similar to A's frame but not hidden. After each guess, A answers in the following way:

(*a*) Opposite to each completely correct pin, she puts a white mark.

(*b*) Opposite to each pin whose color is correct, but position is not, she puts a black mark.

(*c*) Other positions remain empty.

Taking into account A's answers, B must infer the correct solution in a minimum number of guesses.

Write a program which reads A's play, builds the pin set of B and B's first play, and simulates the complete game until B has a play identical to A's. Use the following constant and type definitions:

```
const maxpins = 4; maxcolor = 6;
   nbpins = 24 {maxpins * maxcolor};
type pin = (red, green, yellow, blue, brown, pink, void);
   mark = (white, black, none);
play = array[1..maxpins] of pin {for A's or B's play};
thepins = array [red..pink] of 0..maxpins {for B's set};
```

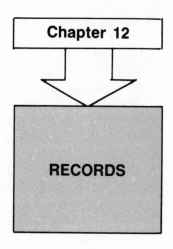

Chapter 12

RECORDS

12.1 CARTESIAN PRODUCTS AND SIMPLE RECORDS

The simplest and most general means for structuring an object is to group several objects of any type (possibly structured objects), and to consider the group as a unique object. For example, a complex number is an ordered pair of reals, which are its real part and its imaginary part, respectively. Polar coordinates in a plane are another pair of reals, representing a modulus and a polar angle. A person may be described by several characteristics: first name and last name (character sequences), date of birth (a structured object), sex, marital status, etc.

This corresponds to what mathematicians call a *cartesian product*, the abstract structural method that we consider now. Given a product type P of types $T1, T2, \ldots, Tn$, an object of type P has n components of type $T1$, $T2, \ldots, Tn$, respectively. We denote $p < x1, x2, \ldots, xn >$ an object of type P whose components are $x1$ (of type $T1$), $x2$ (of type $T2$), $\ldots$, xn (of type Tn). All objects of type P may be built using this constructor.

To refer to any one of the components of a cartesian product, we must name these components, since their order carries no meaning. Moreover, these components may be of different types—if we used the same notation as for arrays, we could not know the type of $p[i]$ (p being of type P) without computing i. Consequently, the definition of a product type P must include its component names $c1, c2, \ldots, cn$. If $x = p < x1, \ldots, xn >$, then $x.c1 = x1$, $x.c2 = x2, \ldots, x.cn = xn$. The dot notation $x.ci$ constitutes the *component selector* for a cartesian product.

The same problem as for mappings will appear; i.e., we need a notation for selective modification of one component of a record. The same solution is used; i.e., the component selector may appear in the left part of an assignment statement. More formally, with the same type and component names as above,

$x.c1 := x1$ is equivalent to $x := p < x1, x.c2, \ldots, x.cn >$; $x.c2 := x2$ is equivalent to $x := p < x.c1, x2, \ldots, x.cn >$; and so on.

The preceding rules suffice to define the cartesian product as an abstract structure, as was done for the sequence in Chap. 8 and for the mapping in Chap. 10. An important difference, however, is that the cartesian product is such a simple structure that it may be implemented in a completely straightforward manner. The realization of this abstract concept needs no particular restriction. It is only for historical reasons that the name of the concrete structural method is not "cartesian product," but *record*.

A record structure is a random-access one, like an array structure, with a fixed and finite number of components, named *fields*, each being separately accessible. In contrast to the array structure, different components may be of different types, which implies that they must be individually named in a fixed way so that the type of a selected component may be known at compile time; the name of a field of a record cannot be computed. A record type in Pascal has the syntax shown in Fig. 12.1. Temporarily, we shall consider a field list to be simply a list of record sections separated by semicolons. The actual definition, which is much more complex, will be given in Sec. 12.3. A record section has the same appearance as a list of variable declarations; its syntax is shown in Fig. 12.2. The syntax of a record type is somewhat permissive, since it allows an optional semicolon before the **end**, and the field list may be absent. The legal type whose description is simply **record end** is an empty record, of very limited usefulness (but see Sec. 12.3).

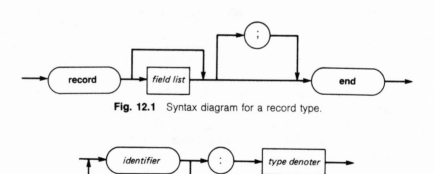

Fig. 12.1 Syntax diagram for a record type.

Fig. 12.2 Syntax diagram for a record section.

Example 12.1: Record-Type Definitions

type *complex* = **record** *realpart, imagpart*: *real* **end**;
    string = **packed array**[*1..stringlength*] **of** *char*;

sextype = (*male, female*) {defined so that male < female};
datetype =
  record *day: 1..31; month: 1..12; year: 1800..2000* **end**;
nametype =
  record *firstname, lastname: string; middlename: char* **end**;
begettertype = (*father, mother*);
civilstatus = **record**
    name: nametype;
    birthdate: datetype;
    parents: **array**[*begettertype*] **of** *datetype;*
    childnumber: 0..maxchildren;
    child: **array**[*1..maxchildren*] **of record**
      birthdate: datetype;
        sex: sextype;
        firstname: string **end**;
    sex: sextype **end** {type civilstatus};

REMARKS

1. The proper layout of record-type definitions is mainly a matter of context and of taste, and no general rules may be stated. One can put the whole definition on one line, if it fits, and even on the same line as the defined name. On the other hand, an indented layout may be used, with a variety of rules for indenting and ending lines. The only important thing is that the definition be readable and easy to understand.

2. A type which is used only once may be defined in-line, and remain anonymous, as already seen in Chap. 3. This could have been done for *begettertype*; no definition of the type itself would appear, and the type denoter for the field *parents* in the type definition of *civilstatus* would appear as **array**[(*father, mother*)] **of** *datetype*. However, no variable of type *begettertype* could be declared afterwards. Thus all references to one parent or the other would be made only with a constant index, making the array itself almost useless. Generally, many different names must be invented by a Pascal programmer, with some care and foresight. If the type of a name is called *name*, no name may be called "name," which is irritating. This explains the frequency of type names ending with *type*, but it reveals an important failure in those non-*Standard*-conforming compilers that consider only the first *n* characters of an identifier to be significant, *n* generally being 8. With this convention, *begettertype* could not be distinguished from *begetter* on many compilers. It is a pity that, for reasons of portability, many programmers accustomed to a *Standard*-conforming compiler must refrain from using its capabilities in this respect.

3. Type *civilstatus* exhibits two different ways to define hierarchically structured records, i.e., records with some fields of record types. Fields *name* and *birthdate* are records whose type is defined in-line (and which contain yet another field of a record type).

4. With regard to the possible number of children, type *civilstatus* is not the best possible implementation of the concept to be represented. If constant *maxchildren* is small (say, 3 or 4), some situations cannot be represented. If this constant is large (say, 15 or 20), much storage is wasted for almost all objects of this type. A better solution will be given in Chap. 14.

5. All combinations of field values are legal in a given record type, even those which are conceptually absurd. For example, February 29 exists for all possible years in type *datetype*, and even February 31 (see Example 12.3).

12.2   USE OF RECORDS

A field designator, which is another case of a variable access, has a very simple syntax (see Fig. 12.3). The record variable is a variable access to some record, and the field identifier must be the identifier of a field which appears in this record. In fact, field identifiers are declared by their occurrence in a record-type definition, but they are local to it, with no conflict with other identifiers declared outside. If several record definitions are embedded, an internal field may be accessed by using a chain of field designators.

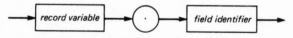

Fig. 12.3   Syntax diagram for a field designator.

Example 12.2:   Record Variables and Field Designators

{This example uses the record-type definitions of Example 12.1.}
var *date: datetype*; *name: nametype*; *firstname: string*;
    father, mother, son, daughter: civilstatus;
    parish: **array**[*1..maxfamilies*] **of** *civilstatus*;
    i: 1..maxfamilies; *j: 0..maxchildren*;
    currentyear: 1800..2000;
begin
   ---
   for *i* := *1* **to** *maxfamilies* **do** {for each family head}
     for *j* := *1* **to** *parish*[*i*]*.childnumber* **do** {for each child}

if *parish* [*i*].*child* [*j*].*firstname* = *Clementine*
then *writeln* (*currentyear* − *parish* [*i*].*birthdate* .*year*)

{This statement prints the current age of each family head of some parish who has a child whose first name is the value of Clementine, a variable or constant which probably contains the string 'Clementine', complete with a number of blank spaces sufficient for the type string.};

{parish[i].birthdate.year refers to the year of birth of the family head considered; parish[i].child[j].birthdate.year would refer to the year of birth of the child considered.}

{Some legal assignments follow.}
father := *parish* [*i*]; *parish* [*i* + *1*] := *mother*;
son .*birthdate* := *mother* .*child* [j].*birthdate*;
if *father* .*child* [j].*sex* = *female* then
daughter .*birthdate* := *date*
else *son* .*name* := *name*

---

end

REMARKS

1. The visibility of names inside and outside record types follows exactly the same rules as for procedures and functions. In type *civilstatus*, fields *birthdate* and *sex* each appear twice, but without ambiguity, since these two occurrences are not at the same level. Similarly, the identifier *name* is used both as a variable and as a field name.

2. No abbreviation is allowed in complicated references, nor is any alternative notation, even if there is no ambiguity (this is in sharp contrast with Cobol and PL/I). For example, there is no other way to refer to the year of birth of the *j*th child of the *i*th family head of the parish than *parish* [*i*].*child* [j].*birthdate* .*year*. The only problem is the length of this reference and the cost of its computation, and a shortcut will be explained below.

3. Like any other structured object (files excepted), a record object may be assigned as a whole to a record variable of the same type. However, the rules of assignment compatibility show that these records must be of exactly the same type, and not, for example, of two different types which happen to have the same structure and the same names and types for all their fields.

It is now time to make a brief comparison with Cobol and PL/I, with respect to the record structure. It is left as an exercise for the reader to translate into one of these languages the definition of type *civilstatus*. If syntax details are considered to be unimportant, the main difference is that the hierarchy of embedded record structures is indicated in Pascal by the embedding of several record-type definitions, instead of level numbers. In fact, a minimal amount of syntax has been added to Pascal because of the availability of type definitions. Other differences are the following:

- All references to fields of records must be complete in Pascal, while Cobol and PL/I allow some abbreviations if there is no ambiguity.

- There is no "assignment by name" in Pascal. Either the record types are the same and assignment is global, or they are different and each field must be assigned individually.

- The detailed implementation of the record fields cannot be specified in Pascal. Only packing may be specified for the whole record, which means that the compiler should try to economize storage in some way, instead of systematically padding up to word limits, as when packing is not specified.

A shortcut was promised for avoiding the cost of complicated field designators, in writing as well as in computing. It is the **with** statement, which has the syntax shown in Fig. 12.4. Its semantics is explained by the following deduction rule:

If x is of type **record** $f1: T1; f2: T2; \ldots; fn: Tn$ **end**
then the statement **with** x **do** is equivalent to
$$\text{statement} \quad \begin{array}{l} f^1, f^2, \ldots, f^n \\ x.f_1, x.f_2, \ldots, x.f_n \end{array}.$$

This means that the **with** statement "opens" the record definition, and makes all field names of the record definition directly accessible within the controlled statement, as if they were declared at its beginning. Possible name conflicts are solved in the same way as name conflicts in embedded procedures or functions.

For example, in the statement controlled by **with** $parish[i].child[j]$ **do** ..., the variable *firstname* is no longer accessible, because of conflict with the like-named field, and *birthdate* refers to $parish[i].child[j].birthdate$. However, $parish[i].birthdate$ remains accessible using its complete designator.

If several record variables appear after **with**, the meaning is exactly the same

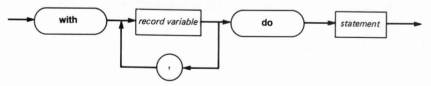

Fig. 12.4 Syntax diagram for a **with** statement.

as with embedded **with** statements: **with** *x1, x2, . . ., xm* **do** . . . is equivalent
to

> **with** *x1* **do**
> > **with** *x2* **do**
> > > . . .
> > > **with** *xm* **do**

For example, in the statement controlled by

> **with** *parish*[*i*], *child*[*j*] **do** . . .

sex refers to the field of this name for the *j*th child, and *name* refers to the
name of the *i*th family head of the parish.

An important remark must be made: it is forbidden, and it would be an
error, to modify the variable access(es) of the **with** construct within the statement controlled by the construct. For example, within the statement controlled by **with** *parish*[*i*].*child*[*j*] **do**, it would be an error to modify *i* or *j*,
either directly by an assignment statement or indirectly by calling a procedure
which modifies *i* or *j*. This restriction is made for reasons of clarity and
efficiency.

Example 12.3   Validation of a Date

```
var today: datetype {type defined in Example 12.1};
    feb: 28..29;
begin . . .
    with today do
        case month of
        4, 6, 9, 11: if day > 30 then Error;
        2: begin {a leap year or not?}
            if (year mod 4 = 0) ∧ (year mod 100 ≠ 0)
            ∨ (year mod 400 = 0) then feb := 29
            else feb := 28;
            if day > feb then Error
           end {February};
        1, 3, 5, 7, 8, 10, 12: {always legal}
        end
```

REMARK

In this example, the **with** statement serves only as an abbreviation, and it has
no influence on the work done by the program, since a reference to a field of
a record may be evaluated at compile time and, consequently, costs nothing
during execution.

Example 12.4

{The following is a rewriting of the two embedded for statements appearing in Example 12.2}

for *i* := *1* **to** *maxfamilies* **do**
  with *parish*[*i*] **do**
    for *j* := *1* **to** *childnumber* **do**
      if *child*[*j*].*firstname* = *Clementine* **then**
        writeln(*currentyear* − *birthdate*.*year*)

REMARKS

Since the bounds of a **for** loop are evaluated only once, the **with** statement would not be useful if the reference to *parish*[*i*] (which needs some computation) did not appear inside the controlled statement, in addition to its occurrence in the upper bound of the loop on *j*.

12.3 TYPE UNIONS AND VARIANT RECORDS

All objects in Pascal must have a definite type, but it is sometimes useful to be able to consider a type as the union of several other types, or to consider these other types as variants of the first one. For example, some type *coordinates* may consist, depending on circumstances, of cartesian coordinates or of polar coordinates. Operations on type components must take into account the particular variant in effect, but operations on the object as a whole are not affected. To indicate what particular variant has been chosen for some object of a union type, this object must contain an indicator as a component, which is called in Pascal a *tag field*. Because of this field, it is rather natural to consider the concept of a united type as a generalization of the record structure. The complete syntax of a record type is therefore much more complicated than the provisional one that appeared in Sec. 12.1, and Fig. 12.5 gives the syntax of the field list. In these rules, the tag field is an identifier, the tag type is an ordinal type identifier, and the case constant is a constant of the same type as the tag type. Similarities between this syntax and that of the **case** statement must not cause the differences to be forgotten. The important remarks to be made here are:

- The fixed part of the record, which may be considered as containing those fields present in all variants, must appear first, if ever.

- There is only one variant part in a given record type, but a given variant is in fact a field list, which can contain a further variant part. As a consequence, a hierarchy of variants may be built.

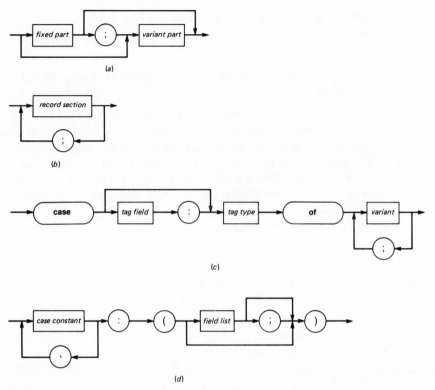

Fig. 12.5 Syntax diagram for a field list: (*a*) field list; (*b*) fixed part; (*c*) variant part; and (*d*) variant.

- The field list of a variant is delimited by parentheses as a means of suggesting that it does not begin another level of declaration: field identifiers appearing in a variant are at the same level as those which appear in the fixed part. As a consequence, all field identifiers must be distinct, even if they appear in different variants (at the same level).

- The upper-level variant part ends with the **end** symbol of the record type; a lower-level variant part ends with the right parenthesis that closes the variant in which it is embedded.

- Several possible values of the tag field may lead to the same variant. Moreover, all possible values of the tag field must appear as case constants.

- A variant is syntactically described as a list of **case** constants, followed by a field list enclosed in parentheses. However, the field list may be omitted, as in the definition of a complete record (see Sec. 12.1). In that case, the possibility of an empty variant is useful and is frequently used. It constitutes a justification of the existence of empty records, for orthogonality.

- The type of the tag field cannot be defined in-line: it must be defined and named before.

- The tag field itself may be omitted. The official definition of the language supposes that, in such a case, everything works as if a hidden tag field were present; i.e., the implementation must be able to determine at run time what variant is in effect for every variant record. Contrary to this definition, many implementations take omission of the tag field as a way of allowing "unsafe" conversions, i.e., of considering some piece of storage from different points of view, as with the Fortran EQUIVALENCE or the PL/I RENAMES option.

Example 12.5:   Variant Record-Type Definitions

```
type register = 0..15;
     form = (immediate, normal, shift, jump);
     twentybits = -1048576..1048575;
     twelvebits = -2048..2047;
     tenbits = 0..1023;
     sixbits = -32..31;
     fifteenbits = 0..32767;
     onebit = 0..1;
     instruction = packed record {description of a machine instruction}
        indirect: Boolean;
        operator: 0..127;
        reg1: register;
        case form of {No tag field appears in the instruction.}
        immediate: (immedop: twentybits);
        normal: (index, base: register;
            displacement: twelvebits);
        shift: (shifttag: register;
            filler: tenbits;
            shiftamount: sixbits);
        jump: (jumptag: register;
            jumpfiller: onebit;
            address: fifteenbits)
        end {type instruction};
     coordform = (cartesian, polar);
     coordinates = record
        case form: coordform of
```

cartesian: (*x*, *y*: *real*);
polar: (*rho*, *theta*: *real*)
end {type coordinates};
figure = **record** {description of a geometric figure}
  position: coordinates;
  case *round: Boolean* **of**
  true: (*diameter: real*);
  false: (*orientation*, *side*: *real*;
      case *rectangular*: *Boolean* **of**
      true: (*width*: *real*);
      false: (*angle1*, *angle2*: *real*)
)
  end {type figure};

REMARKS

1. The description of the type *instruction* assumes that the compiler packs exactly as many bits in a word as possible, and that the host computer has 32-bit words. Of course, this is an example of a nonportable type description.

2. In this type, fields *shifttag* and *jumptag* must have different names, because they occur at the same level. To avoid this, embedded variants would be necessary, as in the type *figure*.

3. There must be no tag field in the type *instruction* because it does not exist in the computer instruction to be described. However, there probably is some relation between the value of the operator and the form of the instruction. The legality of the references will not be verified by most compilers.

4. Type *coordinates* is an example of a record without a fixed part.

A record type with variants describes several different records, all united in one type. However, an object of such a type must take one variant and only one at the same time; i.e., only the fields that appear in the fixed part and in the current variant are defined. The current variant is determined by the current value of the tag field, if present. When there is no tag field, one must consider that the hidden tag field is implicitly assigned each time a reference is made to a field of a particular variant which is not the current one. Since it is very difficult and very costly for a given implementation to verify the correctness of all references to fields of variants, programmers must be very cautious. A useful suggestion is to refer to variant fields only within a **case** statement, following the same pattern as the variant part of the record (if possible). This will be illustrated in several examples in subsequent chapters.

12.4 COMPOSITE STRUCTURES

Records are the third structural method of Pascal that we describe, and they can be used in combination with the two preceding ones, with the restriction (already seen) that files cannot have components which contain other files. For example, one can not only define and use structured types which are records with array or record fields (see Example 12.1), but also arrays whose components are records, or files whose components are records, these records themselves containing array or record fields, and so on. The present section will illustrate this point with some examples of such composite structures, examples that are revisions of examples from preceding chapters.

Example 12.6: Maximum Sales (Revisited)

{This example is the same as Example 7.6, but the abstract idea of a sequence of integer numbers with various meanings is replaced by a concrete file of variant records.}

type *itemtype* = *1000..99999* {An integer codification, but an alphanumeric one would be equally acceptable.};

monthtype = *1..12* {no more need for a zeroth month};

yeartype = *1970..2000*;

{The file to be processed is a sequence of year sequences, each beginning with a record which gives the year number and followed by a sequence of month sequences. A month sequence begins with a record which gives the month number and is followed by a sequence of item records, ordered in increasing item numbers.}

recordtype = (*yearrecord*, *monthrecord*, *itemrecord*);

salesrecordtype = **packed record**

    case *category*: *recordtype* **of**

      yearrecord: (*year*: *yeartype*);

      monthrecord: (*month*: *monthtype*);

      itemrecord: (*item*: *itemtype*;

        qty, tnvr: integer)

    end;

salesfile = **file of** *salesrecordtype*;

procedure *MaxSales*

    (**var** *f*: *salesfile* {the file to examine};

    y: *yeartype* {the year to examine};

    i: *itemtype* {the item of interest};

    var *q, t*: *integer* {maximum qty and corresponding turnover};

    var *m*: *monthtype* {corresponding month}

    );

    var *curmonth*: *monthtype* {current month};

    curqty, curtnvr: *integer* {current maximum qty and tnvr};

status: (*searching, found, absent, yearend*);
procedure *FindTheYear*
{Initialize f, and position it in frontof the year sequence of interest.};
begin {FindTheYear}
reset(*f*); *status* := *searching*;
repeat {Search the year sequence of interest.}
  if *eof*(*f*) **then** *status* := *yearend* **else**
  begin
    if *f*↑.*category* = *yearrecord* **then**
      if *f*↑.*year* = *y* **then** *status* := *found*;
    get(*f*) {Pass the current record.}
  end {¬eof(f)}
until *status* ≠ *searching*
end {FindTheYear};
procedure *FindNextMonth*
{Position f in front of the next month sequence, if it exists.};
begin {FindNextMonth}
status := *searching*;
repeat {Search a month sequence or the end of the current year sequence.}
  if *eof*(*f*) **then** *status* := *yearend* **else**
  with *f*↑ **do**
    case *category* **of**
      yearrecord: *status* := *yearend*;
      monthrecord:
        begin *status* := *found*; *curmonth* := *month*;
          get(*f*) {Pass the month record.}
        end;
      itemrecord: *get*(*f*)
    end {case}
until *status* ≠ *searching*
end {FindNextMonth};
procedure *FindTheItem*
{Position f on the record of the current month sequence that refers to item i, if this
    record exists.};
begin {FindTheItem}
status := *searching*;
repeat {Search the item record of interest.}
  if *eof*(*f*) **then** *status* := *yearend* **else**
  with *f*↑ **do**
    case *category* **of**
      yearrecord: *status* := *yearend*;
      monthrecord: *status* := *absent*;
      itemrecord:

> **if** *item* = *i* **then** *status* := *found*
> **else if** *item* > *i* **then** *status* := *absent*
> **else** *get*(*f*) {Pass the record.}
> **end** {case}
> **until** *status* ≠ *searching*
> **end** {FindTheItem};
> **begin** {MaxSales}
> *FindTheYear*; *curtnvr* := 0;
> *curqty* := 0; *FindNextMonth* {Thus initialize curmonth.};
> **repeat** {Process the item of interest in each month of the year.}
> *FindTheItem*;
> **case** *status* **of**
> *found*:
> **with** *f*↑ **do**
> **begin if** *qty* > *curqty* **then**
> **begin** *curqty* := *qty*; *curtnvr* := *tnvr*;
> *m* := *curmonth*
> **end**;
> *FindNextMonth*
> **end**;
> *absent*: *FindNextMonth*;
> *yearend*: {Do nothing.}
> **end** {case}
> **until** *status* = *yearend*;
> *q* := *curqty*; *t* := *curtnvr* {Pass the result.}
> **end** {MaxSales}

REMARKS

1. It may be interesting to compare this example with Example 7.6 and to consider how a change in the structure of the input file has been reflected in a change of structure in the procedure itself. The behavior of this procedure, especially with limit conditions, is exactly the same as that of Example 7.6. However, the three auxiliary procedures, all modeled along the same pattern, proceed in a completely different way because of the structure of the file.

2. Much care has been taken never to refer to a nonexistent field. For example, in procedure *FindTheYear*, it would be illegal to write

> **if** (*f*↑.*category* = *yearrecord*) ∧ (*f*↑.*year* = *y*) **then**
> *status* := *found*,

since $f\uparrow.year$ only exists if $f\uparrow.category = yearrecord$, and one cannot assume that the second part of the boolean expression is evaluated only if the first part is true. In other circumstances, fields of variants are only referred to in **case** statements where the discrimination is made by the tag field of the record.

Example 12.7:   Sequential Update

program *SequentialUpdate(oldfile, newfile, commands, messages)*
{This program updates a file of records describing car models, identified by a numeric key, according to a file of update commands. It produces as output an updated file, and possibly some error messages. Update commands provide for addition, suppression, and replacement of records. The file is not a textfile, so it must be built by a preceding program. Example 9.5 was similar but used only textfiles.};
const
  alphalength = 30;
type
  alphatype = **packed array** *[1..alphalength]* **of** *char;*
  description = **record**
    key: 1..99999;
    model, color: alphatype;
    year: 0..99/
  end;
var
  oldfile, newfile: **file of** *description;*
  messages: text;
  commands: **file of**
    record *commtype: char; item: description* **end**;
  currentrecord: description;
  found, copy: Boolean;
procedure *CopyRecord*
  {Advance one record on oldfile and newfile. If the global flag copy is true, copy the current record on newfile.};
begin {CopyRecord}
  if *copy* **then** *write (newfile, currentrecord);*
  copy := true; get(oldfile);
  if $\neg eof$ *(oldfile)* **then** *currentrecord := oldfile* $\uparrow$
end {CopyRecord};
procedure *Error(i: integer)* {Write an error message.};
begin {Error}
  with *commands* $\uparrow.item$ **do**
    writeln(messages,

```
        'Error number ', i: 1, ' on command ',
        key: 5, model: alphalength + 1,
        color: alphalength + 1, year: 3)
end {Error};
begin {program SequentialUpdate}
    reset(oldfile); reset(commands);
    rewrite(newfile); rewrite(messages);
    currentrecord := oldfile↑; copy := true;
    while ¬eof(commands) do
        with commands↑ do {Process one command.}
        begin found := false;
            {Copy oldfile onto newfile until the desired key.}
            while ¬eof(oldfile) ∧ (item.key > currentrecord.key) do
                CopyRecord;
            if eof(oldfile) then found := false
            else found := item.key = currentrecord.key;
            {desired key found or absent}
            if commtype = 'A' then {Add a record.}
                if found then Error(1) {Duplicate record.}
                else begin newfile↑ := item; put(newfile) end
            else if commtype = 'S' then {Suppress a record.}
                if found then begin copy := false; CopyRecord end
                else Error(2) {missing record}
            else if commtype = 'R' then {Replace a record.}
                if found then
                    begin currentrecord := item; copy := true; CopyRecord
                    end
                else Error(3) {missing record}
            else Error(4) {illegal command};
            get(commands) {Get the next command.}
        end {of processing one command};
    while ¬eof(oldfile) do CopyRecord
        {Flush remaining records.};
end {SequentialUpdate}.
```

REMARKS

1. This sort of program should be familiar to a Cobol programmer, who will note with interest some programming differences, especially the additional flexibility provided in Pascal by the required function *eof*.

2. The only validation that is made in the program is for the character that denotes the command. The preparation of the file *commands* should

ensure that only valid records are written. In that sense, this program is much simpler than that of Example 9.5.

3. This example does not try to pretend that Pascal can do everything Cobol does. It simply demonstrates that a business-oriented program is not necessarily long, verbose, and unstructured, and that Pascal may be seriously considered for simple and straightforward applications in this area.

Example 12.8: Concordance of a Text (Revisited)

program *TextConcordance*(*input*, *output*)
{This program is a revision of Example 10.5. A count of the occurrences of each word is taken and is printed at program termination.};
   const *wordlength* = *20* {maximum useful length of words};
   dictlength = *1000* {maximum length of the dictionary};
   type *wordtype* = **packed array**[*1..wordlength*] **of** *char* {a string};
   worditem = **record** *w*: *wordtype*; *count*: *1..maxint* **end**;
   var *dictionary*: **array**[*1..dictlength*] **of** *worditem;*
   word: *wordtype* {the current word};
   dictsize, index: *0..dictlength* {two indices in dictionary};
   function *IsALetter*(*ch*: *char*): *Boolean*; . . .{See Example 10.3.};
   procedure *ReadAWord*; . . . {See Example 10.5.};
   procedure *SearchAndEnter*
     {In addition to what is done in Example 10.5, here the number of occurrences of each word is computed.};
     var *left, middle, right*: *0..dictlength*;
     currentitem: *worditem*;
     begin {SearchAndEnter}
       if *dictsize* = *0* **then** {dictionary empty, insert the word}
       begin *dictionary*[*1*].*w* := *word*; *dictisize* := *1*;
         dictionary[*1*].*count* := *1*
       end
       else
       begin {general case}
         left := *1*; *right* := *dictsize;*
         while *left* $\leq$ *right* **do** {binary search}
         begin
           middle := (*left* + *right*) **div** *2*;
           currentitem := *dictionary*[*middle*];
           if *currentitem*.*w* $\leq$ *word* **then** *left* := *middle* + *1*;
           if *currentitem*.*w* $\geq$ *word* **then** *right* := *middle* − *1*
         end;

```
        if currentitem.w = word then {word already found}
          dictionary[middle].count := currentitem.count + 1
        else {word not found; insert it if possible}
          if dictsize < dictlength then {It fits.}
          begin dictsize := dictsize + 1; right := dictsize;
            if dictionary[middle].w < word then
              {but dictionary[middle + 1] > word}
              middle := middle + 1;
            for right := dictsize downto middle + 1 do
              dictionary[right] := dictionary[right − 1];
            with dictionary[middle] do
              begin w := word; count := 1 end
          end
        end {general case}
    end {SearchAndEnter};
  begin {program TextConcordance}
    --- {See Example 10.5.} ---
    for index := 1 to dictsize do
      with dictionary[index] do
        writeln(output, w, count: 3)
  end {TextConcordance}.
```

The only differences between this program and Example 10.5 are the addition of the number of occurrences for each word, the use of **for** and **with** statements when applicable, and the addition of an auxiliary variable *currentitem*, in order to avoid, when possible, repeated references to *dictionary[middle]*.

EXERCISES

12.1   Stock Management

A commercial shop has a file of its items in stock. A record on this file contains the following information: (1) item code, as a six-digit integer; (2) item designation, as a string of 30 alphanumeric characters; (3) quantity in hand, as an integer; (4) tax rate, as a real number; (5) if the item is only sold by unit, its unit price, as a real number; if the item is only sold in one lot, the number of items in this lot, and the lot price; if the item is sold in packages of various sizes (at most five), the number of items in each package, the package prices, the possible package discounts (already included in the prices), and the delivery time.

Describe the corresponding Pascal file. Write a procedure which prints all item codes of items sold in packages of a hundred units, with the possible discount.

12.2   Table Processing

As in Exercise 10.2, a fixed-length table *tb*, with *tblength* components, contains entries made of an alphanumeric key, and some information of type *T*. In order to improve access to this table, an entry with index *i* is such that $i = f(keyi)$; *f* is a so-called hash function, which delivers a result between 1 and *maxhash* (*maxhash* < *tblength*), given any possible key in the table. *f* is such that two different keys may cause collisions; i.e., $f(keyn) = f(keym) = i$. In this case, all entries that collide in the same place are linked in an overflow list; this makes a third item of information in every entry necessary.

The heading of *f* is **function** *F*(*key*: *keytype*): *fastindex*, with *keytype* = **packed array**[*1..keylength*] **of** *char*, and *fastindex* = *1..maxhash*. Describe the data structure of table *tb*. In the case of a collision, the overflow list is searched linearly. Write the function:

function *Search*(*key*: *keytype*; **var** *info*: *T*): *Boolean*

which returns in *info* the information corresponding to a key, if it exists (then *Search* = true, else *Search* = false).

12.3   Game of Patience

This game uses a 32-card deck. Twenty-eight cards are put on the gaming table, face down, in four rows (one for each color) of seven cards (corresponding to the seven values: 7, 8, . . ., queen, king). Four cards are left in a stack. The game begins when the player takes a card from the stack. (1) If this card in hand is an ace, it is thrown aside, and another card is taken from the stack; (2) if the card in hand is not an ace, it is put on the table in the position corresponding to its color and value, and the card turned down in that position is taken in hand; (3) steps (1) and (2) are repeated until no cards remain in the stack. The game is won if all cards on the table are face up.

Given the following types:

valuetype = (*seven, eight, nine, ten, jack, queen, king, ace*);
colortype = (*clubs, diamonds, hearts, spades*);

define representations for a card, the gaming table with its 28 cards, and the stack. Write a program which simulates this game, using a procedure *ReadGameTable* which initializes the gaming table and a procedure *ReadCardStack* which initializes the stack. Print the game status after placing every new card on the table.

Hints: (1) The two reading procedures set the global boolean variable *error* in case of an error. (2) On output, code a card with two characters denoting its color and value (for example, '8s' = eight of spades, and 'Qh' = queen of hearts).

12.4 Sort a Cobol File

The file-sorting algorithm used in Chap. 8 is programmed in Example 8.7 for the case of Pascal files. One wants to define the modifications to be done to this example in order to sort Cobol files, i.e., textfiles structured in lines (Cobol "records"). The program will be parameterized by the constant *maxline*, which gives the maximum admissible length for a record in the Cobol file, and by two variables (read on input), which give the offset of the sorting key from the first character of the record and the length of this key.

Hint: Simulate the behavior of a Pascal file (procedures *reset*, *get* and *put*, and the file buffer) on a textfile structured in lines.

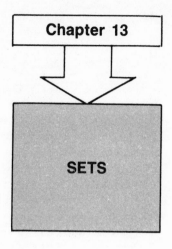

Chapter 13

SETS

The concept of the set is one of the most basic and the most powerful in all mathematics. It is so basic that there is no satisfactory definition of what a set is that does not, to some extent, rely on the reader's intuition. It is so powerful that is often considered to be the basis of "modern math." In programming, it would be useful to be able to define and process sets of any objects, even sets whose elements may be of different types. Such an idea, however, is generally considered to be much too complicated to allow efficient implementation, and the concept of the set in Pascal is much more restricted and less powerful. In fact, the reader may be somewhat disappointed when discovering the difference between the abstraction of set and its realization in Pascal. What is worse, some implementations increase this disappointment by setting restrictions more stringent than necessary, for the sake of efficiency and ease of implementation.

A set in Pascal is not exactly a structured object, since it is not an object made of individual components. Rather, a set is a collection of representatives for objects all of the same type; i.e., a set of characters does not contain characters per se, but only representatives for them. We will discuss the concept as if objects themselves were contained in the set, but this fundamental idea of representatives is the justification for the most basic restrictions imposed upon Pascal sets.

A set type is defined by its structure and by the base type of the set, i.e., the type from which the elements of the set are taken. Its syntax is very simple, as shown in Fig. 13.1. The base type must be an ordinal type. An object of a given set type may be considered as a set of distinct objects of the base type. Every object of the base type either occurs in the set (i.e., the set contains a representative for it), or it does not; two objects with the same

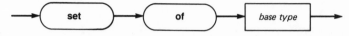

Fig. 13.1 Syntax diagram for a set type.

value have the same representative. Consequently, no object can occur more than once; this is one of the two fundamental differences between abstract mathematical sets and their Pascal implementation. The other one is that only ordinal types are allowed for the base type. One cannot define a set of arrays or a set of records, for example, because that would make it necessary to define different representatives for every possible value in the array type or the record type.

As a consequence of these restrictions, it would not be useful to define an abstract structure first and then describe its realization in Pascal, as we did for other structured types. Rather, we shall describe at the outset all the capabilities of this new concept. The most necessary feature is a way to build sets, i.e., a set constructor. This is not necessary for other structured types, because files, arrays, and records *contain* objects, and tools are given for appending components to files or for selectively updating components of arrays or records.

A set constructor has the syntax shown in Fig. 13.2. An important problem is that the type of the constructor is not specified in this denotation. All expressions must be of the same ordinal type (remember that an expression is never of a subrange type, any subrange variable being automatically expanded to its host type; see Secs. 3.1 and 4.1), and the constructed set is of a canonical set type whose base type is this ordinal type. A set constructor contains a list of member designators, separated by commas and set between square brackets. A member designator made of a unique expression specifies the value of this expression as an element of the constructed set. Two expressions separated by a horizontal colon specify that all values within the indicated subrange are elements of the constructed set. If the subrange is empty (the first expression being greater than the second), it specifies no element at all. A given element occurs only once in the constructed set, even if it is specified several times. The set constructor that specifies no element (containing no member designator) has a value which is an empty set of an indeterminate type, compatible with any set type.

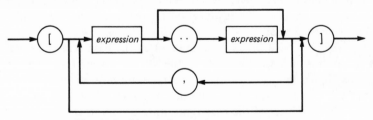

Fig. 13.2 Syntax diagram for a set constructor.

Example 13.1:   Set Types and Set Constructors

type *primarycolor* = (*red*, *yellow*, *blue*);
   floor = (*underground*, *groundfloor*, *mezzanine*, *firstfloor*);
   error = (*off*, *empty*, *parity*, *default*, *cramming*);
   color = **set of** *primarycolor*;
   elevatorcalls = **set of** *floor*;
   readerstatus = **set of** *error*;

   {[red, yellow] is of the canonical type set of primarycolor, compatible with type color;
   it probably represents color orange. [red] represents color red, and is exactly the same color as [red, red, red]. Type elevatorcalls may represent the
   set of floors from which an elevator is called. [empty, parity, cramming] is
   a status descriptor for a card reader, which clearly calls for operator inter-
   vention. [ ] denotes an empty set, of an indeterminate set type, compatible
   with the three defined set types.}

There are no true constants of any set type, but a set constructor whose constituent expressions reduce to constants may be evaluated at compile time by a reasonably good compiler. However, the set constructor cannot occur in a constant definition.

Operations on sets are defined as follows:

Assignment: It works as usual. A set expression is always of the canonical set type of some base type. It may be assigned to a set variable of some set type with the same base type, or a subrange of this base type, provided all elements of the constructed set lie within the bounds of the base type of the set variable it is being assigned to. This is similar to the rules for subrange type assignment, and it results from the concept of assignment-compatibility (see Sec. 2.6).

Set membership: The binary operator **in** has some (canonical) set type as its right operand, and some value of the corresponding base type as its left operand. It delivers a value of type *Boolean*, and it has the same precedence as comparison operators.

Comparison: Operators are defined for equality or inequality of two operands of compatible set types. Two sets are equal if they contain the same elements.

Inclusion: Tests for set inclusion exist for two operands of compatible set types. Only two operators are defined and denoted, $\leq$ and $\geq$. *set1* < *set2* must be written (*set1* $\leq$ *set2*) $\wedge$ (*set1* $\neq$ *set2*). This is because an operator like < would be costly to implement, and not very useful.

Set union, set intersection, and set difference: They are denoted by the operators +, *, and −, respectively. These operators have the same precedence as when they denote arithmetic operations (see Sec. 4.1).

These are the only set operations that are defined in standard Pascal, and they were selected because they are useful, of course, but also because they can be efficiently implemented on current computers. In fact, one of the most natural implementations of the set concept of Pascal, if some restrictions are considered acceptable, is to represent it as its characteristic function, in the form of a bit string, of a size natural for the computer, i.e., a whole, small number of consecutive storage units. Some Pascal implementations consider the set only as an abstraction of the concept of a memory word, and consequently they put very severe limitations on the base type of any set: if the memory word has n bits, the base type must be an ordinal type whose lowest value has a zero ordinal number and whose highest value has an ordinal number less than n. Since ordinary values for n range from 16 to 64, an unfortunate consequence is that many useful applications of the set concept are eliminated—for example, the idea of a set of characters.

The ISO *Standard* does not mention the possibility of restricting the range of the base set, and some other implementations accept a set of any ordinal type, even very large integer numbers. The implementation problem is that, since the precise type of a set constructor can only be the canonical set type of the base type used, a set constructor with integer component expressions must build a set type value allowing any integer elements, probably in the form of a dynamic list of elements, although a limited bit string would be much more efficient, and maybe sufficient. This problem may be avoided by giving special significance to the packing of a set type and by distinguishing two canonical set types for the same base type, one packed and the other unpacked. (This possibility is explicitly mentioned by the ISO *Standard*.) The packed type uses a bit string representation, efficient in time and space, but reasonable only for very small components, while the unpacked canonical type uses, for example, a list representation. Note that this is a case where the packing specification reduces both size and time costs in ordinary circumstances, in contrast to what happens with arrays or records.

If both packed and unpacked sets are allowed, the exact nature of the canonical set type delivered by a given set constructor is implicitly decided by the context in which it appears, for example, in assignments or parameter transmissions. In some situations, this exact nature is irrelevant—for example, if the set constructor is used as the right operand of a set membership operator.

Example 13.2:   Sieve of Eratosthenes with Unrestricted Sets

program *PrimeNumbers(output)*
{This program computes the prime numbers less than some integer n, using the old

algorithm known as "the sieve of Eratosthenes." The sieve is represented as a set of integers from 1 to n. See Dahl, Dijkstra, and Hoare (1972, p. 127)};

const n = . . . {some large integer (say, 10000)};

var *sieve, primes*: **set of** *1..n* {the sieve, the set of primes};

    number, next: 1..n;

begin {PrimeNumbers}

  sieve := $[2..n-1]$ {Initially the sieve is full.};

  primes := $[1]$ {And the set of primes is empty, except 1, which is a special

             case.};

  next := 2 {minimum number in the sieve};

  repeat {until the sieve is empty}

    {All primes less than next are in primes.}

    while ¬(*next* **in** *sieve*) **do** {Find the minimum number.}

      next := *succ*(*next*);

    primes := *primes* + [*next*] {This number is a prime.};

    writeln(*output, next*) {Print it.};

    number := *next*;

    while *number* < *n* **do**

    begin {Remove from the sieve all multiples of next.}

      sieve := *sieve* − [*number*];

      number := *number* + *next*

    end

  until *sieve* = [ ]

  {All primes less than n are in primes; they can be used in the sequel of the program,

     if any.}

end {PrimeNumbers}.

REMARKS

1. This program, in any case a scholarly exercise, makes sense only for small values of n: either the Pascal implementation used will not allow sets of more than, say, 32, 64, or even 256 elements, or it will use a very inefficient representation for large sets, thus losing all the benefits of this algorithm, which avoids repeated multiplications.

2. Although the sieve may "contain" n, we do not use this value, since we cannot remove it. If we did, *number* would take the value $n + 1$, which is not in its subrange type. This is another example of an irritating problem in standard Pascal, already mentioned in Sec. 2.4, that is, the lack of "constant expressions": either the base type of both sets should be in $1..n - 1$, or *next* and *number* should be declared on the range $1..n + 1$.

Example 13.3:   Sieve of Eratosthenes with Restricted Sets

program *EfficientPrimeNumbers(output)*

{This program solves the same (scholarly) problem as Exercise 13.2, but it uses some knowledge of the supporting implementation. We suppose that packed sets, for which all set operations are very efficient, are allowed only on base types whose ordinal numbers are in the subrange 0..maxset, maxset being some implementation-dependent, predefined constant. We represent a large set as an array of small sets. Each small set is a packed set of the maximum allowed size. The number of components of the array is m = (n + 1) div maxset + 1. Indices number and next become a composite, with a part which selects the needed set and another which selects the needed number in this set.};

const $n = \ldots$; $maxset = \ldots$; $maxsetp1 = \ldots$ {maxset + 1};
  $m = \ldots$ {(n + 1) div maxset + 1};
var
  sieve, *primes*: **array**[0..*m*] **of packed set of** *0..maxset*;
  numberset, *nextset:* *0..m* {indices in the arrays};
  numbernb, *nextnb:* *0..maxsetp1* {numbers in the sets};
  done: *Boolean* {true if the sieve is empty};
begin {EfficientPrimeNumbers}
  for *numberset* := *0* **to** *m* **do**
  begin {Initialize both arrays.}
    sieve[*numberset*] := [*0..maxset*];
    primes[*numberset*] := [ ]
  end;
  nextset := *0*; *sieve*[*0*] := *sieve*[*0*] − [*0, 1*]; *done* := *false*;
  repeat {until the sieve is empty}
    nextnb := *0*;
    while ¬(*nextnb* **in** *sieve*[*nextset*]) **do**
      {Find the first present number.}
      nextnb := *succ*(*nextnb*);
    {(nextset, nextnb) represents the next prime number.}
    primes[*nextset*] := *primes*[*nextset*] + [*nextnb*] {Record it.};
    {The value of the prime just found is: currentprime = nextset * maxsetp1 + nextnb; it is not necessary for the rest.}
    numberset := *nextset*; *numbernb* := *nextnb*;
    while *numberset* < *m* **do**
    begin {Remove all multiples.}
      sieve[*numberset*] := *sieve*[*numberset*] − [*numbernb*];
      {The next value of numberset is: numberset + (currentprime + numbernb) mod maxsetp1, which is calculated more efficiently by the two following statements.}
      numberset := *numberset* + *nextset*;
      if *numbernb* + *nextnb* > *maxset* **then**

numberset := *succ*(*numberset*);
{The next value of numbernb is: (numbernb + currentprime) mod maxsetp1,
which is equivalent to the following statement.}
numbernb := (*numbernb* + *nextnb*) **mod** *maxsetp1*
end {while numberset < m};
while *sieve*[*nextset*] = [ ] **do** {Find the first nonempty set, or stop.}
    if *nextset* < *m* **then** *nextset* := *nextset* + *1*
    else *done* := *true*
until *done*
{Primes now contains all prime numbers less than n.}
end {EfficientPrimeNumbers}.

REMARKS

1. This program is a good example of a general fact: an efficient implementation of a simple algorithm may be much more complicated than expected.

2. This program illustrates another problem: to predict the exact subrange that will be necessary for some variables is somewhat difficult. In fact, the program is incorrect, because *numberset* will take values outside its defined subrange (note that it is incremented by increasing steps). A simple "solution" would be to declare it as an integer, but it is a confession of powerlessness if a programmer is unable to anticipate the behavior of the program. Another solution would be to replace the assignment statement that increments *numberset* with the following statement:

    if *numberset* + *nextset* > *m* **then**
        numberset := *m*
    else *numberset* := *numberset* + *nextset*

A third solution, the most difficult one, would be to predict exactly the maximum value that could be taken by this variable, and to use it in the declaration of *numberset*. This program probably computes more primes than are needed, since it stops only when the last set (*sieve*[*m*]) is empty, and not when *currentprime* equals *n*.

3. Here again, the lack of constant expressions in standard Pascal is a hindrance. Comments state the relations that must exist between the various constants defined, but nothing can enforce these assertions.

4. The idea of a set may also be implemented using a packed array of booleans; the presence or absence of a given element is denoted by the boolean value corresponding to this element, taken as an index in the array. Using this idea, the preceding program could be written with no

sets at all, and in fact it would be somewhat shorter. However, it would also be less readable, and overall much more inefficient, because the operations of set union and set difference (especially efficient when one of the operands is a singleton, i.e., a set with only one element) would be replaced by repeated accesses to individual components of packed arrays.

5. The preceding program was written so as to be easily readable, assuming a reasonably good compiler that can recognize the use of constant expressions within loops. For example, the set constructor [0..*maxset*] is used *m* times in the **for** loop at program beginning, or *sieve*[*nextset*] is used in the second **while** loop, which does not modify *nextset.*

6. Although it was explained in the heading comment that *number* and *next* are now composite indices, they are replaced by four new variables, related only by their names. A neater solution would be to declare:

number, next: **record** *word*: 0..*n*; *bit*: 0..*maxsetp1* **end**

However, this would make the program more cumbersome to write and to read, with very little benefit.

The two preceding examples of the use of sets may be considered somewhat contrived. In fact, it is difficult to demonstrate the use of sets in simple examples, and more significant uses will be found in the exercises. However, one usage of sets is extremely frequent, and it has the remarkable property that it appears even in programs which do not declare any variable of set types. The operator for set membership may be used as a favorable substitute for many complicated comparisons. For example:

- If the values involved are small ordinal values, the boolean expression $(a \leq x) \wedge (x \leq b)$ may be replaced by x **in** [*a..b*], which is clearer and probably more efficient if *a* and *b* are constants. This is exactly the case when one wants to know whether some given character is a digit: write

  if *c* **in** ['0'..'9']

  instead of

  if ('0' $\leq$ *c*) $\wedge$ (*c* $\leq$ '9')

  or better, declare a variable

  digits: **set of** '0'..'9'

Initialize it with

$digits := ['0'..'9']$

and write

if c **in** $digits$ **then** . . .

Of course, $digits$ must be considered in the program as a constant.

* The case is even better with a more complicated comparison:

$('a' \leq c) \wedge (c \leq 'i') \vee ('j' \leq c) \wedge (c \leq 'r') \vee ('s' \leq c) \wedge (c \leq 'z')$

is advantageously replaced by

c **in** $['a'..'i', 'j'..'r', 's'..'z']$

(see Example 10.3), or even better by

c **in** $letters$

the variable $letters$ being defined, initialized, and used as $digits$ in the preceding case. If one wants to write a program which is guaranteed to work with any character set, one can even write:

$letters := ['a', 'b', 'c', 'd', 'e', 'f', 'g', 'h', 'i', 'j', 'k', 'l', 'm', 'n', 'o', 'p', 'q', 'r', 's', 't', 'u', 'v', 'w', 'x', 'y', 'z']$ {!}

This simple use of sets, which has been avoided in the preceding chapters because the concept was not yet available, will be used liberally in the remaining chapters.

EXERCISES

13.1 Game of Patience (Continued)

In Exercise 12.3, procedures *ReadGameTable* and *ReadCardStack* were supposed to have been already written. It is now time to build them, using the following specifications:

procedure *ReadGameTable*

{ Initializes gametable, by reading 28 character triples: a color, coded as 'C', 'D', 'H', or 'S', standing for clubs, diamonds, hearts and spades, respectively; a value, coded as '7', '8', '9', 'X', 'J', 'Q', 'K', or 'A'; a space separating successive cards. The global boolean variable error is set if an error occurs during reading.};

procedure *ReadCardStack*

{ initializes cardstack, by reading four character triples, coded as before; may also set error};

190 PASCAL FOR PROGRAMMERS

13.2   Mister Mind (Improved)

In Exercise 11.3, you probably used a boolean array variable which memorizes the colors eliminated from the solution. Implement this variable using a set. Is there any other set which may be introduced in your program in order to make it simpler?

13.3   Railway Reservation

A European railway company uses cars divided in 10 so-called compartments. A compartment in a first-class car contains two seats near the window, two seats near the corridor that serves all compartments, and two seats in the middle. In a second-class car, there are four middle seats in each compartment. The computer reservation system allows the customer to ask for:

(a) First class or second class

(b) Car type (smoking, nonsmoking)

(c) Seat type (window, corridor, middle)

(d) Seat direction (forward, backward)

Describe the representation of a car in the reservation file. Write a boolean function which searches for a given car and ascertains if there is a compartment free to accept a group of n people who want to travel together and who express precise requirements for their seats. Input parameters are:

(a) The car to inspect

(b) The chosen class

(c) The chosen car type

(d) The number of persons in the group

(e) The type and direction of the requested seats

Output parameters are:

(a) The number of the compartment found, if the function returns true

(b) The set of detected errors on input parameters, if the function returns false

Hint: There can be no detected error even if the function returns false (i.e., when there is no free compartment).

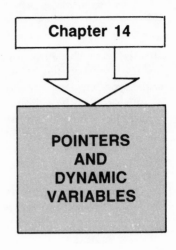

Chapter 14

POINTERS
AND
DYNAMIC
VARIABLES

14.1 RECURSIVE TYPES

Among the four data structures considered so far, only one, the sequence (or
its implementation, the sequential file), allows the definition of structured
objects with a variable number of components. Moreover, the chosen concretization of this method was to use an external storage medium. In the case of
mappings, sets, or cartesian products, the object structure is fixed at declaration time and cannot vary during an execution of the program, or even from
one execution to another. A variable declared to be of a given structured type
may refer to various objects, but all these objects bear the same structure. Even
in the case of type unions, where several different structures are possible, they
must be chosen in a given set, which cannot change during program execution.
It is because of this fundamental property that a fixed storage area may be
assigned to every declared variable, thus avoiding repeated object construc-
tions and allowing selective updating. These objects bear a *static structure*, and
they are associated with so-called *static variables*.

In many circumstances, statically structured objects do not suffice, and
dynamic structures are necessary, structures which change during program
execution. It is no longer possible to allocate a fixed storage area to such
dynamic objects, since their size is unknown at compile time and varies during
execution. Static variables are no longer usable, and some way must be provided for referring to these dynamic objects. Note, however, that any given
dynamic data structure can be finally broken down into elementary objects of
a static structure.

The most natural, high-level, and disciplined way to define dynamic data
structures is to allow the definition of *recursive types*; i.e., types whose definition contains one or more occurrence of themselves, either directly or in-

191

directly. Of course, since any recursion must stop somewhere, the type definition itself must contain some conditional part which controls the recursive use of the type. The simplest way to allow the definition of recursive types would be to generalize the notion of a type union, or its concretization, the *variant record*. For example, a type used to describe the ascending genealogy (the pedigree) of any given individual could be defined in the following way (which is not legal Pascal):

```
type pedigree =
  record firstname,lastname: string;
    father, mother: record case known: Boolean of
      true: (p: pedigree);
      false: ( )
    end
  end
```

or in another way, maybe simpler to use:

```
type pedigree =
  record case known: Boolean of
    true: (firstname, lastname: string;
           father, mother: pedigree);
    false: ( )
  end
```

Consequently, to allow recursive types in Pascal would not necessitate any syntactic addition to the language, and it would appear as both a powerful and a simple generalization. However, it would have so many inconveniences that it can be considered only as an abstraction, whose implementation would make necessary some lower-level feature. Let us note some of the hindrances of the idea of a recursive type in a language like Pascal, where it is considered absolutely fundamental to know the type of any object at compilation time and where the concept of a type involves its structure and its size, as well as many other properties.

- When declaring a variable of a recursive type, it would be impossible to know its structure, since that would depend on the depth of recursion. As a consequence, some object constructors would become necessary, and they should be recursively usable.

- If object constructors were allowed, selective updating of object components could not generally be permitted, since they could change the structure of the updated object.

- Recursive types constitute only a very limited way of building dynamic structures: they can describe only treelike structures, with no common branches. For example, it would be impossible to describe a situation somewhat frequent in pedigrees (especially for selected breed animals), i.e., common ancestors in different branches. It would be equally impossible to describe a circular structure, for example, a list of elements where the successor of the last one is the list head.

For these reasons, and others, recursive types exist only in so-called typeless languages, where every object is dynamically allocated each time it is necessary. In typed languages, like PL/I or Pascal, recursive types are impossible, and another feature is provided, the *pointer*. There is nothing in Basic, Fortran, or Cobol for defining dynamic data structures, and they must be awkwardly simulated or entirely avoided.

14.2 POINTERS AND DYNAMIC ALLOCATION

The tools in Pascal for building dynamic structures (of which recursive structures constitute a simple and clean case) are a new type constructor, the *pointer*, and dynamic allocation for pointed objects. While static objects can be automatically and implicitly allocated when the variables that name them are declared, and de-allocated when these variables no longer exist (i.e., when the subprogram to which they are local is terminated), dynamic objects must be explicitly allocated and de-allocated, using suitable predefined procedures. They cannot be named by ordinary variables, since their number is unknown at compile time; in addition, their existence is not bound to the embedding of subprogram declarations and activations. When a dynamic object is allocated, a pointer value of the suitable type is thus returned; this value may be used later for (indirectly) referring to the object. In order to implement a recursive data structure, one uses a pointer to replace the recursive occurrence of the object type in one of its fields, referring to another copy of the pointed object type.

A pointer type has the syntactic form shown in Fig. 14.1. The domain type may be any simple or structured type, although it is most often a record type. The pointer type is thus bound to its domain type, and a pointer can refer only to objects of this type. As a consequence, the most fundamental property of Pascal types is maintained; i.e., the type of the pointed object may be known at compile time. The domain type must be a type identifier; consequently, the type of the pointed objects must be defined elsewhere. However, a problem occurs in the case of recursive types when the domain type must contain some

Fig. 14.1 Syntax diagram for a pointer type.

component of the pointer type. The general rule, presented in Chaps. 2 and 5, is that any identifier must be textually defined or declared before its first use. This is clearly impossible if the domain type of a pointer type must contain a reference to the pointer type. Consequently, an exception is made to the rule, only for this case: the type identifier that appears in the definition of a pointer type must have been defined when the end of the type-definition part is reached. In the case of a recursive reference, the pointer type must appear first, to be used in the definition of the domain type (see Example 14.1).

There are only two ways to generate a value for a pointer type:

- The universal constant **nil** is a value of any pointer type, and points to nothing. Any pointer may be assigned the value **nil**.

- The predefined procedure $new(p)$, given a parameter p of some pointer type, dynamically allocates an object of the pointed type, and assigns to p a pointer to the created object. Consequently, there is no way to obtain a pointer to a static object. This fundamental property of Pascal pointers avoids the severe dangers which would arise if it were possible to access a static object using different names.

It should be clear that the Pascal pointer concept is not equivalent to the low-level idea of an address, although pointers are normally implemented using addresses. While machine language programs allow one to obtain the address of any object, including an address in the middle of an object or even in the program itself, a Pascal pointer can refer only to a dynamic object of the suitable type. The pointers of PL/I are much closer to machine language, with all the inherent insecurities, since the compiler cannot check that an object is actually of the correct type.

There are very few operators dealing with Pascal pointers. Assignment, and comparison for equality or inequality, are only permitted between two pointers of the same type. There are no arithmetic operations on pointers, nor any order relations. The only remaining tools dealing with pointers are the access to the pointed object and the two predefined procedures *new* and *dispose*. However, a function may return a result of a pointer type.

A pointed variable is another case of a variable access, a notion which may now, and at last, be entirely described. See Fig. 14.2. A pointer variable is a variable access of some pointer type. A pointed variable is a variable access of the domain type to which the pointer type is bound. It is an error if the pointer variable has no defined value, or equals **nil**. Although the second error is generally caught during execution in most implementations, the first one is more complicated and costly to detect, and is consequently the most serious peril of the pointer concept. An illegal pointer value may jeopardize a complete program.

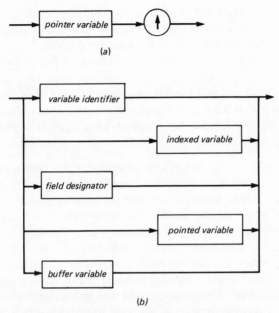

Fig. 14.2 Complete syntax diagram for variable access:
(a) pointed variable and (b) variable access.

The predefined procedure *new* may be called in two forms:

1. Whatever the domain type to which *p* is bound, the form *new*(*p*) creates a new object of this type, and assigns to *p* a pointer referring to this object. This new object is undefined; in particular, if the domain type is a record type with variants, no particular variant is chosen, and all are possible (i.e., *new* allocates a storage area of the size necessary for the largest variant).

2. If the domain type is a record type with (possibly embedded) variants, the form *new*(*p,c1*, . . ., *cn*) creates a new object of this type, with variants corresponding to the case constants *c1*, . . ., *cn*. These constants are enumerated in the order of increased embedding of variants, but constants may be missing at the end of the list. For all variants to which a case constant corresponds, the particular variant taken by the record type is the specified variant, but the tag field, if any, is not set by the call to *new*, and it must be explicitly assigned in the program. Variants for which no constant exists are in the same case as the first form of the call to *new*.

The ISO *Standard* does not state what happens if no more storage is available when *new* is called, in the same manner as it does not specify what happens if the program is too long, or too complicated, and so on. In some implementations, *new* returns the **nil** value in such a situation, while in other implementations it simply constitutes a terminal error.

The predefined procedure *dispose* may also be called in two forms:

1. *dispose(p)* destroys (de-allocates) the dynamic object referred to by *p*. Of course, it is an error if *p* is undefined or equals **nil**. After this call, *p* must be considered to be undefined, since it points to something which no longer exists.

2. *dispose(p,c1, . . ., cn)* is the opposite of the corresponding call to *new*. This form must be used if the object pointed to by *p* was created using the second form of *new*, and the number of case constants must be equal to the number used in the call to *new*. This is easily explained: the second form of *new* is used for allocating an object of the exact size needed, generally smaller than the maximum size of all possible variants of the record type; consequently, it would be a disaster to specify with *dispose* a size larger than that actually allocated. Moreover, since the exact size of an object created using the second form of *new* cannot be known at compile time, it is not legal to use this object in any context which requires knowledge of its size: this includes its use as a pointed variable on both sides of an assignment statement and as a procedure parameter, whatever its transmission mode. In fact, objects created using the second form of *new* cannot be handled globally, only componentwise.

Since *dispose* makes the pointed dynamic object disappear, all references to this object that still exist (by means of other pointer variables having the same value as the parameter of *dispose*) lapse, and are consequently undefined. It would be a severe error if this situation occurred while the dynamic object was in use, so it is not legal to dispose of a dynamic object while it is an actual variable parameter or inside a **with** statement in the variable record list of which it appears. The following fragment is thus incorrect:

```
with pvar ↑ do
begin
    . . . {statements using fields of the object pointed to by pvar} . . .
    dispose(pvar);
    . . .
end
```

Pointers constitute a very powerful device, giving the programmer the capability of building dynamic structures of any shape and complexity. As already noted, this is much more powerful than the idea of a recursive type, and thus more useful. However, pointers are also a very undisciplined device, of a much lower level than all other data structures in Pascal, even if they are a higher-level concept than that of an address. The pointer concept bears some resemblance to the **goto** statement, in the sense that it allows one to construct structures of unmastered complexity, about which no useful assertion may be made. It is not by accident that **goto** statements and pointers are the two Pascal features for which we did not give any deduction rules or axioms. Although some formal semantic rules may be given [see (Alagič and Arbib (1978)], they are so complicated that they cannot be easily used, and are thus more of a hindrance than a help. Moreover, the fact that a pointer result may be returned by a function is further evidence of the very particular properties of pointers —they can be used to build structured objects, even though they are not structured objects themselves.

It has been stated in the preceding paragraphs that some uses of pointers will cause errors, or are forbidden. The big problem is that these situations cannot be detected at compile time (except in very infrequent cases, using a compiler capable of doing a complete flow analysis of the program) and are very difficult and costly to detect at run time. Consequently, the number of such possible errors which will remain undetected in most implementations is very large, and pointers constitute a crucial factor of unreliability in programs. This means that they should be used only if really necessary, and with the utmost care.

14.3 EXAMPLES

Example 14.1: Pedigree Printing

```
type
    name = packed array[1..maxlength] of char;
    parent = ↑pedigree {a pointer type, bound to type pedigree};
    pedigree = {No variant part is necessary.}
        record firstname, lastname: name;
        father, mother: parent
        end;
procedure PedigreePrinter(person: parent; indent: integer)
    {Given some person, this procedure prints his/her pedigree, by printing, under every
        person's name, the names and pedigree of his/her parents, indented one
        character more than the current indentation. The male branch, if available,
        is printed before the female branch. For remembering a female branch while
        printing the corresponding male branch, a stack is used.};
    const stacklength = 20 {sufficient for 20 generations, i.e., at least 400 years};
    var stacktop: 0..stacklength;
        nomorefatherinthisbranch: Boolean;
        stack: array[1..stacklength] of
```

```
    record p: parent; i: integer end;
begin {PedigreePrinter}
  {First initialize the stack with the given person.}
  stacktop := 1;
  with stack[stacktop] do
  begin p := person; i := indent end;
  repeat {until the stack is empty}
    with stack[stacktop] do {Remove the root of the branch to print.}
    begin person := p; indent := i end;
    stacktop := stacktop − 1;
    nomorefatherinthisbranch := false {since we have some person};
    repeat {until nomorefatherinthisbranch}
      with person ↑ do
      begin
        writeln(output,' ': indent, firstname,' ', lastname);
        if mother ≠ nil then
        begin {Remember her.}
          stacktop := stacktop + 1;
          with stack[stacktop] do
          begin p := mother; i := indent + 1 end
        end;
        if father ≠ nil then
        begin {Process him.}
          person := father; indent :=indent + 4
        end
        else nomorefatherinthisbranch := true
      end {with person}
    until nomorefatherinthisbranch
  until stacktop = 0
end {PedigreePrinter}
```

REMARKS

1. Note the order in which type definitions are made: *parent* precedes *pedigree*, although it uses it, because it is the only admitted exception to the rule of definition before use, as explained in Sec. 14.2. Type *parent* is necessary because it is used in the parameter list of procedure *PedigreePrinter*, and also because two variables declared in different places with the type denoter ↑*pedigree* would not be of the same type, and consequently would not be compatible, even for assignment.

2. Another, much simpler version of this procedure, using recursion, will appear in Chap. 15. The present version makes explicit the stack mecha-

nism used in recursive procedures, but it also avoids one useless recursion in the male branch of each printed person.

3. A check should be done when *stacktop* is incremented, for preventing stack overflow. However, this error will be caught by the normal mechanism for type checking, and normally the program will immediately stop, which is probably the most sensible action. This is one more argument demonstrating the importance of run-time checks.

4. The data structure used in this example is capable of representing pedigrees with common ancestors. The procedure will print them with no problem, but with repeated branches.

Example 14.2: String-Handling Package

{Many different implementations are possible for strings, depending upon the operations that are considered useful. The choice in the present example is simple and flexible, but inefficient in time and space. A string is a list of characters.}

```
type natural = 0..maxint;
    varstringtype = ↑stringelement {variable length string};
    stringelement = {The list head contains no useful information.}
        packed record ch: char; next: varstringtype end;
{Only a few possible operations are defined here. Many others could be programmed in
        the same way.}
function Size(varstring: varstringtype): natural
    {returns the number of characters in varstring};
    var s: natural;
begin s := 0;
    while varstring↑. next ≠ nil do
    begin s := s + 1; varstring := varstring↑.next end;
    Size := s
end {Size};
function StringToVarstring
        (var string: packed array[lb..ub: natural] of char
            {the string to convert}
        ): varstringtype
    {Convert a Pascal string to a variable length string.};
    var i: natural; varstring: varstringtype;
begin {StringToVarstring}
    new(varstring); StringToVarstring := varstring; i := lb;
    repeat {Copy one character.}
```

```
    new(varstring↑.next); varstring := varstring↑.next;
    varstring↑.ch := string[i]; i := i + 1
  until i > ub;
  varstring↑.next := nil
end {StringToVarstring};
function Concatenation(first, second: varstringtype): varstringtype
    {returns a new variable length string which is equal to the concatenation of its two
    parameters};
  var varstring: varstringtype;
begin {Concatenation}
  new(varstring); Concatenation := varstring;
  while first↑.next ≠ nil do
  begin {Copy one character from the first string.}
    new(varstring↑.next); varstring := varstring↑.next;
    first := first↑.next; varstring↑.ch := first↑.ch
  end;
  while second↑.next ≠ nil do
  begin {Copy one character from the second string.}
    new(varstring↑.next); varstring := varstring↑.next;
    second := second↑.next; varstring↑.ch := second↑.ch
  end;
  varstring↑.next := nil
end {Concatenation};
function Section
            (varstring: varstringtype {the string to consider};
             i {beginning of the section},
             j {end of the section}: natural
            ): varstringtype
    {returns a substring of varstring, from character i to character j, if it exists; otherwise,
            returns the null string, represented by a list with only its head};
  var sec: varstringtype; k: natural;
      status: (copying, terminated, endofstring);
begin {Section}
  new(sec); Section := sec; k := 0;
  while (varstring↑.next ≠ nil) ∧ (k < i) do
  begin varstring := varstring↑.next; k := k + 1 end;
  if k = i then {Character i exists in varstring.}
  begin status := copying;
    repeat {until status ≠ copying}
      if k > j then status := terminated
      else {Copy one character.}
      begin new(sec↑.next); sec := sec↑.next;
```

```
            sec↑.ch := varstring↑.ch; k := k +1;
            varstring := varstring↑.next;
            if varstring = nil then status := endofstring
        end
    until status ≠ copying
end;
sec↑.next := nil
{Section is nonnull only if 1 ≤ i ≤ j ≤ Size(varstring)}
end {Section};
function Index
        (subject {the variable string in which to search},
         object {the variable string to search in subject}: varstringtype;
         i: natural {Search begins at ith character of subject.}
        ): natural
    {If object appears as a substring of subject, on or after its ith character, Index returns
        the position in subject of the first character of object. Otherwise, Index
        returns zero.};
    var subj, obj: varstringtype; j: natural;
        status: (searching, achieved, aborted);
        result: (comparing, found, notfound, impossible);
begin {Index}
    j := 0; {Advance in subject until character i.}
    while (subject↑.next ≠ nil) and (j < i) do
    begin subject := subject↑.next; j := j + 1 end;
    if i = j then {Character i exists.}
    begin status := searching;
        repeat {until status ≠ searching}
            subj := subject; obj := object↑.next; result := comparing;
            repeat {until result ≠ comparing}
                if obj = nil then result := found
                else if subj = nil then result := impossible
                else if subj↑.ch = obj↑.ch then
                    begin subj := subj↑.next; obj := obj ↑.next end
                else result := notfound
            until result ≠ comparing;
            case result of
                found: status := achieved;
                impossible: status := aborted {There are not enough characters left in
                    subject.};
                notfound: {Advance one character in subject.}
                    begin subject := subject↑.next; j := j + 1 end
            end {case result}
```

until *status* $\neq$ *searching*;
if *status* $=$ *achieved* **then** *Index* $:= j$
else *Index* $:= 0$
end {if i = j}
else *Index* $:= 0$
end {Index};
{The preceding operations could be used in the following piece of program, which replaces in some string the first occurrence of 'computer science', if any, with 'informatics':
var oldname, subject: varstringtype; length, position: natural; ....
oldname := StringToVarstring ('computer science');
length := Size(oldname); position := Index(subject, oldname, 1);
if position $\neq$ 0 then subject :=
    Concatenation(
      Concatenation(Section(subject, 1, position − 1),
      StringToVarstring('informatics')),
    Section(subject, position + length, Size(subject)));}

REMARKS

1. The particular implementation of the string concept chosen in the preceding example has good qualities and defects. Its best quality is that it is simple and easy to process; with an implementation using a list of fixed-length strings (see Exercise 14.4), functions *Concatenation* and *Index* would be much more complicated and difficult to understand. However, the method shown here is inefficient, both in time and space. To use one pointer for each string character needs about three times the space needed for a fixed-length string, and even more if packing is ignored by the Pascal implementation. To scan every list element in order to find the last one is extremely inefficient in time, and to build a new string for each operation is very costly. These various defects are compensated for, if an intensive use of the package is not intended, by the simplicity and naturalness of the functions, as shown in the example.

2. One more element is added as a list head for every *varstring*, although it contains no useful information. This avoids a special representation for the null string and greatly simplifies all operations, since it can be assumed, although a *varstring* is in fact a pointer, that it is never **nil**. The list head could be used for remembering information about the list—for example, its length and a pointer to its last element. This would make the whole package more efficient, but also more difficult to program, since this information should be examined and set whenever necessary.

3. List elements are allocated by the predefined procedure *new*, but never disposed. A de-allocation operation could be defined as a supplementary

procedure, but it could not be used in the last assignment of this example, since *varstring*s are created and immediately used, but never assigned to variables. Anyway, a de-allocation procedure should probably not use the standard procedure *dispose,* since list elements all are of the same size and a simple list of available elements could be used for a very efficient allocation strategy (see Exercise 14.2).

4. The use of functions returning *varstring*s allows very natural operations. It is possible because pointers may be returned by functions, while structured objects are forbidden. However, note that a pointer-returning function is not allowed everywhere a pointer is allowed, because a function designator is an expression and not a variable access. In the right-hand sides of assignments or as actual value parameters, this makes no difference, but the pointer returned by the function cannot be immediately dereferenced, and an auxiliary variable must be used. This restriction was probably made for syntactic reasons, since the exact nature of an assignment statement, whose left part would be a dereferenced function call, could be determined only very late in statement parsing. Consider the statement:

   Section(*subject*, *position* + *length*, *Size*(*subject*))↑.*next* := ...

5. Other useful operations could be defined for *varstring*s, in about the same way as in the preceding example. For example, this could include reading and writing procedures (from or into textfiles), comparison predicates, scanning operations more complicated or general than *Index*, and so on.

6. Note the use of the two status indicators, *status* and *result*, in function *Index*. They make the construction of loops much simpler, more efficient, and easier to understand than if only boolean flags had been used.

Example 14.3:   Cross-Reference Index

program *CrossReference*(*input*, *output*)
   {This program augments the program of Example 10.5, by printing each word that
      appears in the input text along with the list of the line numbers where it
      appears. The input text is first printed with these line numbers.};
   const *wordlength* = *20* {maximum useful length of words};
      dictlength = *997* {maximum number of different words; this must be a prime
         number};
      maxlineno = *9999* {maximum line number};
   type *wordtype* = **packed array**[*1..wordlength*] **of** *char*;
      index = *0..dictlength*;
      linenotype = *0..maxlineno*;
      elementptr = ↑*element*;

```
element { of the reference list of a word} =
  packed record
    lineno: linenotype; next: elementptr
  end;
var
  dictionary: array[index] of
  packed record
    name: wordtype {the word};
    listhead, listtail: elementptr {its reference list};
    empty: Boolean {occupation of this entry}
  end;
  entryno: index;
procedure BuildTheDictionary
  {Read the input text, print it with line numbers, and build the word dictionary with
    references.};
  var letters: set of char;
    word: wordtype {the word just read};
    linenumber: linenotype {the current line number};
    linebegin: Boolean {true if just before the beginning of a new line};
    charread: char {the character just read};
    currententry: index {for scanning the dictionary};
  procedure NextChar
    {Read the next character, print it, and process new lines.};
  begin {NextChar}
    if linebegin then
    begin {We are in front of a new line.}
      writeln(output) {Terminate the preceding line.};
      linenumber := linenumber + 1; linebegin := false;
      write(output, linenumber: 5, '    ')
    end;
    read(input,charread);
    if ¬eof (input) then
    begin {Otherwise charread and eoln are undefined}
      write (output, charread);
      if eoln(input) then linebegin := true
    end
  end {NextChar};
  procedure ReadAWord
    {very similar to the homonym procedure in Example 10.5, except for the use of
      NextChar and of the set letters};
  var
    wordread: array[1..wordlength] of char;
    k: 0..wordlength;
```

```
begin {ReadAWord}
  k := 0;
  repeat {charread in letters}
    if k < wordlength then
    begin
      k := k + 1; wordread[k] := charread
    end;
    NextChar
  until ¬ (charread in letters);
  for k := k + 1 to wordlength do
    wordread[k] := ' ';
  pack(wordread,1,word)
end {ReadAWord};
procedure SearchAndEnter
  {Search the word in the dictionary, enter it if not present, add the current linenum-
    ber to its reference list. The dictionary is organized as a hash table with
    quadratic search for collision handling.};
var
  hash, step: index;
  reference: elementptr;
  found: Boolean;
  i: 1..wordlength;
begin {SearchAndEnter}
  {Compute the hash index.}
  hash := 1;
  for i := 1 to wordlength do
    if word[i] ≠ ' ' then
      {Avoid undue influence from spaces.}
      hash := hash * ord(word[i]) mod dictlength;
  found := false; step := 1;
  new(reference);
  with reference↑ do {Initialize the new list element.}
  begin lineno := linenumber; next := nil end;
  repeat {until an entry is found}
    with dictionary[hash] do
    if empty then
    begin {The word may be inserted here.}
      found := true; name := word; empty := false;
      listhead := reference; listtail := reference
    end else
    if name = word then
    begin {The search word has been found.}
      found := true;
```

```
        listtail↑.next := reference;
        listtail := reference
     end {word already present}
     else
     begin {collision; search elsewhere}
        hash := (hash + step) mod dictlength;
        if step = dictlength then Error('Table full')
           {Procedure Error is not defined here.}
        else step := step + 2 {Thus successive attempts are at quadratically
           increasing distances.}
        end {collision}
     until found
  end {SearchAndEnter};
begin {BuildTheDictionary}
  {initialization}
  for currententry := 0 to dictlength do
     dictionary[currententry].empty := true;
  letters := ['a'..'i', 'j'..'r', 's'..'z',
             'A'..'I', 'J'..'R', 'S'..'Z'];
  linenumber := 0; linebegin := true;
  NextChar;
  {Process the text (nonempty).}
  repeat {until eof(input)}
     if charread in letters then
        begin {of a word}
           ReadAWord {not (charread in letters)};
           SearchAndEnter
        end else NextChar
  until eof(input)
end {BuildTheDictionary};
procedure SortTheDictionary
  {Sort the dictionary in ascending order of words. Leave all used entries at the beginning
     of the dictionary and set entryno to the number of used entries.};
begin {The body of this procedure is not defined here; see Example 15.4 for a very
     efficient sorting procedure.}
end {SortTheDictionary};
procedure PrintTheDictionary
  {Since the dictionary is already sorted, its printing is a trivial task.};
  const linelength = 120 {length of a print line};
     digitnumber = 6 {width of a reference number, with leading spaces; related to
        maxlineno};
  var linepos: 0..linelength {current position in the print line};
```

reference: *elementptr* {for scanning a reference list};
    currententry: *index* {for scanning the dictionary};
begin {PrintTheDictionary}
    page(*output*);
    writeln(*output*,'*Cross-reference index of the preceding text*');
    writeln(*output*); *writeln*(*output*);
    for *currententry* := *0* **to** *entryno* **do**
    with *dictionary*[*currententry*] **do**
    begin {Print one entry and its reference list.}
        write(*output*, *name*) {Name is a character string.};
        linepos := *wordlength*; *reference* := *listhead*;
        repeat {linepos = current position in the line; reference points to the current
            reference}
            if *linepos* + *digitnumber* > *linelength* **then**
            begin {The next reference number does not fit.}
                writeln(*output*); *write*(*output*,' ': *wordlength*);
                linepos := *wordlength*
            end {The next reference number now fits.};
            write(*output*, *reference*↑.*lineno*: *digitnumber*);
            linepos := *linepos* + *digitnumber*;
            reference := *reference*↑.*next*
        until *reference* = **nil**;
        writeln(*output*)
    end {of processing one entry}
end {PrintTheDictionary};
begin {program CrossReference}
    BuildTheDictionary;
    SortTheDictionary;
    PrintTheDictionary
end {CrossReference}.

REMARKS

1. The preceding program is an example of one whose structure represents
   the way in which it is built and the hierarchy of its different processes.
   Global names (constants, types, or variables) are names which are used
   in more than one of the different parts. If a variable is used in different
   procedures, but has no meaning outside these procedures, it is declared
   locally twice, instead of being global (see, for example, *reference* or
   currententry). Such a method is extremely general, and it allows an easy
   replacement of every procedure by a completely different one which
   achieves the same task. As a borderline case, if *BuildTheDictionary* left

the dictionary already sorted, *SortTheDictionary* would become void. The cost of the definition and use of procedures called only once is entirely negligible with a reasonably good implementation.

2. Since name collisions are handled by placing the conflicting name elsewhere in the dictionary, the dictionary size sets a definite limit to the number of different words that can be processed, hence the call to *Error* in *SearchAndEnter*. *Error* should probably immediately terminate the program—for example, using a **goto** leading to a label just before the end of the program. Another way of handling collisions would be to make each entry in the dictionary the head of a list of all names with the same hash index.

3. The two pointers to a reference list provide an easy way to build the list and print it in the same order (as a queue). With only one pointer, the list would be a stack, and it would be reversed before printing.

4. The use of the "constant" set *letters* is a simple, efficient, and readable way to avoid function *IsALetter* of Example 10.5. The set constructor conforms to the peculiarities of the EBCDIC character set, but it works also for the ISO-ASCII set.

5. The hashing function used in *SearchAndEnter* is somewhat inefficient, but machine-independent. In machine language, one could consider the word as a group of a few machine words, thus reducing the number of multiplications. Blanks are skipped, in order to avoid giving them too much importance in short words.

6. *SortTheDictionary* is necessary because the principle of a hash table is to enter the keys in a pseudorandom order, not suitable for the final printing. Many different sorting algorithms could have been chosen here, but we prefer to postpone the choice until Chap. 15, where we can use the algorithm that is the best of all known in normal situations and with a limited amount of supplementary storage.

7. In the final printing, reference numbers are printed at regular intervals, forming columns for a word used many times. A different choice would have been to print numbers with only the necessary length, and to separate them with commas. The automatic field extension made by the standard procedure *write* would do the job, but it would be somewhat difficult to keep track of the current position number in the line.

8. As in the preceding examples, *dispose* is not used in this program, although it is a really complete program. This is a frequent situation, which explains why *dispose* is sometimes not implemented at all: in many programs, dynamic allocation is used for permitting an optimal partition

of the memory between different structures of unpredictable size, but the memory requirements only increase during program execution.

EXERCISES

14.1 Message Processing

A meteorological station is linked to numerous transmitter stations, either fixed and permanent (survey stations with human attendants), or fixed but not permanent (automatic beacons), or moving and intermittent (ships cruising in the region). At some fixed time, each transmitter sends to the station a message containing the readings of the main parameters that have an effect upon weather. A message is divided into packets, consisting of a fixed number of characters, preceded by a number identifying the transmitter. The character '.' ends the message, which may be of any length. Messages are assumed to arrive at the station on the same transmission line (it may be likened to a sequential file). The order of arrival for the different packets from a given transmitter is the same as the order of transmission. However, packets from different transmitters may arrive interspersed at the station (i.e., they may overlap).

Write a procedure for handling the message file, which rebuilds the messages transmitted. Since the number of transmitters is variable, active transmitters are organized in a list, sorted by their identifying number. Each list element contains, among other things, the head and tail of the list of packets for the message being transmitted. As soon as the end of a message is encountered, the corresponding message is printed, and the storage space needed by the packed list and the transmitter descriptor is recovered.

14.2 Package for Stack and Queue Handling

A package for handling stacks and queues of elements of a given type T contains the following utilities: create and destroy a stack or a queue, push and pop a stack, add to and remove from a queue. In order to minimize the storage space needed by these structures, and the time needed to process them, they are organized in lists, and created using the following method:

(a) Initially, the package does not allocate any structure but a list head (see d).

(b) When creating a structure, the package dynamically creates a descriptor for it.

(c) When pushing a stack or adding to a queue, the package dynamically creates a stack or queue element.

(*d*) When popping a stack, removing from a queue, or destroying a structure, the package inserts all forsaken elements in a list of free elements. Subsequent allocations, needed by a creation, a push, or an addition, use this list until it is empty, then come back to dynamic allocation.

Specifications of the package follow:

type *itemptr* = ↑*item*;
  item = . . . {descriptor for a stack or queue element};
procedure *CreateStack*(**var** *s*: *itemptr*) {creates a stack, denoted by s};
procedure *DeleteStack* (*s*: *itemptr*) {deletes the stack s};
procedure *Push*(**var** *s*: *itemptr*; *elem*: *T*) {pushes elem on top of stack s};
procedure *Pop* (**var** *s*: *itemptr*; **var** *elem*: *T*; **var** *empty*: *Boolean*)
    {pops elem from the top of stack s, or sets empty if s is empty};
procedure *CreateQueue* (**var** *q*: *itemptr*) {creates a queue, denoted by q};
procedure *DeleteQueue* (*q*: *itemptr*) {deletes the queue q};
procedure *AddTo* (**var** *q*: *itemptr*; *elem*: *T*) {adds an elem at end of q};
procedure *RemoveFrom* (**var** *q*: *itemptr*; **var** *elem*: *T*; **var** *empty*: *Boolean*)
    {removes elem from the front of queue q, or sets empty if q is empty};

14.3   Sparse Matrices

A representation of a large sparse matrix (i.e., a matrix with most elements not denoting information) as an array structure leads to a huge waste of storage. Other methods, generally using lists of the only significant elements, are needed. Design a representation for such matrices, satisfying the following requirements:

(*a*) Matrices are square but with variable dimensions.

(*b*) Operations on matrices are always made either on all elements of a row in increasing column indices, from a given column index, or on all elements of a column in increasing row indices, from a given row index.

(*c*) A matrix element is of a given type *T*; an element of such a type may be read from a textfile using procedure *ReadT* (**var** *x*: *T*).

Given that it is desired to speed up the access to matrix elements when they are used in the normal frame described above, design the necessary data structures, and program the following procedures:

(a) *InitRowTraversal* and *InitColumnTraversal*, given a matrix m, a row i or a column j, a starting index bi or bj, prepare for traversing a row or a column of m (three parameters: m, i or j, bj or bi).

(b) *NextInRow* and *NextInColumn*, given a matrix m, yield the value v of the next element in the initialized row or column, as well as its column or row indices; booleans *endofrow* or *endofcolumn* are set if there is no such element (four parameters: m, v, j or i, *endofrow* or *endofcolumn*).

(c) *InitMatrix* initializes a matrix m from triples (i, j, v) read in a textfile.

14.4 String-Handling Package (alternative solution)

In Example 14.2, variable-length strings were represented as lists whose elements contained only one character. In Exercise 14.1, messages (which are actually strings) are transmitted as lists of packets, a packet being a fixed-length string. By combining these two ideas, it is possible to represent a variable-length string as a list of packets, the last one being possibly incomplete. Design the necessary data structures for this representation, and write the procedures and functions of Example 14.2, i.e., *Size*, *StringToVarstring*, *Concatenation*, *Section*, and *Index*, and in addition, the procedure *PrintVarstring* (*vs*: *varstring*), which prints on *output* the variable-length string *vs*.

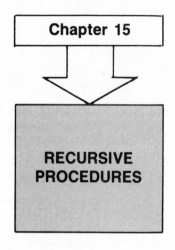

Chapter 15

RECURSIVE PROCEDURES

A concept is recursive if it contains itself partly or is partly defined using itself. Recurrent definitions, common in mathematics, are recursive, as is the syntax of Pascal. This can be seen, for example, in the definition of an expression (Chap. 4) or a statement (App. II). We have already considered the use of a recursive concept to describe dynamic data structures. In this chapter, we apply recursion to actions, using recursive procedures or functions.

A recursive definition allows one to define an infinite number of objects with a finite number of rules; for example, one can define the set N of natural numbers with the two rules: 1 is a natural number, and the successor of a natural number is a natural number. Similarly, a recursive program (i.e., a program which uses recursion) allows us to describe an infinite number of processes with a finite number of statements, even without using iterative or repetitive statements. In fact, these latter statements may always be described in a recursive way. In contrast, a recursive statement may not always be described (at least in a completely general way) using iterative or repetitive statements. This means that recursive programming adds enormous power to the set of tools provided by the programming language.

However, the power given by recursion may be misused, as we shall see: it can lead to extremely inefficient programs when an iterative solution would be much simpler. As a general rule, we note that a recursive solution may be interesting and useful only if the problem to be solved, or the function to be defined, or the data to be processed are defined in a recursive way.

Allowing recursion in a programming language does not require any additional syntactic mechanism, provided a way exists to name a given statement (generally a compound one). This capability is inherent in the concept of a subprogram (a procedure or a function), and a subprogram is recursive if it calls itself, either directly or indirectly (by calling another subprogram). If this is allowed, the remaining problems are only matters of semantics and implementation.

Semantics must provide a means to store data used in one activation of the subprogram independently from data pertaining to other activations. The corresponding mechanism is provided in Pascal by local variables, which are created at the beginning of activation of the subprogram and exist during the complete activation. If several activations of the same subprogram exist simultaneously during recursive calls, a distinct set of local variables is attached to each activation. Thus, the context of each activation is saved and restored at suitable points, and there is no communication between different activations of the same subprogram.

The implementation must guarantee that such a mechanism works both correctly and efficiently. In fact, the problem of implementing recursive subprograms is now perfectly mastered by implementors, and it is included in the general solution given to the problem of implementing local variables and subprogram calls. Recursion adds no particular cost to the implementation of subprograms, and subprograms themselves are implemented very efficiently on present-day computers. As a consequence, lack of implementation efficiency should never be an excuse for avoiding recursion; the choice between an iterative and a recursive solution, in Pascal, is guided only by the properties of the algorithm being programmed.

This was not always the case in older programming languages. The official definition of Fortran did not prescribe any choice for the relation between the existence of a variable and the activation of the subprogram in which it was defined. However, all compilers have made the same choice, which is now considered de facto a part of Fortran: all variables exist during the whole program, they are not related to a particular activation, and consequently, recursion is impossible. Cobol officially made the same choice, and recursion for a long time has been considered an entertainment for academics. The authors of PL/I at last recognized the importance of recursion, which had been known a long time (it was used in Algol 60), but they feared inefficiencies in its implementation and made it an optional feature. In fact, the use of recursion in PL/I is generally discouraged because of its perceived prohibitive cost.

We said before that no special syntactic mechanism is needed in order to allow recursive procedures. In fact, there is one minor problem in the case of mutual recursion, i.e., when two procedures call each other. Since the declaration of any identifier must precede all its uses, some trick must be performed when procedure A calls B, which itself calls A. The solution is given by the standard directive, *forward*, already explained in Sec. 5.1. Procedure A, for example, is first predeclared; i.e., only its heading appears, and its block is replaced by *forward*. Procedure B may then be declared completely, and it can use A, which is already declared. The body of A appears afterward, completing the declaration of A; it may use B, which is already declared. Remember that, when the body of a procedure is separated from its heading, it is preceded by a simple procedure identification; the procedure parameters, if any, are specified only once, in the heading. In the case of several mutually recursive procedures, furthermore, a neater organization is to first predeclare all the procedures that bear this mutual relationship, accompanied with suitable comments, and then to declare their corresponding blocks, in any order.

The remaining part of this last chapter will be devoted to examples of recursive programs: first, two examples showing situations where recursion is not a good choice, since an iterative solution is much more efficient, and is easy to find. After that, more useful examples will demonstrate how recursion may be used as an elegant, simple, and efficient tool in various situations.

Example 15.1:   Recursive and Iterative Factorials

```
function RecursiveFactorial(n: natural): natural;
begin {RecursiveFactorial}
  if n = 0 then RecursiveFactorial := 1
  else RecursiveFactorial := n * RecursiveFactorial(n − 1)
end {RecursiveFactorial};
function Factorial(n: natural): natural;
  var f, i: natural;
begin {Factorial}
  i := 0; f := 1;
  while i ≠ n do {f = i!}
  begin i := i + 1; f := i * f end {f = n!};
  Factorial := f
end {Factorial}
```

REMARKS

1. The first version of this function that computes a factorial is directly deduced from the recurrent definition given by mathematicians. By reversing the order in which the successive factorials are computed, one obtains the second version. The first one is apparently simpler, since it needs no local variable and contains no iteration. In fact, an iteration is hidden by the recursive call, and n activations need to exist at the same time in order to compute the nth factorial. The cost in time is probably not really prohibitive if subprogram calls are correctly implemented, but the cost in storage space is huge since the activation stack must store the function context n times.

2. The recursive version exhibits a situation where recursion may be avoided very simply, i.e., when there is only one recursive call in the subprogram and it is followed by no other action. In all similar cases, an

iterative version is very easy to obtain and dramatically reduces the cost of the subprogram.

3. Note the different meanings of the occurrences of the function name in its body in the case of functions *RecursiveFactorial* and *Factorial*. In only two situations does this occurrence not imply a call to the function: in the function heading (of course) and as the left-hand side of an assignment statement. That explains the need for the local variable *f* in function *Factorial*.

Example 15.2: Recursive and Iterative Fibonacci Numbers

function *RecursiveFibonacci*(*n: natural*): *natural*
{This function computes the nth Fibonacci number, defined by the following recurrence relation: F(i + 1) = F(i)+ F(i − 1) for i > 0; F(1) = 1; F(0) = 0};
begin {RecursiveFibonacci}
　　if *n = 0* **then** *RecursiveFibonacci* := *0*
　　else if *n = 1* **then** *RecursiveFibonacci* := *1*
　　else *RecursiveFibonacci* :=
　　RecursiveFibonacci(*n − 1*) + *RecursiveFibonacci*(*n − 2*)
end {RecursiveFibonacci};
function *Fibonacci*(*n*: *natural*): *natural*;
　　var *fib, lastfib, temp, i*: *natural*;
begin {Fibonacci}
　　i := *1*; *fib* := *1*; *lastfib* := *0*;
　　if *n = 0* **then** *fib* := *0* **else**
　　while *i ≠ n* **do**
　　begin {fib = Fibonacci(i); lastfib = Fibonacci(i − 1)}
　　　　temp := *fib*; *i* := *i + 1*;
　　　　fib := *fib + lastfib*; *lastfib* := *temp*
　　end {fib = Fibonacci(n); lastfib = Fibonacci(n − 1)};
　　Fibonacci := *fib*
end {Fibonacci}

REMARKS

1. Here again, the recursive version is immediately deduced from the recurrence relations. In contrast, the iterative version is less evident, since there are two recursive calls of the function, following each other. However, reversing the order in which the successive values are computed suffices.

2. The recursive version is extremely bad, because of the depth of recursive calls necessary and also because of the repeated computations of results

already computed. For example, *F5* needs *F4*, then *F3* and *F2*, and so on, with a total number of 15 function calls in order to compute only four different values. The maximum depth of function calls is n, and the number of recursive calls about k^n, with $k \cong 1.67$ for the first integer values of n.

The lesson of the two preceding examples may be summarized in the following rule. Given some problem for which a recursive solution is available, this solution must be discarded for the benefit of an iterative one in two situations:

1. The iterative solution is evident.

2. A study of the recursive solution shows that the maximum depth of recursion is of the order of n or more, or the number of recursive calls is of the order of $n \log_2 n$ or more, and an iterative solution is found.

In some situations, a recursive solution and an iterative one for the same problem may have comparable advantages and shortcomings; it is difficult to assert that one solution is simpler, clearer, more efficient, more elegant, and more understandable than the other, all at the same time, and the choice between these two possibilities is mainly a matter of taste. This is the case for the following example.

Example 15.3: Recursive and Iterative Writing of Integers

```
procedure WriteInteger(var f: text; n: integer)
    {This procedure writes on f a decimal representation of the integer number n, on
        the minimum number of characters.};
    const maxdigits = 7 {maximum number of digits in an integer;
            maxdigits = log₁₀ maxint + 1};
        base = 10;
    var digits: array[1..maxdigits] of '0'..'9';
        index: 0..maxdigits;
    begin {WriteInteger}
        index := maxdigits;
        if n < 0 then {Write the negative sign.}
        begin write(f, '−'); n := − n end;
        {0 ≤ n < 10 maxdigits}
        repeat {until no more digits to compute}
            digits[index] := chr(n mod base + ord('0'));
            n := n div base; index := index − 1
        until n = 0;
```

```
repeat {until no more digits to write}
    index := index + 1;
    write(f, digits[index])
until index = maxdigits
end {WriteInteger};
procedure RecursiveWriteInteger(var f: text; n: integer);
const base = 10;
begin {RecursiveWriteInteger}
    if n < 0 then {Write the negative sign.}
    begin write(f, '−'); n := − n end;
    if n ≥ base then {Write the first digit(s).}
        RecursiveWriteInteger(f, n div base);
    write(f, chr(n mod base + ord('0'))) {the last digit}
end {RecursiveWriteInteger}
```

REMARKS

1. A value parameter is local to the procedure, while a variable parameter denotes the corresponding actual parameter. Thus, in procedure *RecursiveWriteInteger*, there is one copy of n for each activation, while the reference to the actual textfile parameter is the same at all levels of recursion.

2. The recursive version needs a depth of recursion equal to the number of digits to write, but the iterative version needs a local array because digits cannot easily be obtained in the order in which they are to be written. Moreover, the iterative version is clearly more complicated. However, the recursive version would lose appeal if the specification of the procedure was changed in order to require the integer to be right-justified in a field of a given length, as does the predefined procedure *write*.

The three following examples show situations in which a recursive solution is not only conceptually simple, but also efficient. This occurs in many different contexts, and other cases will form the subject of exercises.

Example 15.4: Quicksort

```
procedure Quicksort(var table: array[lower..upper: integer] of T)
    {This procedure has the same specifications as procedure Shellsort in Example
        11.3, but it uses the best algorithm known for internal sort, credited to
        C. A. R. Hoare. See Wirth (1976).};
    procedure Partition(left, right: integer {left < right};
            var first, second: integer)
        {This local procedure makes a partition of the subarray table[left..right] around
```

positions first and second, given as results; i.e., it permutes table components until the following relations hold:

first < second

table[i] ≤ table[j] for i in left..second − 1 and j in first + 1..right

This implies that there exists some x such that

table[i] < x for i in left..first

table[i] = x for i in first + 1..second − 1

table[i] > x for i in second..right

Consequently, table elements between first and second are already in their final position.};

var *x, z*: *entrytype*;
begin {Partition}
   x := *table*[(*left* + *right*) **div** *2*] {Choose the middle component as the axis of the partition.};
   first := *right*; *second* := *left*;
   repeat {until second > first}
      {table[i] ≤ x for i in left .. second − 1,
      table[i] ≥ x for i in first + 1 .. right,
      second < first}
      while *LessThan*(*table*[*second*], *x*) **do** *second* := *second* + *1*;
      while *LessThan*(*x*, *table*[*first*]) **do** *first* := *first* − *1*;
      if *second* ≤ *first* **then** {table[second] ≥ x, table[first] ≤x}
         begin {Exchange table[second] and table[first].}
            z := *table*[*second*]; *table*[*second*] := *table*[*first*];
            table[*first*] := *z*;
            second := *second* + *1*; *first* := *first* − *1*
         end
   until *second* > *first*
end {Partition};
procedure *Sort* (*left, right*: *integer* {left < right})
   {This local procedure, which is the recursive one, sorts the subarray table[left..right] by repeatedly calling Partition.};
   var *newleft, newright*: *integer*;
begin {Sort}
   Partition(*left, right, newright, newleft*)
      {table[left..newright] and table[newleft..right], if nonempty, may now be sorted independently. table[newright + 1 .. newleft − 1] is already in its final state.};

```
       if left < newright then Sort(left, newright);
       if newleft < right then Sort(newleft, right)
       {table[k] ≤ table[l] for all k < l such that k and l are in left..right}
   end {Sort};
begin {QuickSort}
   Sort(lower,upper)
end {QuickSort}
```

REMARKS

1. A complete study of this algorithm is outside the subject of the present book. Note, however, that *Quicksort* has two important shortcomings:

   a. Its mean performance is excellent ($n \log_2 n$ comparisons), but it becomes frankly bad if the given array is already sorted, or almost sorted.

   b. The resulting sorting is not stable; i.e., two equal components cannot be guaranteed to appear in the sorted array in the same order as they did initially. This can be annoying if type T contains some fields which do not intervene in the order relation given by *LessThan*, but must be sorted in some secondary order.

2. An important improvement can be made very easily by using recursion only for the shortest subarray given by *Partition*, and using an iteration for the longest. This reduces the maximum depth of recursion, which otherwise is, at worst, equal to the length of the array. Procedure *Sort* becomes:

```
procedure Sort(left, right: integer);
var newleft, newright: integer; finished: Boolean;
begin {Sort}
   finished := false;
   repeat {until finished}
      Partition(left, right, newright, newleft);
      if newright − left ≤ right − newleft then
      begin {The left subarray is the shortest.}
         if left < newright then Sort(left, newright);
         if newleft < right then left := newleft
         else finished := true
      end else
      begin {The right subarray is the shortest.}
         if newleft < right then Sort(newleft, right);
         if left < newright then right := newright
```

```
        else finished := true
    end
  until finished
end {Sort}
```

With this improvement, the maximum depth of recursion is $\log_2$ of the length of the array, which is quite acceptable.

Example 15.5: Pedigree Printing (Improved)

{Given the type definitions of Example 14.1, the following procedure is a general tool for applying some process to every person in a given genealogy. The person is processed first, followed by the father branch, followed by the mother branch.}

```
procedure PedigreeTraversal
    (person: parent {the pedigree to be processed};
    procedure ProcessANode {the process to apply}
        (node: parent {the node to process};
        depth: natural {the recursion depth, possibly useful}
        )
    );
    procedure Traverse {in the order node-father-mother}
        (node: parent; depth: natural);
    begin {Traverse}
        if node ≠ nil then
        begin {The node exists.}
            ProcessANode(node, depth);
            with node↑ do
            begin {recursive calls for the father and mother branches}
                Traverse(father, depth + 4);
                Traverse(mother, depth + 4)
            end
        end
    end {Traverse};
begin {Pedigree Traversal}
    Traverse(person, 4)
end {Pedigree Traversal};
```

{The procedure of Example 14.1 can now be written extremely easily. It does not need its second parameter.}

```
procedure PedigreePrinter(person: parent);
    procedure PrintANode(node: parent; indent: natural)
        {This auxiliary procedure does the job needed for each given node.};
    begin {PrintANode}
        with node↑ do {node ≠ nil, thanks to Traverse}
```

writeln (output, ' ': indent, firstname, ' ', lastname)
  end {PrintANode};
begin {PedigreePrinter}
  PedigreeTraversal (person, PrintANode)
  end {PedigreePrinter}

REMARKS

1. The procedure *PedigreeTraversal* is completely general, in the sense that it can apply any process to the pedigree, except one which would erase it. Although the first parameter is a value parameter, it can be used to modify the tree structure of the pedigree, which is not recommended. By changing the respective order of the call to *ProcessANode* and the two recursive calls to *Traverse* in procedure *Traverse*, one can change the order in which the tree is visited.

2. The procedure *PedigreeTraversal* exhibits a general characteristic that is found in many recursive solutions and that appeared also in the preceding example: the main procedure serves only to call a local recursive procedure, which does all the work. This is the simplest way to make the necessary initializations.

Example 15.6:   Desk Calculator

{The following incomplete example simulates a desk calculator by reading and directly interpreting assignment statements with a simplified syntax. The following procedures are assumed to be available:

- NextSymbol reads the next significant symbol keyed in by the user, ignoring spaces, tabulations, carriage returns, and so on. This symbol is assigned to the global character variable named symbol.

- Constant(var value: real) reads a real constant and assigns it to its parameter.

- Error prints an error message and stops the treatment.

All variables are of type real, and named by one of the 26 lowercase letters. The global variable
   varvalue: array['a'..'z'] of real
contains the current values of all variables. The syntax accepted by each of the following procedures is indicated in the comment that follows its predeclaration. The square brackets enclose an optional entity, while the angle brackets enclose an entity which may be repeated zero or more times.}

procedure *Assignment*
  {assignment = variable '=' expression ';'}; *forward*;

procedure *Expression* (**var** *value*: *real*)
{expression = ['+' | '-'] factor < ('+' | '-') factor > };
forward;
procedure *Factor*(**var** *value*: *real*)
{factor = term < ('*' | '/') term > };
forward;
procedure *Term* (**var** *value*: *real*)
{term = variable | constant | '(' expression ')'};
forward;
procedure *Assignment*;
   var *name*: *char*;
begin {Assignment}
   if ¬(*symbol* **in** *letters*) **then** *Error*
   else begin *name* := *symbol*; *NextSymbol* **end**;
   if *symbol* ≠ '=' **then** *Error*
   else *NextSymbol*;
   Expression (*varvalue* [*name*]);
   if *symbol* ≠ ';' **then** *Error*
   else begin *writeln* (*output*, *varvalue* [*name*]: 8: 2); *NextSymbol*
   end
end {Assignment};
procedure *Expression* {See predeclaration.};
   var *rightoperand*: *real*; *operator*: *char*;
begin {Expression}
   if *symbol* **in** ['+', '-'] **then** {initial sign}
   begin *operator* := *symbol*; *NextSymbol* **end**
   else *operator* := '+';
   Factor(*value*);
   if *operator* = '-' **then** *value* := − *value*;
   while *symbol* **in** ['+', '-'] **do** {additive operator}
   begin *operator* := *symbol*; *NextSymbol*;
      Factor(*rightoperand*);
      if *operator* = '+' **then** *value* := *value* + *rightoperand*
      else *value* := *value* − *rightoperand*
   end {additive operator}
end {Expression};
procedure *Factor* {See predeclaration};
   var *rightoperand*: *real*; *operator*: *char*;
begin {Factor}
   Term (*value*);
   while *symbol* **in** ['*', '/'] **do** {multiplicative operator}
   begin *operator* := *symbol*; *NextSymbol*;
      Term (*rightoperand*);

if *operator* = '*' **then** *value* := *value* * *rightoperand*
else *value* := *value* / *rightoperand*
end {multiplicative operator}
end {Factor};
procedure *Term* {See predeclaration.};
begin {Term}
  if *symbol* **in** *letters* **then**
  begin *value* := *varvalue*[*symbol*]; *NextSymbol* **end**
  else if *symbol* **in** *digits* **then**
    begin *Constant*(*value*); *NextSymbol* **end**
  else if *symbol* = '(' **then**
  begin *NextSymbol*; *Expression*(*value*);
    if *symbol* ≠ ')' **then** *Error*
    else *NextSymbol*
  end
  else *Error*
end {Term};

REMARKS

Writing such a set of mutually recursive procedures is remarkably straightforward. The only problem is the processing required in the case of errors. By comparison, an equivalent program not using recursion would be much less readable and much more complicated, for probably equivalent performance. In fact, most Pascal compilers are written in Pascal and use a generalization of this method.

EXERCISES

15.1 Cross-Reference Index (Revisited)

The problem to solve is the same as in Example 14.3, but the word dictionary is organized in such a way that it is sorted after every insertion of a new word. The fixed-length table (variable dictionary) and its organization as a hash table is abandoned: the table is dynamically built and is structured as a binary tree. An element of the table has the following type:

type *itemptr* = ↑*item*;
  item = **record**
    name: *wordtype* {the word};
    listhead, *listtail*: *elementptr* {its reference list};
    before, *after*: *itemptr* {subtrees preceding or following *name* in lexical
        order}
  end;

All items occurring in the subtree with *before* (resp. *after*) as a root contain names less (resp. greater) than the name in the item.

Write procedures *SearchAndEnter* and *PrintTheDictionary* with these new specifications, modifying program *CrossReference* as a result (note that procedure *SortTheDictionary* is no longer necessary). Does this solution, which resembles the binary search in an array, yield a result generally as good as a binary search?

15.2 Best Choice

A shop wants to give an identical package to all its customers as a New Year's gift. The package will have several items taken from a set of possible items. Each item has three characteristics: its cost, its attractiveness as a gift, and a list of items incompatible with it, i.e., items that cannot be added to the package if the item is already there.

Write a program which, from data giving the set of possible items numbered from *1* to *n*, and their characteristics, finds the set ideal for the shop, i.e., that set with a price less than or equal to a given *maxprice*, which has the maximum attractiveness for customers.

15.3 Message Dispatch

In Exercise 14.1, a set of meteorological transmitter stations were sending to a main receiving station variable-length messages in the form of packets of a fixed length *l*. We are interested in the transmission of packets and the handling of possible transmission errors on the communication line. The chosen protocol is very simple: a transmitter sends a packet as a sequence of characters, but it waits before sending the next character until an echo of the character sent has been returned by the receiving station. If the echo returned is wrong, an error is detected, and the transmitter sends a delete character (for example "#"), then repeats the right character. Given the following procedures:

procedure *SendChar*(*ch*: *char*) {Send ch on the line.}
procedure *ReceiveChar*(**var** *ch*: *char*) {Receive ch from the line.}

write the procedure

procedure *SendPacket*(*p*: *packet*)

which transmits the packet *p* according to the preceding protocol, given the following type definition:

type *packet*: **array**[*1..l*] **of** *char*

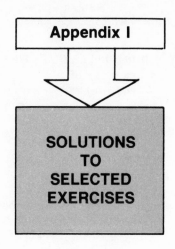

Appendix I

SOLUTIONS TO SELECTED EXERCISES

6.2 Print a Title

procedure *PrintTitle*(*title* : *char*)
{prints a personal title, identified by the character title};
begin {PrintTitle}
  case *title* **of**
    'L' : *write*(*'Lady'*);
    'D' : *write*(*'Madam'*);
    'T' : *write*(*'Mistress'*);
    'M' : *write*(*'Miss'*);
    'S' : *write*(*'Sir'*);
    'P' : *write*(*'Professor'*);
    'R' : *write*(*'Mister'*)
  end {case title}
end {PrintTitle}

REMARKS

If the parameter title is not guaranteed to have only a legal value, the **case** statement should be protected against illegal values; otherwise the program will abort. An **if** statement could be used :

  if (*title* = *'L'*) ∨ (*title* = *'D'*) ∨ . . . ∨ (*title* = *'R'*) **then**
    case *title* **of** . . .
    end {case title}
  else *write*(*'erroneous title'*)

It would be better to use a constant set constructor (see Chap. 13), as in the following **if** statement :

```
if title in ['L','D','T','M','S','P','R'] then
  case title of . . .
  end {case title}
else write('erroneous title')
```

7.3   Function Root

```
procedure HeronRoot
      (xzero: real {initial approximation of the root};
      function F(x: real): real {the function itself};
      function Fprime(x: real) : real {its derivative};
      epsilon: real {the desired relative precision};
      var convergence: Boolean {true if the desired precision is obtained before the
            limit of iterations is reached};
      var solution: real {the desired root if convergence}
      )
   {Compute the root of f(x) = 0 using the method of Heron of Alexandria};
   const maxiteration = 20 {limit to number of iterations};
   var xi, xiplus1: real {two consecutive values of the computed root};
       status: (computing, goodprecision, toomanyiterations);
       iterationnumber: integer;
begin {HeronRoot}
   xiplus1 := xzero; iterationnumber := 0;
   status := computing;
   repeat {until status ≠ computing}
      xi := xiplus1; iterationnumber := iterationnumber + 1;
      xiplus1 := xi − (F(xi) / Fprime(xi));
      if abs((xiplus1 − xi) / xi) < epsilon then
         status := goodprecision
      else if iterationnumber = maxiteration then
         status := toomanyiterations
   until status ≠ computing;
   case status of
      goodprecision: convergence := true;
      toomanyiterations: convergence := false
   end;
   solution := xiplus1
end {HeronRoot};
```

REMARKS

Note the use of the variable status, as in Example 7.6, for separating the two
possible exit conditions after termination of the loop.

8.1 File List

procedure *Listing*(**var** *f*: *fileofinteger*; *month*, *year*: *integer*)
{Give the list of all item codes in f whose unit price has not been updated since (month, year).};
var *itemcode*, *unitprice*, *quantity*, *m*, *y*: *integer*
{the five components describing an item};
function *NotUpdated*: *Boolean*
{true if (m, y) precedes (month, year)};
begin {NotUpdated}
  NotUpdated := (*y* < *year*) ∨
    (*y* = *year*) ∧ (*m* < *month*)
end {NotUpdated};
begin {Listing}
  reset(*f*);
  {f↑ is the first item code if ¬eof(f).}
  writeln('***Listing of all item codes whose unit',
  ' price has not been updated since', *year*, ' / ',
  month, '***');
  while ¬*eof*(*f*) **do**
  begin {Process an item.}
    read(*f*, *itemcode*, *unitprice*, *quantity*, *m*, *y*);
    if *NotUpdated* **then** {List it.}
    write(*itemcode*)
      {If y was the last integer of f, eof(f) is true.}
  end;
  writeln
end {Listing};

REMARKS

1. In the case of invalid data (integers on *f* are not logically grouped in fives), this procedure causes an error, since the end-of-file is tested only after reading a complete set of five. A better solution would be to structure *f* as a file of records (see Chap. 12).

2. The layout of the results is poor because we cannot use yet the tools that will be presented in the next chapter.

9.5 File Comparison

procedure *CompareFiles*
    (**var** *ref*, *verif*: *text*;
    var *newref*: *text*
)
{Compare the reference file ref with verif and produce a new reference file newref.};

```
var refno, newrefno, verifno: integer
    {line numbers on the three files};
procedure Initialize
    {Set all variables, including files, in their initial state.};
begin {Initialize}
    reset(ref); reset(verif); rewrite(newref);
    newrefno := 0;
    writeln(output, '*** Comparison of two files ',
    'by procedure CompareFiles ***')
end {Initialize};
procedure ReadNo (var f: text; var lineno: integer)
    {Read the line number lineno on the file f, if any.};
begin {ReadNo}
    {We are at the beginning of a new line or at end of file.}
    if ¬eof(f) then read(f, lineno)
end {ReadNo};
procedure Deletion
        {Delete one line from ref file and list it onto output with an appropriate mes-
        sage.};
begin {Deletion}
    writeln(output, 'line number ', refno: 1, ' is deleted. This line is: ');
    while ¬eoln(ref) do
    begin
        output↑ := ref↑; put(output); get(ref)
    end;
    readln(ref); writeln(output)
end {Deletion};
procedure Insertion
    {Insert one line on newref and list it onto output.};
begin {Insertion}
    writeln(output, 'At line ', refno: 1, ' of the ',
    'reference file, the following line ', 'is inserted');
    while ¬eoln(verif) do
    begin output↑ := verif↑; put(output);
        newref↑ := verif↑; put(newref);
        get(verif)
    end;
    readln(verif); writeln(output)
end {Insertion};
procedure WriteNo
    {Update and write the line number onto the newref file.};
begin newrefno := newrefno + 1;
    write(newref, newrefno: 5, ' ')
```

end {WriteNo};
procedure *CompareLines*
    {Compare characters of ref and verif files and copy those of verif file onto newref;
    after the first mismatch, trailing characters of each files are listed onto
    output.};
  var *ccountref, ccountverif*: *integer*
    {character counts of ref and verif files};
    status: (*match, mismatch, endoflines*);
begin {CompareLines}
  ccountref := *1*;
  {ref↑ and verif↑ are the first characters to compare.}
  status := *match*;
  while *status* = *match* **do**
    {lines matching so far}
    if *eoln*(*ref*) **then**
      if *eoln*(*verif*) **then** *status* := *endoflines*
      else *status* := *mismatch*
    else if *ref*↑ ≠ *verif*↑ **then** *status* := *mismatch*
    else
      begin {matching one character more}
        newref↑ := *verif*↑; *put*(*newref*);
        get(*ref*); *ccountref* := *ccountref* + *1*;
        get(*verif*)
      end;
  if *status* = *mismatch* **then**
  begin
    writeln(*output*, 'Mismatch in line ', *refno*: 1, 'beginning at the ',
      ccountref: 1, 'th character');
    ccountverif := *ccountref*;
    writeln(*output*, 'Rest of the ref line is: ');
    while ¬*eoln*(*ref*) **do**
    begin *output*↑ := *ref*↑; *put*(*output*);
      get(*ref*); *ccountref* := *ccountref* + *1*
    end;
    readln(*ref*); *writeln*(*output*);
    writeln(*output*, 'Rest of the verif line is: ');
    while ¬*eoln*(*verif*) **do**
    begin {Copy onto output and newref.}
      output↑ := *verif*↑; *put*(*output*);
      newref↑ := *verif*↑; *put*(*newref*);
      get(*verif*); *ccountverif* := *ccountverif* + *1*
    end;
    readln(*verif*); *writeln*(*output*);

```
        writeln(newref); writeln(output, 'difference ',
          'of length between the two lines = ',
          abs(ccountverif − ccountref));
      end {if status = mismatch}
      else {complete match}
      begin readln(ref); readln(verif) end
      {The end of line is set on newref and read from ref and verif.}
      end {CompareLines};
    begin {CompareFiles}
      Initialize;
      ReadNo(ref, refno); ReadNo(verif, verifno);
      while (¬eof(ref) ∧ ¬eof(verif)) do
          {beginning of a line after the line number on ref and verif and before the line number
            on newref}
        if refno = verifno then
        {perhaps a modification inside the current line}
        begin WriteNo; CompareLines;
          ReadNo(ref, refno); ReadNo(verif, verifno);
        end
        else if refno < verifno then {Delete one line.}
              begin Deletion; ReadNo(ref, refno) end
              else if verifno = 0 then {Insert one line.}
                    begin WriteNo; Insertion;
                      ReadNo(verif, verifno)
                    end;
      {In all cases, we are at the beginning of a line on ref and verif files after the line
        number or end-of-file is true.}
      {Perhaps one of the two files is not exhausted.}
      while ¬eof(ref) do
      begin Deletion; ReadNo(ref, refno) end;
      while ¬eof(verif) do
      begin WriteNo; Insertion; ReadNo(verif, verifno) end;
      writeln(output, '*** End of the comparison ***')
    end {CompareFiles};
```

REMARKS

1. The preceding procedure is long and complex. It is recommended that the body of the main procedure be read before reading the local procedures it calls.

2. To solve a complex problem, it is very useful to break it down into several subproblems. Thus, the procedure *ReadNo* contains only one statement for solving the delicate problem of the end-of-file.

3. The comparison is sufficiently simple to do because of the nature of the files to be compared. It would be very different if lines were not numbered; to discover the first discrepancy would be easy, but to find the end of the differing sequences would be impossible without trying several different solutions, with comebacks to the text for verification.

10.2 Table Processing

The table *tb*, each entry of which contains two values (a key of type *keytype* and an item of information of type *T*) is divided in two parallel tables: *tb* contains information of type *T*, and *tbkey* contains the keys, in such a way that the information with key *tbkey*[*i*] is in *tb*[*i*].

To access the table *tbkey* with a key of length *l*, a linear search is made among entries with the same key length. Thus it is necessary to know for each key length the index of the first corresponding entry. These key-length indices are stored in an array *accesstotb*, such that, if nb_j is the number of entries for keys of length *j*, the following relations hold:

$accesstotb[1] = 1$
$accesstotb[2] = 1 + nb_1$

. . .

(1) $accesstotb[j + 1] = accesstotb[j] + nb_j$

As a particular case, if $nb_j = 0$, then $accesstotb[j + 1] = accesstotb[j]$. For searching in *tbkey* a key of length *j*, a linear search will be made between *tbkey*[*accesstotb*[*j*]] and *tbkey*[*accesstotb*[*j* + 1] − 1]. When *j* = *keylength*, this uses *accesstotb*[*keylength* + 1], in which case relation (1) yields:

$$accesstotb[keylength + 1] = accesstotb[keylength] + nb_{keylength}$$
$$= 1 + \Sigma_{j=1}^{keylength} nb_j$$

or (2) $accesstotb[keylength + 1] = tblength + 1$
The management module for *tb* is specified with the following declarations:

```
const
    keylength   = . . . {maximum length of a key};
    accesslength = . . . {keylength + 1};
    tblength    = . . . {number of entries in tb};
    maxaccess   = . . . {tblength + 1};
type
    keytype = packed array[1..keylength] of char;
    index   = 1..tblength;
var tb: array[index] of T;
```

```
tbkey: array[index] of keytype;
accesstotb: array[1..accesslength] of 1..maxaccess;
procedure Build(var tbfile: text)
   {Construct tb, tbkey, and accesstotb; it is assumed that the textfile tbfile contains a
   sequence of tblength couples (key, information of type T), which are ordered
   on the length of the keys, and that the procedure ReadT reads on tbfile an
   item of information of type T. There is a blank character after every item.};
   var
      numberofkeys: array[1..accesslength] of 0..tblength
         {nb of formula (1)};
      i: 0..keylength; j: 0..tblength;
      key: keytype;
   begin {Build}
      reset(tbfile); i := 0;
      repeat {Initialize numberofkeys.}
         i := i + 1; numberofkeys[i] := 0
      until i = keylength;
      j := 0;
      repeat {Initialize tb and tbkey; compute numberofkeys.}
         j := j + 1; i := 0;
         repeat {Read the key.}
            i := i + 1; key[i] := tbfile↑; get(tbfile)
         until tbfile↑ = ' ';
         numberofkeys[i] := numberofkeys[i] + 1;
         while i < keylength do {Fill with blanks.}
         begin i := i + 1; key[i] := ' ' end;
         tbkey[j] := key; ReadT(tb[j])
      until j = tblength;
      {Compute accesstotb with numberofkeys.}
      accesstotb[accesslength] := maxaccess
         {formula (2)};
      i := keylength;
      repeat
         accesstotb[i] := accesstotb[i + 1] - numberofkeys[i]
            {formula (1)};
         i := i - 1
      until i = 0
   end {Build};
   function Search(key: keytype; var k: index): Boolean
      {If true, tb[k] is the item whose key is key; if not, tb[k] is undefined.};
      type lengthofkey = 1..keylength;
      var leng: lengthofkey; status: (searching, found, exhausted);
      i, j: 1..maxaccess;
```

function *Length*: *lengthofkey*
{Compute the used length of key; it is assumed that a blank character follows
the last character of a key whose length is < keylength.};
   var *status*: (*searching, blank, exhausted*); *i*: *0..keylength*;
begin {Length}
   status := *searching*; *i* := *1*;
   repeat {*key*[*j*] ≠ ' ' *for j* = 1 . . . *i*}
     if *i* = *keylength* **then** *status* := *exhausted*
     else if *key*[*i* + *1*] = ' ' **then** *status* := *blank*
     else *i* := *i* + *1*
   until *status* ≠ *searching*;
   Length := *i*
end {Length};
begin {Search}
   {accesstotb[1] = 1 and accesstotb[accesslength] = tblength + 1}
   leng := *length* {1 ≤ leng ≤ keylength};
   i := *accesstotb*[*leng*] {1 ≤ i ≤ tblength + 1};
   j := *accesstotb*[*leng* + *1*] − *1* {1 ≤ j ≤ tblength};
   status := *searching*;
   repeat {until status ≠ searching}
     if *i* > *j* **then** *status* := *exhausted*
     else {1 ≤ i ≤ tblength}
       if *tbkey*[*i*] = *key* **then**
         status := *found*
       else *i* := *i* + *1*
   until *status* ≠ *searching*;
   Search := *status* = *found*; *k* := *i*
end {Search};

REMARKS

1. The function *Length*, which is called only once, is not really necessary. However, the statement *leng* := *Length* in the function *Search* avoids the corresponding computation, which would mask somewhat the actual problem solved by *Search*. Remember that the call of a parameterless subprogram is normally very cheap in a good Pascal implementation.

2. The several assertions stated in *Search* should be examined carefully. They demonstrate that the lower bound *i* of the linear search may well be greater than the upper bound *j*; a **while** loop is consequently necessary. This situation occurs, for example, when the table *tbkey* does not contain any key with a length greater than some value *kmax* < *keylength* and when a call to *Search* is made with a key longer than *kmax*. In that case,

accesstotb[*kmax*] = *accesstotb*[*kmax* + 1] = . . . = *accesstotb*[*accesslength*] = *accesslength*.

3. The procedure *Build* aborts if the number of couples on *tbfile* is greater than *tblength*, or if a key is longer than *keylength*.

4. Type *keytype* could have been defined in another way, so as to associate a length to the key. Function *Length* would become useless. Such an association will be easy using record types (see Chap. 12).

11.1 Evaluation of a Polynom

function *PolynomValue*
    (var *a* : **array**[*lb..ub* : *integer*] of *real*; *x* : *real*
) : *real*
    {Compute a[n]x^n + a[n−1]∗x^{n-1} + . . . + a[1]∗x + a[0]; lb = 0, ub = n};
    var *i* : *integer*; *p* : *real*;
begin {PolynomValue}
    p := *0.0*;
    for *i* := *ub* **downto** *lb* **do** *p* := *p* ∗ *x* + *a*[*i*];
    PolynomValue := *p*
end {PolynomValue}

REMARKS

1. This function uses the well-known Horner scheme, which avoids the computation of x^i, thanks to the following formula :

$$P = (. . .((a[n]*x + a[n-1])*x + a[n-2])*x + . . . + a[1])*x + a[0]$$

2. The type of the control variable of the loop must be the type of the bound identifiers. These are not constants, so *i* cannot be declared in the interval *lb..ub*, which would be an erroneous type denoter.

12.3 Game of Patience

program *GameOfPatience*(*input*, *output*);
    const *numberofcards* = *28*;
        cardsinstack = *4*;
    type
        valuetype = (*seven*, *eight*, *nine*, *ten*, *jack*, *queen*, *king*, *ace*);
        colortype = (*clubs*, *diamonds*, *hearts*, *spades*);
        cardtype = **record** *color*: *colortype*; *value*: *valuetype* **end**;
    var
        error: *Boolean*;

gametable: **array**[*colortype, seven..king*] **of** *cardtype*;
uncodedgametable: **array**[*colortype, seven..king*] **of**
record *c, v*: *char* **end** {game table for printing};
cardstack: **array**[*1..cardsinstack*] **of** *cardtype*;
currentcard: *cardtype*;
cardnb: *0..cardsinstack* {number of cards remaining in the stack};
faceupcards: *0..numberofcards* {number of face up cards on the game
    table};
status: (*stackexhausted, won, playing*);

. . .

procedure *InitGameTableForPrinting*
  {Initialize uncodedgametable for printing: all cards are face down; i.e., their character
      values are two periods.};
  var *color*: *colortype*; *value*: *valuetype*;
begin {InitGameTableForPrinting}
  for *color* := *clubs* **to** *spades* **do**
    for *value* := *seven* **to** *king* **do**
      with *uncodedgametable*[*color, value*] **do**
        begin *c* := '.'; *v* := '.' **end**
end {InitGameTableForPrinting};
procedure *DecodeACard*(*card*: *cardtype*; **var** *uncodedcolor*,
        uncodedvalue: *char*)
  {Decode card yielding two characters.};
begin {DecodeACard}
  with *card* **do**
  begin
    case *color* **of**
      clubs : *uncodedcolor* := 'c';
      diamonds : *uncodedcolor* := 'd';
      hearts : *uncodedcolor* := 'h';
      spades : *uncodedcolor* := 's'
    end;
    case *value* **of**
      seven: *uncodedvalue* := '7';
      eight: *uncodedvalue* := '8';
      nine: *uncodedvalue* := '9';
      ten: *uncodedvalue* := 'X';
      jack: *uncodedvalue* := 'J';
      queen: *uncodedvalue* := 'Q';
      king: *uncodedvalue* := 'K';
      ace: *uncodedvalue* := 'A'
    end
  end
end {DecodeACard};

```
procedure PrintCard(card: cardtype)
  {Print two characters for card.};
  var c, v: char;
begin {PrintCard}
  DecodeACard(card, c, v);
  writeln(output, c, v)
end {PrintCard};
procedure RecordCard(card: cardtype)
  {Record uncovered card in uncodedgametable.};
begin {RecordCard}
  with uncodedgametable[card.color, card.value] do
      DecodeACard(card, v, c)
end {RecordCard};
procedure PrintGameTable
  {Print uncodedgametable.};
  var color: colortype; value: valuetype;
begin {PrintGameTable}
  for color := clubs to spades do
  begin
    for value := seven to king do
      with uncodedgametable[color, value] do
          write(output, c, v, ' ');
    writeln(output)
  end
end {PrintGameTable};
begin {GameOfPatience}
  InitGameTableForPrinting; InitData;
  ReadGameTable; writeln(output);
  ReadCardStack; writeln(output);
  if error then
    writeln(output, 'There is something wrong in the data')
  else begin
    writeln(output, 'Beginning of the Game of Patience');
    writeln(output); PrintGameTable; writeln(output);
    faceupcards := 0; status: = playing;
    cardnb := cardsinstack;
    repeat {until not playing}
      currentcard := cardstack[cardnb];
      writeln(output, 'card taken in the stack is:');
      PrintCard(currentcard);
      while currentcard.value ≠ ace) ∧ (faceupcards ≠ number of cards
          ) do
      begin
          RecordCard(currentcard); PrintGameTable;
```

```
    writeln(output);
    currentcard := gametable[currentcard.color, currentcard.value];
    faceupcards := faceupcards + 1
  end
  if faceupcards = numberofcards then status := won
  else begin {take a card in the stack, if any}
    cardnb := cardnb ≠ 1;
    if cardnb = 0 then status := stackexhausted
  end
  until status ≠ playing;
  case status of
    won: writeln(output, 'The Patience is won')
    stackexhausted: writeln(output, 'The Patience is lost', 'with', num-
        berofcards - faceupcards: 3, 'face down cards')
  end
end {no error in data}
end {GameOfPatience}.
```

REMARKS

1. The type of a card is very simple: it is a couple [*colortype*, *valuetype*]. The game table is a matrix whose rows are colors and whose columns are subsets of values.

2. All the procedures in this program, except *ReadGameTable* and *ReadCardStack*, are auxiliary procedures for printing the cards. Thus, in parallel with the variable *gametable*, which contains the color and value of each card, the variable *uncodedgametable* contains the status of the game at a given time, in a printable form: a couple of characters if the card is uncovered or two dots if it is face down.

3. The codification of cards, with the two enumerated types *colortype* and *valuetype*, allows quick scans with **for** loops of the arrays *gametable* and *codedgametable*. This would have been impossible with the character codification used for printing, since the characters are not consecutive.

4. Procedure *DecodeACard* uses a **case** statement where an array would be more usual) **array** [*colortype*] **of** char and **array** [*valuetype*] **of** char). There is almost no difference, in time and storage, between the two solutions, except that the use of a codification array would make necessary to explicitly initialize all components.

13.1 Game of Patience (Continued)

var {Add the following variable to the global variables of Exercice 12.3.}
    data: **array**[*colortype*] **of set of** *valuetype*

{for verifying data};
. . .
procedure *ReadACard*(**var** *card*: *cardtype*)
{Read (and write) triple characters, verify whether these characters are correct, code
    the card, and set the global boolean error if characters are not correct and
    if the card has been read.};
var
  cch, *vch*, *separator*: *char* {the triple};
  procedure *EncodeACard*
  {Produce card from cch and vch.};
  begin {EncodeACard}
    with *card* **do**
    begin
      case *cch* **of**
        'c': *color* := *clubs*;
        'd': *color* := *diamonds*;
        'h': *color* := *hearts*;
        's': *color* := *spades*
      end;
      case *vch* **of**
        '7': *value* := *seven*;
        '8': *value* := *eight*;
        '9': *value* := *nine*;
        'X': *value* := *ten*;
        'J': *value* := *jack*;
        'Q': *value* := *queen*;
        'K': *value* := *king*;
        'A': *value* := *ace*
      end
    end
  end {EncodeACard};
begin {ReadACard}
  read(*input*, *cch*, *vch*, *separator*);
  write (*output*, *cch*, *vch*, ' ');
  if (*cch* **in** ['c', 'd', 'h', 's']) ∧
    (*vch* **in** ['7', '8', '9', 'X', 'J', 'Q', 'K', 'A']) **then**
  begin {no error in the triple}
    EncodeACard;
    if *card.value* **in** *data*[*card.color*] **then** {duplicated card}
      error := *true*
    else {Record card in data.}
      data[*card.color*] := *data*[*card.color*] + [*card.value*]
  end else {error in the triple}
    error := *true*

end {ReadACard};
procedure *InitData*
  {Initialize data to the empty set: no card read.};
  var *c*: *colortype*;
begin {InitData}
  error := *false*;
  for *c* := *clubs* **to** *spades* **do** *data*[*c*] := []
end {Initdata};
procedure *ReadGameTable*
  {Initialize gametable by reading 28 char triples: a color, a value, and a blank separator;
      print the data and set the global variable error if characters have erroneous
      values or if the set of cards is erroneous.};
  var *ci*: *colortype*; *vi*: *valuetype;*
    card: *cardtype*;
begin {ReadGameTable}
  writeln(*output*, 'cards read for the game table');
  writeln(*output*);
  for *ci* := *clubs* **to** *spades* **do**
  begin
    for *vi* := *seven* **to** *king* **do**
      ReadACard(*gametable*[*ci*, *vi*]);
    writeln(*output*)
  end {for all colors}
end {ReadGameTable};
procedure *ReadCardStack*
  {Initialize cardstack by reading four char triples, as in procedure ReadGameTable.};
  var *ci*: *colortype*; *vi*: *valuetype;*
    i: *1*..*cardsinstack*;
begin {ReadCardStack}
  writeln(*output*);
  writeln(*output*, 'cards read for the stack');
  writeln(*output*);
  for *i* := *1* **to** *cardsinstack* **do**
    ReadACard(*cardstack*[*i*]);
  writeln(*output*)
end {ReadCardStack};

REMARKS

1. There is no difficulty in reading the data: the procedure *ReadACard* is the counterpart of the procedure *DecodeACard* of Exercise 12.3. Error detection is more critical and is divided in two parts (see *ReadA-Card*):

a. The detection of coding errors is made with two "constant" sets that contain the only legal characters for coding card colors and values.

b. The detection of illegal names (duplicate cards) is made with the array data, indexed with the four colors, whose elements each contain the set of card values. Initially, these sets are empty (**procedure** *Init-Data*). Upon each card reading (**procedure** *ReadACard*), the couple [*value,color*] is examined: if it has not been read already (i.e., if it is not present in *data*[*color*]), it is added to data.

2. The use of a codification array should be rejected in the present case. An array defined as **array** [*'c'* .. *'s'*] **of** *colortype* may be more space-consuming than the equivalent **case** statement (because of initializations). Moreover, the other codification cannot be defined with less than an **array** [*char*] **of** *valuetype*, if character–set independence is desired.

14.1 Message Processing

const
    charnumber = . . . {number of characters in a packet};
    terminator = '.' {message-ending character};
type
    packet = **packed array**[*1..charnumber*] **of** *char*;
    messagepointer = ↑*messagescrap*;
    messagescrap = **record**
            data: *packet*;
            nextscrap: *messagepointer*
       end;
    stationpointer = ↑*station*;
    station = **record** {transmitter descriptor}
          idstation: *integer* {identifying the transmitter};
          messagehead, *messagetail*: *messagepointer*;
          nextstation: *stationpointer*
       end;
    sendinformation = **record** {basic information sent by transmitters}
          idtransmitter: *integer*;
          information: *packet*
       end;
    messages = **file of** *sendinformation* {interspersed messages};
. . .
procedure *MessageHandler* (**var** *m*: *messages*)
    {Handle file m, which contains interspersed messages from several transmitters.};
    var *activetransmitters: stationpointer* {List head of active transmitters.};
      sp, *previous*: *stationpointer*; *exist: Boolean*;
procedure *IdentifyTransmitter*

(n: *integer* {number of the transmitter};

var *found*: *Boolean* {true if transmitter n is yet active};

var *sp, previous*: *stationpointer* {If found, sp is the pointer on the active transmitter n and previous is its predecessor in the activetransmitters list; if not, transmitter n must be inserted after previous.}
)
{Search for transmitter n in the activetransmitters list.};

var *status*: (*searching, transmitterfound, none*);

begin {IdentifyTransmitter}

  previous := **nil**; *sp* := *activetransmitters*; *status* := *searching;*

  repeat {until not searching}

    if *sp* = **nil then** *status* := *none*

    else if *n* = *sp*↑*.idstation* **then** *status* = *transmitter found*

    else if *n* > *sp*↑*.idstation* **then** *status* := *none*

    else begin *previous* := *sp*; *sp* := *sp*↑*.nextstation* **end**

  until *status* ≠ *searching*;

  found := *status* = *transmitterfound*

  {previous = nil ∧ sp = nil: no active transmitters;

  previous = nil ∧ sp ≠ nil: transmitter n is the first of the list;

  previous ≠ nil ∧ sp ≠ nil: transmitter n is not the first}

end {IdentifyTransmitter};

procedure *InsertTransmitter*

    (n: *integer* {number of the transmitter};

    previous: *stationpointer* {must be inserted after previous};

    var *sp*: *stationpointer* {created transmitter descriptor}
)
{Create a transmitter descriptor and insert it in the activetransmitters list.};

begin {InsertTransmitter}

  new(*sp*);

  with *sp*↑ **do**

  begin

    idstation := *n*; *messagehead* := **nil**; *messagetail* := **nil**;

    if *previous* = **nil then** {insert in head}

    begin *nextstation* := *activetransmitters*;

      activetransmitters := *sp*

    end

    else begin *nextstation* := *previous*↑*.nextstation*;

      previous↑*.nextstation* := *sp*

    end

  end

end {InsertTransmitter};

procedure *InsertPacket*(*p*: *packet*; *sp*: *stationpointer*)

  {Insert packet p in the message of transmitter sp.};

```
    var mp: messagepointer;
begin {InsertPacket}
    new(mp);
    with mp↑ do begin data := p; nextscrap :=nil end;
    with sp↑ do
      if messagehead = nil then {firstpacket}
      begin messagehead := mp; messagetail := mp end
      else {insertion in tail}
      begin messagetail↑.nextscrap := mp;
        messagetail := mp
      end
end {InsertPacket};
procedure EditMessage(sp: stationpointer)
    {Print the message from sp transmitter.};
    var mp: messagepointer; i: 0..charnumber;
      up: array[1..charnumber] of char;
begin {EditMessage}
    writeln(output, '** Message from the transmitter number',
      sp↑.idstation: 4, ' **');
    mp := sp↑.messagehead;
    if (mp ≠ nil) ∧ (sp↑.messagetail ≠ mp) then
      {There are complete packets.}
      while mp ≠ sp↑.messagetail do
      begin write(output, mp↑.data); mp := mp↑.nextscrap end;
    {Print the last packet.}
    i := 0; unpack(mp↑.data, up, 1);
    repeat {There is at least one character in the last packet.}
      i := i + 1; write(output, up[i])
    until up[i] = terminator;
    writeln(output); writeln(output)
end {EditMessage};
procedure Suppress(previous, sp: stationpointer)
    {Suppress message and transmitter descriptor sp.};
    var predpp, pp: messagepointer;
begin {Suppress}
    pp := sp↑.messagehead; predpp := pp;
    while pp ≠ nil do {predpp ≠ nil}
    begin pp := pp↑.nextscrap; dispose(predpp);
      predpp := pp
    end {of deleting message scraps};
    if previous = nil then {Suppress the first transmitter description.}
      activetransmitters := sp↑.nextstation
    else previous↑.nextstation := sp↑.nextstation;
```

```
    dispose (sp)
end {Suppress};
function LastPacket(p: packet): Boolean
      {Yield true if p contains a terminator.};
    const terminator = '.';
    var i: 0..charnumber; found: Boolean;
      up: array[1..charnumber] of char;
begin {LastPacket}
    i := 0; found := false; unpack(p, up, 1);
    repeat {There is at least one character in p.}
      i := i + 1; found := up[i] = terminator
    until (i = charnumber) ∨ found;
    LastPacket := found
end {LastPacket};
begin {MessageHandler}
    reset(m);
    while ¬eof(m) do
    begin
    IdentifyTransmitter(m↑.idtransmitter, exist, sp, previous);
    if ¬exist then
      InsertTransmitter(m↑.idtransmitter, previous, sp);
    InsertPacket(m↑.information, sp);
    if LastPacket(m↑.information) then
      begin EditMessage(sp); Suppress(previous, sp) end;
    get(m)
    end
end {MessageHandler};
```

REMARKS

1. The insertion of a list element pointed by p modifies the value of the preceding element in the list, if the insertion is not at the beginning of the list. In *InsertTransmitter*, the test on the pointer *previous* (the preceding element in the insertion) results from the exit conditions of *IdentifyTransmitter*.

2. In a general way, the number of times an equality or inequality with **nil** is tested should be noticed. Most of the time, it is done to avoid accessing a nonexistent element, or as in *Suppress*, to avoid disposing of a nonexistent dynamic variable.

3. The efficiency of *MessageHandler* could be improved with a memory management similar to that of Exercise 14.2 and by avoiding the inspec-

tion of every packet in *LastPacket*. When transmitting, a flag should be
added to indicate the last packet.

15.3 Message Dispatch

```
const l = . . . ;
type packet = array[1..l] of char;
procedure SendChar(ch: char); . . . ;
procedure ReceiveChar(var ch: char); . . . ;
. . .
procedure SendPacket(p: packet)
        {Send a packet with a very simple protocol.};
    var i: 1..l;
    procedure Transmit(c: char)
            {Send a character and resend it if echo is wrong.};
        var echo: char;
    begin {Transmit}
        SendChar(c); ReceiveChar(echo);
        if c ≠ echo then
        begin Transmit('\') {Delete character.};
            Transmit(c)
        end
    end {Transmit};
begin {SendPacket}
    for i := 1 to l do Transmit(p[i])
end {SendPacket};
```

REMARKS

1. Recursion, used in the procedure *Transmit*, allows elegant and concise
   programming, in which the transmission protocol is applied to all characters, including the delete character.

2. However, this protocol gives poor performance, since the case of echo
   errors is not handled. If the transmission error deals with the echo
   transmission, the transmitter resends a character correctly received. This
   simple case leads only to an increase in the number of characters transmitted, but an error that is impossible to detect may occur if the delete
   character sent by the transmitter is transformed into a normal character
   when it arrives at the receiver.

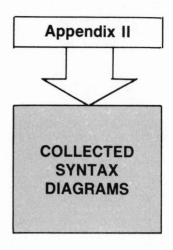

Appendix II

COLLECTED SYNTAX DIAGRAMS

The following diagrams describe in a very concise way the complete syntax of the Pascal language. As explained in Sec. 2.1, these diagrams are not a simple collection of those that appear throughout the chapters of this book, since their goal is different. They are not made for explaining the syntax of a notion being described, but for giving a handy reference, intended for anyone wishing to refresh his or her understanding of the syntax of Pascal.

For example, the various statements of the language are described in several diagrams in the corresponding chapters, but all statements are collected in the same diagram in this appendix.

The same convention used throughout the book is used in this appendix, too: a nonterminal called "something identifier" is not defined elsewhere in the diagrams. It simply represents an identifier, with the additional property that it must be defined somewhere in the program as being "something."

IDENTIFIER

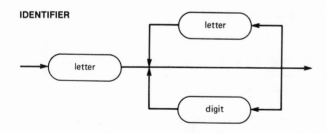

UNSIGNED INTEGER

UNSIGNED NUMBER

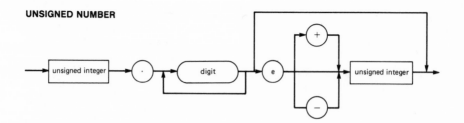

UNSIGNED CONSTANT

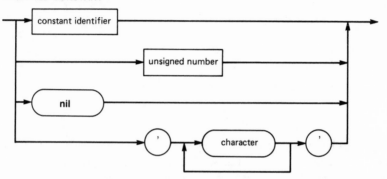

CONSTANT

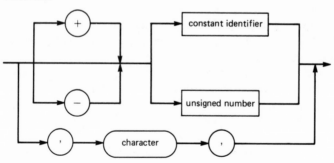

ORDINAL TYPE

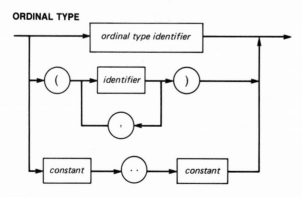

TYPE DENOTER

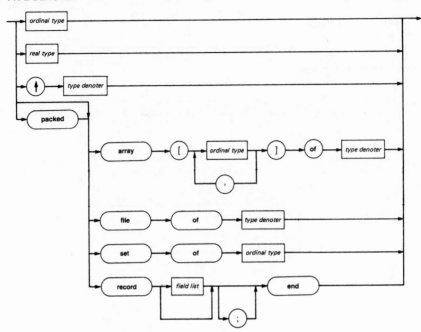

RECORD SECTION

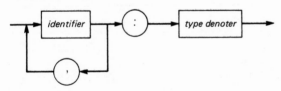

VARIANT

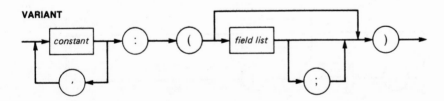

FIELD LIST

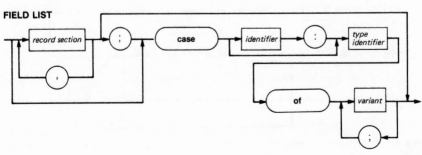

VARIABLE ACCESS

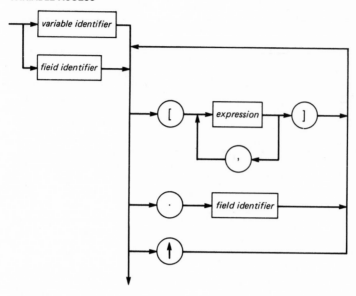

FACTOR

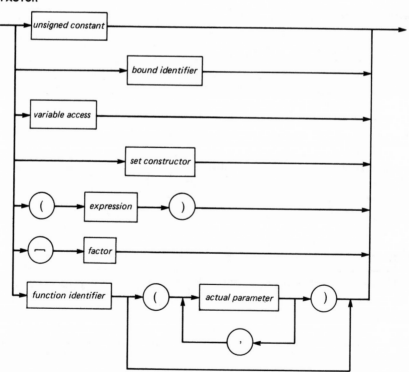

SET CONSTRUCTOR

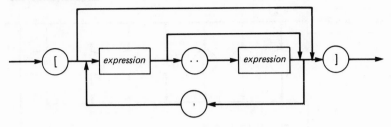

ACTUAL PARAMETER

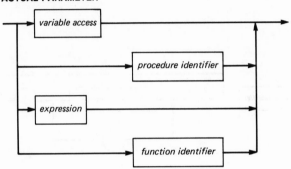

TERM

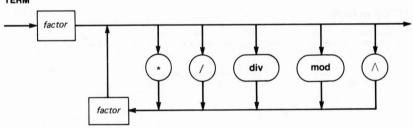

SIMPLE EXPRESSION

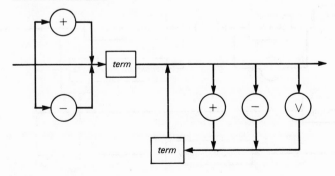

EXPRESSION

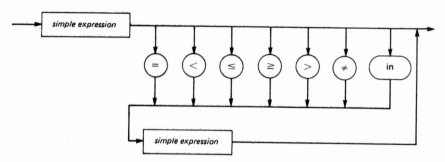

PROCEDURE HEADING

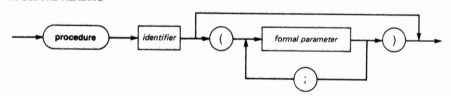

FUNCTION HEADING

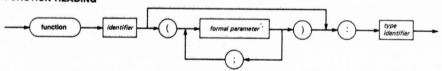

FORMAL PARAMETER

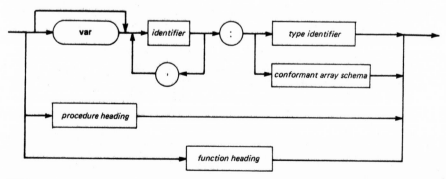

250

CONFORMANT ARRAY SCHEMA

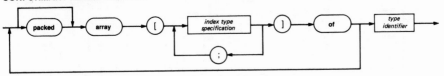

INDEX TYPE SPECIFICATION

STATEMENT

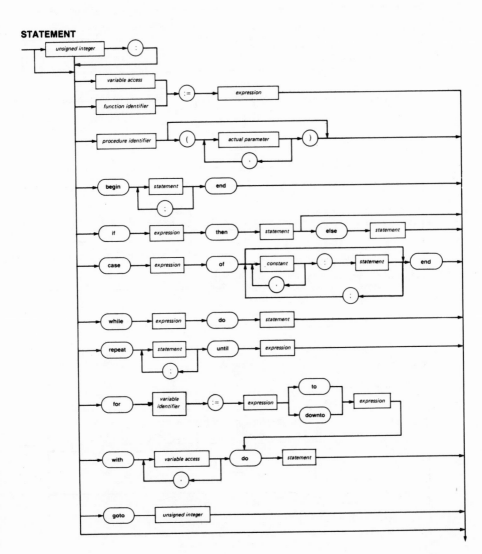

251

BLOCK

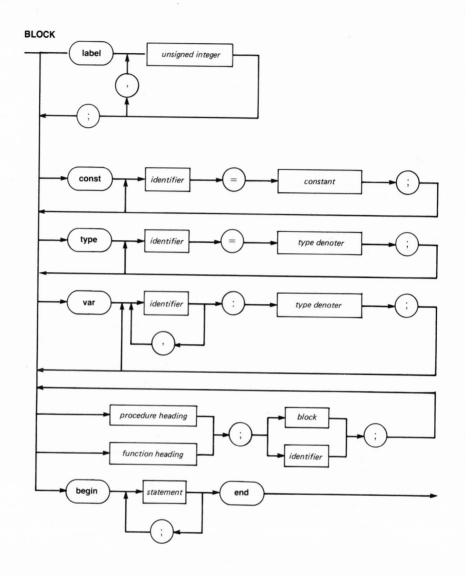

PROGRAM

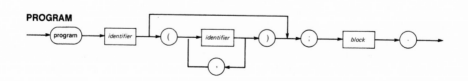

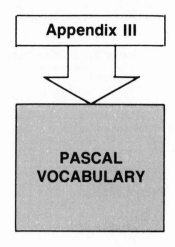

Appendix III

PASCAL VOCABULARY

The complete Pascal vocabulary is described in Sec. 2.2 and is regrouped in this appendix only for easy reference. Two different classifications are used: in the first one, vocabulary elements are classified according to their function, while in the second one, they are classified according to their appearance. Since a few symbols serve several usages, they occur several times in the first classification. Because there are several different representations for a few symbols, the second classification presents not only the representation that is preferred in this book, but also the possible alternatives, and it is consequently somewhat redundant.

Basic Symbols of Pascal

Standard representation	Alternative representations	Class
a . . . z	Any other case, font, or style	Letters
0 1 2 3 4 5 6 7 8 9		} Digits
+ − * / div mod		} Arithmetic operators
or and not	∨ ∧ ¬	} Boolean operators

Basic Symbols of Pascal (*Continued*)

Standard representation	Alternative representations	Class
<		
< =	≤	
=		
< >	≠	Relational operators
> =	≥	
>		
in		
(		
)		
[	(.	
]	.)	Brackets
{	(*	
}	*)	
begin		
end		
.		
,		
:		Separators
;		
..		
if then else		
case of end		
while do repeat until		Statement separators
for to downto		
with program		
const type var		Object class specifiers
procedure function		
array file of		
record set end		Structure class specifiers
packed		
:=		
,		
↑	∧ @	Miscellaneous
nil		
goto		
label		

Basic Symbols of Pascal (*Continued*)

WORD-SYMBOLS

and	downto	if	or	then
array	else	in	packed	to
begin	end	label	procedure	type
case	file	mod	program	until
const	for	nil	record	var
div	function	not	repeat	while
do	goto	of	set	with

SPECIAL SYMBOLS

+	<	≠	>	.)	;	..	{	^
−	< =	< >	[	.	↑	:=	(*	∨
*	<	≥	(.	,	^	(	}	¬
/	=	> =	]	:	@	)	*)	

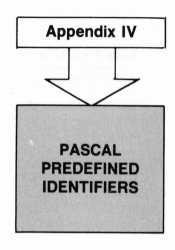

Appendix IV

PASCAL PREDEFINED IDENTIFIERS

Since these identifiers exist as if they were defined or declared in an environment containing the program, they are enumerated below in the form of an informal sequence of definitions and declarations.

const
    $maxint$ = {largest positive integer};
    {true, false are defined with the type Boolean}

type
    $Boolean$ = ($false$, $true$);
    $integer$ = $-maxint$ .. $+maxint$;
    $char$ = {the underlying character set};
    $real$ = {the possible set of real numbers};
    $text$ = **file of** $char$ {with additional properties};

var
    $input$, $output$: $text$ {declared only if they appear as program parameters};

{arithmetic functions}
function abs (x : {integer or real}) : {type of x};
    {absolute value}
function sqr (x : {integer or real}) : {type of x};
    {square of x}
function sin (x : $real$) : $real$;
    {sine of x, expressed in radians}
function cos (x : $real$) : $real$;
    {cosine of x, expressed in radians}
function exp (x : $real$) : $real$;
    {exponential of x}
function ln (x : $real$) : $real$;
    {natural logarithm of x > 0}

function *sqrt* (*x* : *real*) : *real*;
  {square root of x $\geq$ 0}
function *arctan* (*x* : *real*) : *real*;
  {principal value, in radians, of the arctangent of x}

{transfer functions}
function *trunc* (*x* : *real*) : *integer*;
  {0 $\leq$ x $-$ trunc(x) $<$ 1 if x $\geq$ 0, or
  -1 $<$ x $-$ trunc(x) $\leq$ 0 if x $<$ 0}
function *round* (*x* : *real*) : *integer*;
  {trunc(x $+$ 0.5) if x $\geq$ 0, or
  trunc(x $-$ 0.5) if x $>$ 0}
  {ordinal functions}
function *ord* (*x* : {any ordinal type}) : *integer*;
  {ordinal number of x}
function *chr* (*x* : *integer*) : *char*;
  {character whose ordinal number is x, if it exists}
function *succ* (*x* : {any ordinal type}) : {type of x};
  {successor of x, if it exists}
function *pred* (*x* : {any ordinal type}) : {type of x};
  {predecessor of x, if it exists}

{Boolean functions}
function *odd* (*x* : *integer*) : *Boolean*;
  {x is odd}
function *eof* (**var** *f* : {any file type}) : *Boolean*;
  {*right* f is empty}
function *eoln* (**var** *f* : *text*) : *Boolean*;
  {*first right* f is an end-of-line mark, if ¬eof(f)}

{file handling procedures}
procedure *rewrite* (**var** *f* : {any file type});
  {initialize f for generation}
procedure *reset* (**var** *f* : {any file type});
  {initialize f for inspection}
procedure *put* (**var** *f* : {any file type});
  {pass to the next component during generation}
procedure *get* (**var** *f* : {any file type});
  {pass to the next component during inspection}
procedure *write* (**var** *f* : {any file type};
            $x_1, \ldots, x_n$: {type component of f, or other types if f is a text});
  {write values of x₁, . . . , xₙ onto f}
procedure *read* (**var** *f* : {any file type};
            var $x_1, \ldots, x_n$: {type component of f, or other types if f is a text}
            );

{read values of $x_1, \ldots, x_n$ from f}
procedure *writeln* (**var** f : *text*;

$x_1, \ldots, x_n$: {integer, real, char, Boolean, or string});
{write onto f and pass to the next line}
procedure *readln* (**var** f : *text*;

var $x_1, \ldots, x_n$:{integer, real, or char});
{read from f and pass to the next line}
procedure *page* (**var** f : *text*);
{begin a new page on f}

{dynamic allocation procedures}
procedure *new* (**var** p : {any pointer type};

$c_1, \ldots, c_n$: {types of the relevant tag fields});
{allocate a dynamic variable, pointed to by p}
procedure *dispose* (p : {any pointer type};

$c_1, \ldots, c_n$: {types of the relevant tag fields});
{delete the dynamic variable pointed to by p}

{transfer procedures}
procedure *pack* (a : {some unpacked array type};

i : {index type of the type of a};

var z : {packed array type with the same component type as a});
{pack a into z beginning at a[i]}
procedure *unpack* (z : {some packed array type};

var a : {unpacked array type with the same component type as z}
;
i : {index type of the type of a});
{unpack z into a beginning at a[i]}

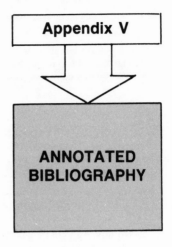

Appendix V

ANNOTATED BIBLIOGRAPHY

A complete bibliography for Pascal would probably include several hundred papers and several dozen books. Moreover, it would be obsolete as soon as it was completed. We have selected here only a very small set of important texts, easily available and listed in the order in which they were published.

Language Definitions

Wirth, Niklaus: "The Programming Language Pascal," *Acta Informatica*, vol. 1, no. 1, 1971, pp. 35–63.

This is the original definition of the language, reprinted later in Wassermann (1980). It is interesting to read for noting the differences between this original version and the revised one. The introductory section is of particular interest.

Hoare, C. A. R., and Niklaus Wirth: "An Axiomatic Definition of the Programming Language Pascal," *Acta Informatica*, vol. 2, no. 4, 1973, pp. 335–355.

This very concise paper contains the almost complete semantics, in axioms, and the complete syntax, in diagrams, of the revised version of Pascal. It too was reprinted in Wassermann (1980).

Jensen, Kathleen, and Niklaus Wirth: *Pascal: User Manual and Report*, Springer-Verlag, New York, 1974.

This small (167 pages) best-seller contains the revised report on Pascal by Niklaus Wirth and the user manual by Jensen and Wirth. For a long time it was the only official reference on standard Pascal. It is not completely satisfactory because of several ambiguities, contradictions, and holes. Slight revisions were made between successive editions and reprints.

ISO (International Organization for Standardization): *Specification for the Computer Programming Language Pascal*, 7185-1983.

This is the current state of the international standard. It is an 80-page paper, somewhat difficult to read and understand, but extremely precise and complete. National standards in ISO member-countries will be (hopefully) exact copies of this international standard.

Language Evaluations and Criticisms

The following four papers have been reprinted in Wassermann (1980).

Habermann, A. N.: "Critical Comments on the Programming Language Pascal," *Acta Informatica*, vol. 3, no. 1, 1973, pp. 47–57.

The main criticisms by Habermann deal with the ambiguities, incoherences, and holes in the defining texts, and with the notion of "type." The paper also contains criticisms that could only arise from misreadings of the texts or from differences of opinion on what should or should not be included in such a language.

Lecarme, Olivier, and Pierre Desjardins: "More Comments on the Programming Language Pascal," *Acta Informatica*, vol. 4, no. 3, 1975, pp. 231–243.

This paper is a reply to the paper by Habermann. It corrects some mistakes in that paper and suggests some improvements to the language.

Wirth, Niklaus: "An Assessment of the Programming Language Pascal," *IEEE Transactions on Software Engineering*, June 1975, pp. 192–198.

The author of the Pascal language examines his work six years later and discusses some apparently controversial choices, showing that most of them are the result of a careful balance between simplicity and power.

Welsh, James, W. J. Sneeringer, and C. A. R. Hoare: "Ambiguities and Insecurities in Pascal," *Software—Practice and Experience*, vol. 7, no. 6, November, 1977, pp. 685–696.

This important paper has been also reprinted in Barron (1981). The careful scrutiny it gave to some difficult aspects of Pascal was extremely useful during the preparation of the ISO *Standard*, which incorporates solutions for almost all problems pointed out.

Other Textbooks

Dahl, Ole-Johan, Edsger W. Dijkstra, and C. A. R. Hoare: *Structured Programming*, Academic Press, London, 1972.

This book is made up of three papers that constitute the cornerstone of structured programming. The second one, "Notes on Data Structuring" by C. A. R. Hoare, contains most of the ideas about data types that were implemented in Pascal.

Wirth, Niklaus: *Systematic Programming: An Introduction*, Prentice-Hall, Englewood Cliffs, N.J., 1973.

This small book on introductory programming uses Pascal as a support tool, without ever naming it, and covers about two-thirds of the language.

————: *Algorithms + Data Structures = Programs*, Prentice-Hall, Englewood Cliffs, N.J., 1976.

This is the logical sequel to the preceding book, suitable for a second course in programming; it too presents Pascal as a support tool. It is an invaluable source of medium-to-fairly-large Pascal programs.

Alagič, Suad, and Michael A. Arbib: *The Design of Well-Structured and Correct Programs*, Springer-Verlag, New York, 1978.

This somewhat theoretically oriented textbook uses Pascal as a tool for demonstrating the construction of programs in parallel with their formal demonstration, using Hoare's axiomatization.

Wassermann, Anthony I. (ed.): *Tutorial: Programming Language Design,* IEEE Computer Society Press, New York, 1980.

This is a collection of previously published papers (with a few exceptions), which contains six of the most important papers about Pascal, along with many others; among them, the papers by Hoare and by Wirth about the design of programming languages are most noteworthy.

Barron, David W. (ed.): *Pascal—The Language and Its Implementation,* Wiley, Chichester, 1981.

This is another collection of papers, but these deal only with Pascal, and most of them were previously unpublished. In particular, it contains reports about Pascal-P, the portable implementation that was used in most of the Pascal implementations, at least in the beginning, and Pascal-S, a Pascal subset especially designed (by Niklaus Wirth) for an extremely compact implementation, described here in Pascal itself.

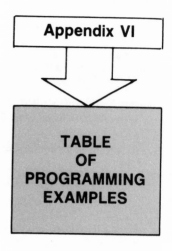

Appendix VI

TABLE
OF
PROGRAMMING
EXAMPLES

The following table includes all programming examples that are sufficiently self-contained—that is, complete programs, procedures, or functions, not partial examples that only demonstrate some simple construction or feature. Solutions to exercises, which appear in App. I, are included in the following table, and are distinguished from the ordinary examples that appear within chapters by the prefix "S."

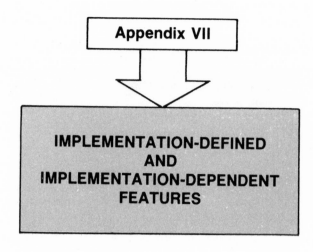

Appendix VII

IMPLEMENTATION-DEFINED AND IMPLEMENTATION-DEPENDENT FEATURES

Several language features cannot be defined without reference to some particular implementation (see Sec. 1.3). The following topics must be *defined* in every implementation:

Predefined Types

- Value of the predefined constant *maxint* (see Sec. 3.4.1)

- Values of type *real,* their range, their precision, the precision of the computations dealing with real values (see Secs. 3.6 and 4.1)

- Values of type *char* and their ordinal numbers (see Sec. 3.4.3)

Files

- Binding of program parameters of file types with the environment (see Sec. 8.4)

- When the physical action implied by a call to the predeclared procedure *get* is actually done (see Sec. 9.2)

- Default values of total width when writing integers, reals, or Booleans on textfiles (see Sec. 9.4)

- Number of exponent digits and case of the letter *e* used for denoting the exponent, when writing reals on textfiles (see Sec. 9.4.3)

- Case of the character string written when writing Booleans on textfiles (see Sec. 9.4.4)

- Effect on the textfile of the predeclared procedure *page* (see Sec. 9.4)

- Effect of calling *reset(input)* and *rewrite(output)* (see Sec. 9.2)

The following topics are *implementation-dependent:*

Host System Interface

- Directives other than *forward* (see Sec. 5.1.1)

- Nature, and binding with the environment, of program parameters that are not files (see Sec. 2.3)

Value or Access Computations

- Order of evaluation and/or access to variables in both parts of an assignment statement (see Sec. 2.6)

- Order of evaluation, and existence of this evaluation, for operands of binary operators (see Sec. 4.1)

- Order of evaluation, access and binding, of actual parameters in a procedure or function call (see Sec. 4.3)

Miscellaneous

- What happens when a textfile to which the predeclared procedure *page* has been applied is reread (see Sec. 9.4)

- Existence of other alternative representations for Pascal symbols (see Sec. 2.2)

For all the points enumerated above, it is absolutely necessary to consult the user's manual, or equivalent documentation, of the Pascal implementation in use.

Index

ABOUT THE AUTHORS

Olivier Lecarme has a Doctorat de Spécialité and a Doctorat d'Etat in computer science. He has taught at the University of Grenoble and at the University of Montreal and is currently a professor of computer science at the University of Nice. His interests include compiling, programming languages, programming methodology, portability, and special-purpose programming languages. He is a member of AFCET and ACM; chairman of the French Pascal working group; chairman of the French committee for the standardization of the Pascal language; and a member of TC 97/ SC5/ WG 4 of ISO (for the standardization of Pascal).

Jean-Louis Nebut is an engineer from the Ecole Supérieure des Travaux Publics. He has a Doctorat de Spécialité in computer science and is currently an assistant professor at the University of Rennes. His interests include programming languages, system programming, and operating system design. He is a member of the French Pascal working group and of the French group BIGRE, dealing with the design and construction of operating systems. He published a textbook about Pascal in 1980: *Théorie et pratique du langage Pascal (Theory and Practice of the Pascal Language).*

Both authors have used and taught Pascal since 1972. Olivier Lecarme's contribution to the definition of the language is acknowledged by Niklaus Wirth, the author of the language, in his preface to *Pascal—User Manual and Report.*